FROM CONCENTRATION CAMP
TO CAMPUS

THE ASIAN AMERICAN EXPERIENCE

Series Editor

Roger Daniels, University of Cincinnati

*A list of books in the series
appears at the end of this book.*

FROM CONCENTRATION CAMP
TO CAMPUS

Japanese American Students
and World War II

ALLAN W. AUSTIN

University of Illinois Press
Urbana and Chicago

© 2004 by the Board of Trustees
of the University of Illinois
All rights reserved
Manufactured in the United States of America
C 5 4 3 2 1

∞ This book is printed on acid-free paper.

Library of Congress Cataloging-in-Publication Data
Austin, Allan W.
From concentration camp to campus : Japanese American
students and World War II / Allan W. Austin.
p.   cm. — (Asian American experience)
Includes bibliographical references and index.
ISBN 0-252-02933-X (alk. paper)
 1. National Japanese American Student Relocation Council.
 2. Japanese Americans—Evacuation and relocation, 1942–
1945. 3. Japanese Americans—Education (Higher)—History—20th century. 4. Japanese American college students—
Social conditions—20th century.
 I. Title. II. Series.
 D769.8.A6A94   2004
 940.53'089'956073—dc22   2003024507

For Vicki

CONTENTS

FOREWORD

Roger Daniels

Of all the contradictions inherent in the incarceration of the Japanese American population of the West Coast during World War II, perhaps none is so striking as the program that took four thousand of the imprisoned people of college age, as Allan W. Austin puts it, "from concentration camp to campus." Although works about that secondary exodus have been published by journalists and scholars from the immediate postwar years to the present, Austin is the first to exploit the archival evidence to show in telling detail just how that liberation was effected.

Despite the fact that Franklin D. Roosevelt quickly approved the notion of release for qualified and admittedly loyal students, bureaucrats, military and civilian, kept inventing reasons for not releasing students and successfully retarded the program. The greatest strength of Austin's compelling book is its detailed analysis of the process of selection and rejection, which went on until almost the end of war. He shows the ways in which the largely Quaker volunteer group—the National Japanese American Student Relocation Council—struggled to overcome bureaucratic opposition and inertia on the one hand and the reluctance of many college officials to stick out their necks and accept students who looked like the enemy on the other. While a few academic leaders, such as Rufus B. von Kleinsmid of the University of Southern California, were openly hostile to Japanese American students, most of those who had to be persuaded to accept the students were afraid of public, alumni, and trustee reactions.

However, as so often is the case, the struggles between the "good guys" and the "bad guys" were paralleled by internecine conflict among the forces supporting students—conflicts about strategy, tactics, ideology, and integrity. To succeed, the council and its agents needed the cooperation of the army and the War Relocation Authority, the civilian agency that ran the camps. This meant not criticizing the government policies that had put the students and other Japanese Americans into concentration camps in the first place, a limitation many were loath to accept.

Austin's analysis of the burdens placed on the students once they were on campus is also telling. They were expected to be models of excellence and propriety and came to feel that they were "ambassadors of goodwill" on whom the fate of an oppressed people depended.

The students were also pioneers; on most Midwestern and East Coast campuses they were the first sizable group of what are now called Asian American students. Those Nisei students, most of whom compiled outstanding records and were successful ambassadors, were the forerunners for the relatively large numbers of native and foreign-born Asian American and Asian students who play such a prominent role on many American campuses today.

Despite the real accomplishments of both the students and the activists who worked so hard for them, this must not be regarded as a happy ending for the nation, even though the wartime experience opened up opportunities for some of the students that they otherwise would not have had. What happened to Japanese Americans in World War II, despite these and other mitigations, was an American war crime, a war crime whose echoes, alas, are with us today.

ACKNOWLEDGMENTS

Although people too numerous to list have provided help as this project has developed, I must first and foremost extend my gratitude to Roger Daniels, who has provided invaluable guidance and support from the initial stages of this book through its final revisions. Professor Daniels, as both an editor and a mentor, has always pushed me to become a better historian. Gary Hess, Thomas Sakmyster, Man Bun Kwan, and two anonymous outside readers made suggestions that strengthened this work considerably. Cathy Turner, a colleague at College Misericordia, has always been supportive while making critical comments on my work and answering innumerable silly questions. Becky Steinberger also deserves thanks for the moral support she provided as we went through this process together.

This book has been made possible by financial support from a number of sources. The University of Cincinnati awarded me a Charles Phelps Taft Graduate Fellowship and a research fellowship, which the History Department generously supplemented whenever necessary. The Balch Institute for Ethnic Studies in Philadelphia provided a resident fellowship. College Misericordia has also provided summer research grants, and Donald Fries and David Wright of the History Department have offered support whenever asked. Financial support of a different sort came from a number of families that generously gave of their time and energy in helping me. The Raybould family in Reston, Virginia, provided me with free lodging, meals, and companionship while I researched at the National Archives. The Berg family in Menlo Park, California, graciously agreed to rent to a desperate graduate student for just one month when they could have more easily and lucratively signed someone else to a one-year lease. The Brogan family also made my stay in California much more enjoyable by taking me in and making me feel like part of the family. Kinji Hiramoto's willingness to share his life with me in the form of his diary is also greatly appreciated.

I must also thank archivists from a variety of institutions for their help. In particular, Carol Leadenham at the Hoover Institution, Karl Krueger at the Balch Institute for Ethnic Studies, Jack Sutters at the American Friends Service Committee Archives, and Aloha South at the National Archives provided invaluable aid. Many more, especially college archivists, responded promptly and informatively to my inquiries. Andrew Wertheimer also deserves thanks for always finding something new for me on his research trips around the country.

Finally, I extend thanks to my family and friends who have supported me throughout the writing of this book. My parents have always cheered me on while helping in any way they could, and this book reflects their lives' devotion to history and writing. Most of all, I must thank Vicki, who has been with me in this from the start, as well as Bobby and Hope, who arrived in time to help me finish. Your love and support have made this book possible. Words cannot express the depth of my love and appreciation for the three of you. Thank you.

ABBREVIATIONS

ABHMS	American Baptist Home Mission Society
AFSC	American Friends Service Committee
ASTP	Army Specialized Training Program
FBI	Federal Bureau of Investigation
JACL	Japanese American Citizens League
NICC	National Intercollegiate Christian Council
NRF	No-Records Folders
PMGO	Provost Marshal General's Office
SSAF	Student Scholarship Aid Fund (Topaz, Utah)
WCCA	Wartime Civil Control Administration
WDC	Western Defense Command
WRA	War Relocation Authority
WSSF	World Student Service Fund
YMCA	Young Men's Christian Association
YWCA	Young Women's Christian Association

INTRODUCTION
"AMBASSADORS OF GOODWILL"

A Japanese American college student incarcerated at the Tanforan camp in 1942 discovered that by climbing a hill he could see a familiar sign that he had driven past countless times on his way to school. From his new vantage point, however, he remembered that it now "'seemed as though [he] was gazing on a strange landmark.'"[1] Although still close to his home, this uprooted student felt a growing psychological distance between himself and a higher education. The shock and trauma resulting from Japan's attack on Pearl Harbor on December 7, 1941, as well as the ensuing exile and incarceration of Japanese Americans, affected this young man and other Nikkei college students in special ways and provoked a range of responses from both Japanese Americans and other sympathetic Americans.[2]

Only on May 5, 1942, five months after the bombing of Pearl Harbor and almost three months after President Franklin D. Roosevelt signed Executive Order 9066, did War Relocation Authority (WRA) director Milton S. Eisenhower begin to try to get some students into colleges for the fall 1942 semester.[3] The National Japanese American Student Relocation Council, created at Eisenhower's urging on May 29, 1942, worked within a context of pervasive wartime racism to facilitate the movement of college students from concentration camps to colleges away from the West Coast.[4] This privately organized and financed agency helped more than four thousand incarcerated students obtain releases to pursue higher education at more than six hundred schools during World War II. The complicated dynamics of student resettlement required the council to work with not just the students but also their parents, civilian and military arms of the government, college administrators, local communities, philanthropic foundations, and church mission boards.[5]

Student resettlement remains an underexamined topic within the widely studied history of the Japanese American wartime experience. The most

comprehensive work on Nikkei educ   nas
James's *Exile Within: The Schooling*   )45
(1987), concentrated on primary and   ari-
ous camps and devoted little attention   :hat
played the central role in efforts to hel   mes
later briefly explored the resettled Japanese American stuaents experiences
in the article "Life Begins with Freedom: The College Nisei, 1942–1945."
Gary Okihiro expanded on James's studies by investigating the effect of
wartime college education on several Nikkei students in *Storied Lives: Japanese American Students and World War II* (1999).

This book embeds the students' stories in a broader social history of the
wartime home front that examines the larger context as well as the development of personal agency that underpinned the students' experiences.
Although constrained by bureaucracy and the tense wartime atmosphere,
the resettled Nikkei had the opportunity to structure the meaning of their
experiences. In viewing student resettlement from a wider perspective, this
work fills an important historiographical gap by explicitly connecting the
Nikkei college students to the government and the society with which they
had to cope. As a result, this study charts the meaning of higher education
and student resettlement for both the students and the wider society.

Furthermore, the administrative history of the council has remained neglected for too long. The council member Robert W. O'Brien published the
only history of the council itself, *The College Nisei*, in 1949. However, O'Brien
failed to systematically examine the mechanisms of student resettlement, providing only fragmentary glimpses of the council's interactions with friendly
agencies such as the WRA; unfriendly agencies such as the army, navy, and
Federal Bureau of Investigation (FBI); and friendly and unfriendly colleges
and universities. O'Brien also ignored the complex internal organization and
problems of the council. Indeed, the contemporary nature of O'Brien's account makes it especially useful today as a primary, not a secondary, source.

From the beginning of its work, the council stressed a familiar theme:
resettled Japanese American students were to serve as "ambassadors of goodwill" in their new communities.[6] When students arrived at many colleges
and in many communities that were unfamiliar with Nikkei, the council
expected them to make a favorable impression. This ambassadorship, the
council believed, helped create a safe environment for the students and, just
as importantly, paved the way for future students. Positive receptions of students in new locales also proved the viability of student resettlement to the
philanthropic organizations and church mission boards on whose funding
the council relied.

Many students did become ambassadors of goodwill, furthering the council's program in other ways. Helen Matsunaga, for example, wanted to study music and sociology at Rockford College in Illinois "to become a leader in culture after the war." After resettling, she wrote the council, "[I am] keenly aware of the responsibilities I bear in accepting your aid. I shall surely strive to show our fellow Americans the hearts of us Americans with Japanese faces."[7] Another student thanked the council "for the wonderful opportunity to help promote a better understanding of the [Nisei]."[8] A farewell party held for two students at Poston drew seventy-five well-wishers and provided an opportunity for the students to assure the group that "they [would] strive to create good will so that in the future, more students [would] be able to leave the relocation camps for educational purposes."[9]

An editorial in the *Santa Anita Pacemaker* reinforced the students' roles as ambassadors of goodwill. Arriving in locales where Nikkei were rare, the editorial explained, the students would be scrutinized and must not be found wanting: "Upon their scholarship, their conduct, their thoughts, their sense of humor, their adaptability, will rest the verdict of the rest of the country as to whether Japanese Americans are true Americans. So, upon the students will be the onus of proving to people to whom they are strangers that the first word in 'Japanese American' is merely an adjective describing the color of our skin—not the color of our beliefs. There is no place for cry-babies or weaklings in this program. The burden must be borne."[10]

The students' exemplary behavior eased the council's relationship with government officials. In general, the council managed to cooperate with the WRA, the civilian agency running the concentration camps, in part because the emphasis on ambassadors of goodwill promoted the WRA's wider program of Japanese American resettlement. Clearly, student resettlement could not succeed without WRA approval.

The students' roles as ambassadors of goodwill may have produced some negative effects in the long run, such as in providing early evidence to support the "model minority" stereotype of Japanese Americans that developed in the mid-1960s. This stereotype was employed both to praise the achievements of Nikkei after the war and to denigrate other ethnic groups that had not similarly achieved "success." While the educational achievements of the Nikkei community had been impressive, the council understandably promoted its program by highlighting the accomplishments of its "best and brightest" students and ignoring those who vacillated about making decisions or dropped out after getting accepted and resettling.[11]

The council's members acted as ambassadors of goodwill as well, even though they did not use that term to describe themselves. If the students had something to prove to Americans outside the concentration camps, the council had something to prove to Nikkei in the camps. Nikkei, in fact, expected a reciprocal ambassadorship; a statement in a camp yearbook declared to America in 1944, "I hope that your faith in me has grown since the last time I saw you [for] that faith must grow for my faith in you to grow."[12] Thus, while the students were demonstrating the virtues of Nikkei to the wider society, the council believed that it was demonstrating that not all the wider society was hostile to Japanese Americans. The council viewed its efforts in the camps as symbolic of American democracy to a group that had been treated in a most undemocratic manner. Robbins W. Barstow, the council's first national director, explained that student resettlement would demonstrate to Nikkei and the world "that America really is a land of opportunity, and of justice, and of democratic integrity." He believed that the American public, by furnishing financial aid and providing warm welcomes to Nikkei students, could "truly reinforce our national unity by wise and generous attitudes and actions with respect to one of the many minorities that all together help to make our nation what it is."[13] The bitterness engendered by the concentration camp experience, the council believed, had to be countered with actions that at least suggested the hope of a better future in which the ideals of democracy might be translated more fully into reality.

The council's difficulties also grew out of nearly a century of anti-Asian prejudice, first directed against Chinese, then against Nikkei when numerically significant Japanese immigrants began to reach the United States in the 1890s from both Japan and Hawaii. The census of 1890 recorded 2,039 Japanese in the United States, but this number increased by about 25,000 over the next decade. An additional 125,000 Japanese arrived between 1900 and 1908, the peak period of Japanese immigration to the United States. Between 1909 and 1924, about 10,000 more Japanese entered the United States annually under the provisions of the Gentlemen's Agreement of 1907–8.[14]

The majority of Japanese immigrants came from the countryside. Before 1907–8, most were single young men who, on average, possessed eight years of education. As Japanese immigration increased, the new arrivals clustered on the West Coast and especially in California, which was home to two-fifths of mainland Japanese Americans in 1900, nearly two-thirds in 1920, and more than seven-tenths in 1940. Slightly less than one-sixth of Japanese Americans lived in Oregon and Washington in 1940; thus, only one Nikkei in nine lived in the other forty-five states in 1940.[15]

New Japanese arrivals typically started on the lower rungs of the American economic ladder, but many made economic gains. In agriculture, which employed about one-half of the Nikkei population by 1919, many Issei moved from being laborers to independent farmers, either as owners or as lessors. They used their skill, energy, and the labor of their families to improve land that whites often considered worthless and to pioneer in developing potato, rice, fruit, and vegetable production. Although few became wealthy, most enjoyed a steady prosperity.[16]

Urban Issei remained a vital part of the Japanese American community. These immigrants, usually starting as either domestic servants or common laborers, also managed to improve their socioeconomic standing. Barred from most skilled occupations because unions would not accept them, many urban Issei established a small business (such as a laundry, a restaurant, or a curio shop), went to work for an established Japanese American businessman, or became purveyors of Nikkei-grown produce. Although some Issei did engage in direct economic competition with whites, for example in commercial fishing, most Issei entrepreneurs, like the agrarian Issei, engaged in complementary economic activities.[17]

Japanese had also come to America as early as the 1860s to pursue an education, often under Japanese government sponsorship. These students typically returned to Japan with technical, legal, or social science training to help their country pursue the developmental course plotted by its leaders. This type of immigration became less important to the Japanese government after colleges in Japan began to produce graduates with the desired skills and knowledge. Some of the Japanese immigrants after 1890 also came to America to pursue an education, often working their way through school as replacements for Chinese domestic servants. Most of the so-called Japanese schoolboys, however, had no connection to higher education; they chose domestic work only as a temporary circumstance while they learned the English language and became accustomed to their new surroundings.[18]

Most Issei lived segregated lives. Although this segregation resulted in part from the typical immigrant desire to live with culturally similar people, the continuing segregation of Japanese Americans should not be blamed on the victims. Japanese immigrants faced almost immediate hostility from whites, largely on the basis of the anti-Chinese tradition and racism. The Naturalization Act of 1870, passed in the aftermath of the Civil War, had limited naturalization to "white persons and persons of African descent," thus making Japanese immigrants "aliens ineligible to citizenship." An anti-Japanese movement became significant in San Francisco and gradually extended its influence to the state, regional, and national levels. The movement's notoriety began in 1906, when the San Francisco school board announced plans to segregate Japanese American students. The Gentlemen's Agreement negotiated by President Theodore Roosevelt defused this crisis momentarily, but anti-Japanese sentiments did not remain muted for long. California passed alien land laws in 1913 and 1920, which attempted to bar aliens ineligible for citizenship—meaning Nikkei—from owning and eventually leasing agricultural land. The anti-Japanese movement eventually had its basic demand met by the provision of the 1924 National Origins Act that barred immigration to the United States by aliens ineligible for citizenship.[19]

At the beginning of the 1940s, Japanese America consisted of two distinct elements, the Issei and the Nisei, or second-generation Japanese Americans. The percentage of native-born Nikkei in the United States rose from 26 percent in 1920 to 62 percent in 1940.[20] Generational conflict developed as the size and influence of the Nisei group increased, in large part because the Nisei, citizens by virtue of their native birth, tended to adopt more aspects of the wider American culture and to be more America-oriented, although they continued to maintain ties to Japanese America through racial and ethnic religious institutions and newspapers. The complexities of identity formation that the Nisei faced resulted in the creation of a Nisei subculture that tapped both American and Japanese American qualities.[21]

Pushed to achieve academically by Issei organizations and their parents, the Nisei became increasingly aware of their marginal place in American society as they approached adulthood. Despite educational achievements that rivaled and often surpassed those of white students, the great majority of Nisei graduates could not find work outside the ethnic community. Limited by racism, many Nisei, Jere Takahashi has noted, continued into higher education in an attempt "to postpone their coming to terms with their problematical circumstances."[22]

Already facing this prejudiced present and ambiguous future, the Nisei students' world all but collapsed after December 7, 1941. The Japanese attack on Pearl Harbor resulted in many Americans viewing Nikkei as the enemy. The war, of course, only further clouded the Japanese American situation. While student strategies for coping after December 7 differed widely, most experienced a common feeling of shock and disbelief in the aftermath of the bombing of Pearl Harbor.

Yoshiko Uchida, a student at the University of California, first heard of the attack on Pearl Harbor from "a frenzied voice on the radio" during a quiet Sunday lunch at home. Her family dismissed the report as false. At worst, they concurred, if an attack had occurred, it must have been "an aberrant act of some crazy irresponsible fool." Not yet contemplating that the attack meant war between the United States and Japan, Uchida later went to the library to study for her final exams. Groups of obviously nervous Nisei were already there, discussing "the shocking event" but also dismissing it as "a freak incident." Uchida returned home that night, however, to find both her family and her world turned upside down. The FBI had earlier broken into the Uchida house, searched it without a warrant, and then later returned to arrest Uchida's father, who worked for a Japanese company. Her mother, hoping that her husband would soon return, left the porch light on and the screen door unlatched before going to bed that night. Her husband did not return that night, and the family did not learn of his whereabouts for five days.[23]

Kenji Okuda, a freshman at the University of Washington, also learned of Pearl Harbor while listening to the radio with his family. He later went to the university and discussed the uncertain situation with both Nisei and whites at the American Friends Service Committee (AFSC) office and the Young Men's Christian Association (YMCA). His father was arrested that night. This development suggested an ominous answer to a question raised in Okuda's previous conversations: "Would things remain normal or would all sorts of disruptions occur?"[24]

Nikkei students at the University of Washington expressed the confusion and anxiety that they shared with Uchida and their classmate Okuda to the *University of Washington Daily* reporter Dick Takeuchi on December 8. The shocked and unbelieving students wishfully hoped that Germany had attacked Pearl Harbor or that the story had been fabricated, like Orson Welles's 1938 "War of the Worlds" broadcast. As reality sank in, some students feared racial violence while others expressed concern for their noncitizen parents. Takeuchi raised the possibility of concentration camps, although he feared this possibility only for the Issei. The Nisei students and Takeuchi feared discrimination and suspicion, not incarceration. Although one Nikkei joked, "[o]ur immediate concern . . . is about final exams," the interviewed students clearly worried about a foreboding future. The students' uncertainty echoed the larger question asked by Frank Miyamoto, an associate in the university's department of sociology, in an article in the *Japanese American Courier.* "Well here we are at last," Miyamoto wrote. "But where do we go from here, in particular where do we Nisei go from here?"[25]

Miyamoto's question was not easily answered, in part because government policy became clear only slowly after December 7. What a presidential commission forty years later called "race prejudice, war hysteria, and a failure of political leadership" led to President Franklin D. Roosevelt's Executive Order 9066 on February 19, 1942. This order allowed the military to designate areas from which some or all persons might be excluded and to transport such persons to camps in new locales. Congress endorsed the executive order on March 21 by providing penalties for those who violated orders in the military areas. The government gave the initial task of rounding up the entire West Coast Nikkei population and cooping them up in temporary assembly centers to the military Wartime Civil Control Administration (WCCA). Executive Order 9066 eventually resulted in the incarceration of 120,313 Japanese Americans, nearly nine out of ten Nikkei in the continental United States. American citizens constituted more than 60 percent of the incarcerated group. Executive Order 9102, issued on March 18, 1942, gave the permanent task of handling the incarcerated Nikkei to a civilian agency, the WRA. The military began to forcibly remove Nikkei from the West Coast in late March 1942. Japanese Americans were exiled from Military Area No. 1 by June 7 and from Military Area No. 2 by August 7.[26]

As mass exile and incarceration loomed, Nikkei students were forced to formulate plans to meet it. Some, of course, chose simply to comply with military orders, perhaps in an attempt to demonstrate their loyalty to the United States, to care for their parents and families, or to surrender to a sense of disillusionment or helplessness. Others, however, began to seek opportunities to continue their education outside the West Coast. Many of these students received help in doing so from sympathetic whites, although such aid in early spring 1942 took the form of only sporadic and uncoordinated efforts at student resettlement.

CREATING THE NATIONAL
JAPANESE AMERICAN STUDENT
RELOCATION COUNCIL

In spring 1942, a sign tacked to a door in the Japanese Student Club house at the University of Washington presented a plaintive plea:

WORKING ON THE FINAL TERM
PAPER OF MY CAREER
PLEASE DO NOT DISTURB
LETS MAKE IT A MASTERPIECE.
Geo. Yamaguchi[1]

Yamaguchi's poignant notice revealed the despair that Nikkei students felt as exile loomed. The despair moved different people in different ways, however. Some Nikkei dropped out immediately after Pearl Harbor. Yamaguchi and others temporarily remained in school but viewed exile and incarceration as the terminal point of their higher education.

Other Nikkei students resisted such fatalism. Nobu Hibino, a senior at the University of California, Berkeley, recalled, "[s]hortly after [Pearl Harbor,] events happened so fast. I finished my exams and went back to register for the second semester. A lot of my classmates chose not to come back, but I only had five months to go and I was just determined to finish." Hibino had to withdraw, however, when the government placed restrictions on Japanese Americans that limited travel to no more than five miles from their homes. She moved with her family to Tanforan and then to Topaz before resettling to Boston University.[2] Refusing to become victims of unjust and unnecessary government policies, Hibino and others decided to continue their college education. Some attempted to resettle immediately; others moved to camps but worked to resettle after helping their families adjust to their new surroundings. Those who wished to continue their education received help from academics, college administrators, civil libertarians, and religious activists.

9

Sporadic Attempts at Student Resettlement

Only after mid-February 1942 did it become clear in an atmosphere permeated by wartime racism that all Nikkei would be forcibly removed from the West Coast. Executive Order 9066, issued on February 19, gave the military the authority to create military areas and to remove people from them, but the Western Defense Command (WDC) was not yet ready to act. Still, calls by an American Legion post in Portland and the Native Sons of the Golden West in early February for the removal of all Japanese Americans from the West Coast did not bode well for the Nikkei. Furthermore, isolated congressional debates and the Tolan Committee Hearings on National Defense Migration held in late February and early March in San Francisco, Portland, Seattle, and Los Angeles suggested widespread support for a program of mass incarceration.

General John L. DeWitt, commander of the WDC, issued Public Proclamation No. 1, which designated military areas in Washington, Oregon, California, and Arizona, on March 2. Although the proclamation ordered no one moved, it was aimed at German and Italian aliens as well as "any person of Japanese Ancestry." An accompanying press release predicted that all Nikkei would eventually be excluded from Military Area No. 1. Although the army suggested that it was not contemplating Nikkei exclusion from Military Area No. 2, this area was also later evacuated.

President Roosevelt created the WRA with Executive Order 9102 on March 18 and gave it responsibility for the uprooted Nikkei, although the specifics of its program remained to be worked out. The reality of concentration camps for Nikkei, alien and citizen alike, was now undeniable. As government policy moved inexorably toward a program of exile and incarceration, attempts to place college students at schools outside the West Coast intensified.[3]

Two questionnaires circulated in early spring 1942 by the National Intercollegiate Christian Council (NICC) and the University of California present an overview of the Nikkei students' situation. The YMCA and Young Women's Christian Association (YWCA) at the University of California reported in early April 1942 that about one-fourth of the university's 435 Nikkei students had withdrawn from school before January 20, 1942, the start of the new semester.[4] They had left either out of concern for the welfare of their families or because of a "general disillusionment and despair with the situation." The drop-out rate increased for similar reasons in the spring term after the first announcements of impending exile. Strained finances exacerbated by the freezing of "alien enemy" funds by the government forced additional students to withdraw.

The YMCA and YWCA representatives believed that morale represented a pressing problem: Nisei students increasingly seemed to give up hope for their future and to feel unwanted in the United States. "Each case," they reported, "seems to be one of unusual hardship." Despite the disenchantment and dejection they described, the white students still believed that most Japanese American students wanted to continue their education if their families were well provided for in the camps.[5]

A separate questionnaire circulated among Nikkei students in the San Francisco Bay Area by the University of California reinforced these impressionistic conclusions and revealed what would become enduring problems. Almost 83 percent of the first 257 students answered that they wanted to continue their college education, but most reported a need for financial assistance to do so. The students, most of whom attended large public institutions on the West Coast (see table 1), also expressed a desire to transfer to large institutions.[6]

College students constituted a relatively small proportion of the 120,313 evacuated Japanese Americans. Robert W. O'Brien, an active participant in and an early chronicler of student resettlement, believed that there were 3,252 Nikkei students enrolled in institutions of higher learning in California, Washington, and Oregon in 1941.[7] An additional 278 Japanese American students were attending institutions of higher learning outside of the West Coast. O'Brien estimated that men comprised two-thirds of the West Coast Nikkei students.[8] Although these students were a relatively small proportion of the total population, they played an important role as a major segment of early Nikkei resettlers.

Sporadic and uncoordinated efforts at student resettlement began on the Pacific Coast in spring 1942 as a variety of interested organizations and individuals stepped forward to help students. The NICC, for example, urged student YMCA and YWCA groups to bring the issue of evacuated college students before their college presidents and to offer their services in helping the administrations meet this crisis. The YMCA and YWCA at Berkeley became quite active in trying to help Nikkei students. In addition to reporting to the NICC, they also invited a number of speakers to a race relations luncheon group to provide information on exile and incarceration and brought pertinent data to the attention of the college newspaper. In extending their efforts off campus, they sent letters to public officials and spoke to church groups.[9]

Table 1. Japanese American College Students at West
Coast Schools and Elsewhere, 1941

Geographical Region	Number of Students
California	
University of California at Berkeley	485
Los Angeles City College	265
University of California at Los Angeles	244
Sacramento Junior College	224
San Francisco Junior College	145
Pasadena Junior College	123
University of Southern California	113
San Jose State	111
Other	857
	2,567
Oregon	
Oregon State College	41
University of Oregon	27
Other	64
	132
Washington	
University of Washington	458
College of Puget Sound	32
Other	63
	553
West Coast total	3,252
Other states and regions	
Arizona	7
Rocky Mountain states	73
Midwestern states	119
Southern states	11
Mid-Atlantic states	48
New England states	20
	278

Source: O'Brien, *College Nisei,* 135–37.

These activities were enhanced by an active and sympathetic university administration. The University of California provost Monroe E. Deutsch was an outspoken advocate for Nikkei students.[10] His boss, President Robert Gordon Sproul, also became an exponent for the students. The conservative Sproul had headed the university since 1930. Although he described exile and incarceration as a "necessary evil" and refrained from direct criticism of government actions, Sproul acted effectively to help Nikkei students. In addition to contacting Midwestern university presidents to explore their willingness to accept Nikkei students, he worked in other ways to help students cope with exile and incarceration. Sproul met with faculty members, students, and church representatives to discuss ways to help the students. The university also granted leaves of absence to Nikkei who requested them and refunded all fees to Nisei students who withdrew before March 21. Loans were made available to Japanese American students facing financial difficulties. The university deans counseled Nikkei students and wrote letters of recommendation to facilitate transfers.[11] Sproul and Deutsch later made a further contribution by successfully lobbying the government to establish a program for student resettlement.

Similar efforts to help Nisei students developed on other West Coast campuses. Under the leadership of President Lee Paul Seig, the University of Washington held a graduation ceremony at the Puyallup Assembly Center. Seig and other interested university personnel used the school's prestige and administrators to aid as many of the institution's 458 Nikkei students as possible. Seig expressed public support for Nikkei and emphasized the loyalty of "the great majority." As exile and incarceration became a reality, Seig wrote to college presidents across the United States, praising the Nisei and urging colleges to accept them as students.

Robert O'Brien, the faculty adviser to the Japanese Student Club, called a meeting on December 12 to discuss the problems, both real and potential, caused by the war. In his testimony before the Tolan Committee on March 2, he defended the Nisei as patriotic and suggested providing federal funds to college students in the case that mass evacuation occurred. O'Brien had previously established a local student relocation group to aid students wishing to resettle.[12]

Seattle students also received assistance from an AFSC counseling program designed to help them resettle. The Quaker Thomas Bodine became involved in student resettlement through these efforts, which were part of a larger program aimed at "extending spiritual handshakes" to West Coast Nikkei.[13] Bodine, born in 1915 in Philadelphia, attended Quaker schools for his primary and secondary education but then chose Wesleyan University because he wanted to see the world outside of Quakerism. He graduated in 1937 and went to work as an investment researcher for Connecticut General Life Insurance in Hartford, Connecticut. While in Hartford, Bodine also worked with German refugees. He joined the AFSC in 1941 when his local draft board came calling. The AFSC chose Bodine to participate in its first training program for overseas work. Bodine's scheduled trip to Shanghai to work with Jewish refugees, however, was scotched by the attack on Pearl Harbor. The AFSC instead sent Bodine to Seattle to monitor the Nikkei situation and then transferred him to San Francisco in June 1942 for student resettlement work. Bodine, who would become a leading and passionate advocate for Nikkei students, recalled in 1991, "when I lived on the east coast and worked in Hartford I had no awareness particularly of the Japanese American community on the west coast." This easterner, who had never met a Nisei until the AFSC sent him to Seattle, played a leading role as an outspoken advocate for the incarcerated students while working for the council.[14]

Uncoordinated efforts like those at the University of California and the University of Washington were repeated along the West Coast and managed to place 216 Nikkei students, including a disproportionate number from the University of Washington and the University of California, by the end of March.[15] Public Proclamation No. 4, effective March 29, ended voluntary Nikkei evacuation from Military Area No. 1. The army, however, sometimes allowed individual students to resettle on a case-by-case basis, and students continued to move east. A total of 630 students managed to transfer directly to new schools without spending time in a concentration camp.[16]

Gyo Obata made the decision to resettle in late April as his family's scheduled evacuation neared.[17] The straight-A architecture student at the University of California told his father, Chiura Obata, a professor of art at Berkeley, that he would not comply with the unconstitutional exile. Instead, the eighteen-year-old wanted to resettle to continue his higher education. His father supported this decision and asked his colleague, Professor Oliver M. Washburn, for help. Washburn, the chair of Berkeley's art department, wrote George R. Throop, president of Washington University in St. Louis, who arranged young Obata's acceptance. By this time, however, even citizen Nisei needed army permission to travel. His first attempt to secure permission was blocked by an army officer. "Okay, Sonny," he recalled being told, "just do like everyone else, Uncle Sammy's gonna take care of you. Just forget about school."

Obata left discouraged, but his father contacted Geraldine Scott, a friend and former student, who had a friend in the judge advocate's section of DeWitt's WDC headquarters. The officer had the case reconsidered and approved. Since the elder Obata's funds were frozen as an enemy alien, Scott hurriedly raised money from friends to buy a train ticket. Because of curfew regulations, she also took Obata to meet his train. "I remember he seemed so young to have to go under these circumstances, where he might not have any friends, to just work," Scott recalled. "He did make friends, of course, and fortunately the hysteria there was not as bad."

With Washburn's help, Obata relocated directly to college while his family reported to an assembly camp. At Washington University, Obata became president of the Architectural Society, served in student government, and worked as art editor for the *Hatchet*. He earned a degree in architecture in 1945 and continued his studies as a graduate student with a scholarship at the Cranbrook Academy of Art in Michigan. Obata went on to a successful architectural career, becoming a partner as well as principal in charge of design with Hellmuth, Obata & Kassabaum (HOK) in St. Louis in 1955. Obata would later plan the Japanese American National Museum in Los Angeles.

Students lacking Obata's connections sometimes managed to resettle. Betty Ikeda, for example, took advantage of her family's move from Berkeley to Dallas before the government's March 27 ban on voluntary evacuation.[18] Eager to continue her education, Ikeda enrolled in Mary Hardin Baylor College in Texas. She fulfilled her role as an ambassador of goodwill at her new college by being voted "Most Charming Girl" by her classmates.

While many private colleges were willing to enroll Japanese Americans soon after Pearl Harbor, most public universities were initially reluctant. One notable exception was the University of Nebraska, which had enrolled Nikkei students since the 1880s and decided on March 28, 1942—two months prior to the creation of a government-sanctioned resettlement agency—to accept students cleared by the FBI who met academic requirements, were loyal citizens, and had sufficient funds.[19] The registrar George Walter Rosenlof played a key role in this decision and soon convinced Nebraska chancellor Chauncey Boucher to raise the school's quota from twenty-five to fifty. Rosenlof felt strongly about exile and incarceration, comparing the army camps to German concentration camps and writing, "[I do not] dare to speak as I feel—suffice it to say that to me it is exceedingly disappointing that the government and the Army officials are not handling this situation as it ought to be handled."

Nikkei students who rushed to take advantage of this opportunity were assisted in their efforts by the Lincoln Japanese Student Relocation Council, which had grown out of a grassroots movement among local clergy. Chaired by Reverend Robert Drew, the university's Methodist minister and a member of the Fellowship of Reconciliation, the Lincoln group sent letters to students who had been admitted, met them as they arrived at the train station, and helped arrange housing.

Although the University of Nebraska's decision met some local opposition, especially from a local commander of the American Legion, the arrival of Nikkei went fairly smoothly. Japanese American students at Nebraska seem to have adopted various strategies upon arrival; some chose to remain inconspicuous while others spoke publicly about exile and incarceration. While

racism occasionally manifested itself and housing became a contentious issue, a student later recalled the "amity and brotherhood" of Nebraskans and
another thanked the university for "restor[ing] my faith in people."[20]

The admissions of Jack Takiguchi and Masao Umino at Ohio University
in summer 1942 did not go as smoothly; their arrival instead provoked rumors of a planned lynching in the fall.[21] The students believed that the danger was exaggerated and described their summer in Athens as "pleasant."
The rumors, however, were rooted in negative feelings in the local community. The mayor and police chief refused permission for additional students
to relocate to Ohio University because of "entirely unsatisfactory" local attitudes that could "easily become dangerous for [Nikkei] students."[22]

B. T. Grover, the university's director of public relations, had not expected
such problems. By September 15, however, he had reversed his initial position to side with the mayor. The university apparently asked Takiguchi and
Umino to transfer but relented and let them stay. Umino suspected that the
university's unwillingness to accept additional Nikkei was based on the trustees' hopes of gaining a naval training unit for their campus. He also believed
that the trustees feared negative reactions from the local community if too
many Nikkei appeared in Athens.

Umino, in the midst of this controversy, assumed the role of ambassador
of goodwill. He wrote the council in February 1943 to offer advice to students considering resettlement. Although some were upset that Nisei were
not being drafted, most townspeople and students had welcomed him
warmly. Umino joined the debate team and pledged a fraternity—despite
not believing in them—to establish more contacts to make it "better for the
[Nisei]." He was also active in a local Presbyterian organization and Sunday evening bull sessions with fellow liberals. Both he and Takiguchi received
invitations to any interracial gatherings that occurred.

Despite noting his "uneasiness" in asking girls out on dates, Umino urged
"scared freshmen" to go to college. "The dangers have been exaggerated,"
he argued, "and the advantages are tremendous." Friendships, freedom, and
escape from the frustrations of camp, in addition to the value of a college
degree, all made student relocation a worthwhile experience. He advised
students to allow time for initially unfriendly communities to "get used to
seeing you and knowing you." Umino concluded his advice by arguing that
Nikkei should not be too assertive. "Jewish students," he suggested in a
stereotyped remark, asserted themselves in an "ostentatious and often ob-
noxious" manner. "Of course stand up for your rights," he suggested, "[but]
present your side of the question in a tactful way."[23]

Most students were unable to resettle before being removed to concentration camps. Although some who dropped out in anticipation of being sent to concentration camps never returned to school, many sent to the camps sought opportunities for higher education, often relying on individuals unconnected with colleges and universities. Roy Nakata, for example, received considerable help from his family's employer, Alice Sinclair Dodge.[24] When the Nakata family was sent to the Santa Anita Assembly Center, it placed its savings into a bank account bearing Dodge's name.

Nakata had rushed to graduate high school prior to exile with the help of sympathetic instructors. He wanted to resettle in order "to continue studying and try my humble part in serving in the best possible manner this great land of America." Bolstered by his parents' support, Nakata hoped to avoid "being sent to an internment camp and wasting away what little knowledge I have gained thus far. . . . It is my sincere hope that I be allowed the privilege of attending an institution of good name so that I may mold myself into a better American and do my part in building an even greater America." Dodge helped Nakata resettle after a period of incarceration to Ohio's Oberlin College in fall 1942.

Despite individual successes, student resettlement occurred only slowly and in small numbers throughout spring 1942. "The anxiety over the future and the fear and despair they face at home," Dick Mills, a field secretary for the regional office of the YMCA, concluded in his first report on exile and incarceration, "makes it impossible for them to study." Many students did not wish to finish out the term if doing so meant being separated from their families. Similarly, many students wanted to see their families safely settled in their postevacuation surroundings before resettling to continue their education.

Although resettlement remained possible in the spring if the student were financially self-sufficient, it had to be done at the student's own initiative. Mills's report contained a number of suggestions for aiding student relocation in this context. The YMCA and YWCA, he suggested, could facilitate resettlement by identifying colleges that would offer scholarships and individuals who would open their homes to Nikkei students. Even with such help, Mills argued, few students would resettle until their families had been safely moved. He thus suggested simply keeping in touch with students and beginning to work in midsummer to place them for the fall term. Mills also suggested that letters be written to government officials involved with the forced evacuation, urging them "to recognize the tremendous importance of education and [to] take steps to have funds provided for the continuance of education among Japanese young [men] and women. In addition, we can present facts to the authorities in our schools and to the town officials with the request that they too bring pressure to see that some provision is made for the continuance of education, either in the resettlement camps, or in direct subsidy from the Government to enable college men and women to continue their education."[25]

Noting that large numbers of Nikkei students had left school, Mills concluded two weeks later that these withdrawals resulted from family situations and from the fact that "uncertainty and tension has made study at present impossible." The relatively uncoordinated efforts advocated in his first report, Mills now implicitly seemed to realize, were proving insufficient to meet the students' needs. Local groups simply could not do a satisfactory job acting independently; some form of coordination was necessary to have a significant effect on students' lives. Mills pointed to an "imperative" need to find one person to coordinate the efforts of the churches and the YMCA and YWCA as well as to interpret the rights of Nikkei to communities overwhelmed by anti-Japanese propaganda.[26]

Early Attempts to Create a Coordinated Program
to Aid Nikkei Students

Two strategies emerged as student resettlement advocates tried to help Nikkei. The first urged the federal government to establish a program for student resettlement. The second facilitated the immediate resettlement of Nikkei students. Proponents of the second strategy hoped that the government would sanction their efforts after a coordinated plan emerged. The strategies were complementary: advocates of the first pointed out the plight of Nikkei students to the federal government while supporters of the second kept the western military authorities aware of the students by helping them resettle. Sproul and the University of California emphasized the former strategy, O'Brien and the University of Washington the latter. The momentum created by the two strategies pushed the government toward creating a student resettlement program.

Paul S. Taylor, a professor of economics at Berkeley, may have been the first to suggest the idea of student resettlement to the federal bureaucracy, in a March 17 letter to Dr. Will Alexander in the Office of Production Management.[27] Taylor's letter suggested placing Nikkei students, after careful selection and with the necessary supervision, in midwestern colleges with the help of government scholarships. He argued that scholarships would help the students overcome the special problems facing them and would cost less than supporting the students in the camps. Such government aid would also help, he noted, to counter arguments that exile and incarceration resulted from "race discrimination." Alexander forwarded Taylor's letter to Secretary of Agriculture Claude R. Wickard soon after receiving it, suggesting in an attached note that the government ought to consider the proposal. Wickard recommended that Taylor's letter be passed on to Milton S. Eisenhower, a former Department of Agriculture staffer and the recently appointed director of the WRA. A good bureaucrat, Eisenhower had not publicly criticized exile and incarceration. However, on April 1, within two weeks of assuming the directorship of the WRA, he did share with Wickard his belief that "when the war is over and we consider calmly this unprecedented migration of 120,000 people, we as Americans are going to regret the avoidable injustices that may have been done."[28] Alexander also sent a copy of Taylor's proposal to Eleanor Roosevelt, who shared it with Undersecretary of State Sumner Welles, who agreed that the plan had "much merit" and reported that the Office of Education was working on the problem.[29]

Midwestern university presidents also discussed how best to deal with Nikkei students. W. C. Coffey of the University of Minnesota wrote seventeen other presidents on March 18 and asked them for advice. Clarence Dykstra, the president of the University of Wisconsin, had served as the first director of the Selective Service and knew Washington, D.C. He suggested that university presidents approach Eisenhower with a plan for student relocation. He believed that most local communities would approve a government-run program that distributed the students widely. Coffey, whose university had already received thirty-two formal applications and had seen a number of students arrive without any assurance of admission, feared the results of too many Nikkei showing up at any one school and wired Eisenhower in early April about the need for just such a systematic plan.[30]

As appeals reached the government for action, concerned West Coast civil libertarians created the Student Relocation Committee to coordinate student resettlement on March 21 at a meeting on the Berkeley campus called by the YMCA and the YWCA. The participants discussed the points Mills raised—before and after the meeting—and chose Joseph Conard, a Quaker involved with the AFSC and a graduate student in economics at the University of California, as executive secretary.[31] As Conard later described it, the participants had concluded "that there was imperative need for a [coordinating] central office. . . . Excellent work was being done by groups in some areas, but lack of information prevented other interested groups from doing likewise. Many jobs were being done in conflicting ways by groups unaware of what the others were doing. Many other needed jobs were not being done at all. Miscellaneous information was 'floating around,' and no one knew what was fact and what was fiction."[32] Although it lasted only a little more than two months, the committee set the agenda for student resettlement throughout the war.

The committee set up three regional groups covering the Pacific Northwest, northern California, and southern California. Each worked largely on its own, but all were coordinated by Conard, executive secretary in the Northern California office. A West Coast committee, functioning primarily by correspondence, formulated policy. A central committee also discussed policy and submitted proposals by mail to the West Coast committee members. Conard justified what he acknowledged as a "complex and unwieldy" organization by arguing that "the large area requires such machinery in order to be representative. Co-operation has been 100% from all concerned."[33]

Pro-resettlement arguments focused on the students, described as "a strategic group among the evacuees," as well as the Nikkei as a group, democracy, and the country's future. Supporters pointed out that the students would be widely scattered, an argument often used to support student resettlement. This dispersal would allow them to feel more like American citizens; if they remained in concentration camps, "their Americanism [would] be sullied by a sense of bitterness."[34] Supporters cited the Tolan Committee and other "[r]esponsible officials" to argue "that the large majority of evacuees are loyal and law-abiding citizens" and insisted that a program of student resettlement would boost the morale of the Nikkei population. Choosing, as Sproul did, not to challenge the policy of exile and incarceration, they also argued that their program represented a test of American democracy. "So far as military necessity permits," they argued, "a democracy must show fair and equal treatment of minority groups in peace and war. It must not deprive persons of freedom without due process of law." Discrimination against these students damaged democracy and created the possibility of future discrimination against other groups. While Nikkei had willingly made sacrifices for the national interest, the committee argued, needless sacrifices should not be asked of them.[35]

Conard reported in April that the most pressing task was to help Nikkei students continue or begin their college education in fall 1942. He warned that planning and financing for student resettlement would be slow but added that "careful procedures now will yield much more favorable results in the end."[36] He explained to the AFSC's C. Reed Cary that the committee's broad purpose was "to constantly survey the needs of the students arising from West Coast evacuation and to see that wherever possible these needs are met."[37]

Conard envisioned meeting this purpose in a variety of ways, including cooperating with and coordinating the work of existing groups as well as encouraging others to become involved. If no organization existed to perform a certain task, the committee would do that job itself. His committee would cease operations when groups were found that could effectively meet all the needs of the students.[38]

Within days of the creation of the committee, government actions further restricted Nikkei. Congress passed Public Law No. 503, which made it a crime to disobey exclusion orders from a military area, on March 21, the same day the organizational meeting was held in Berkeley. On the heels of congressional approval for mass evacuation, the military tightened restrictions on Nikkei. Public Proclamation No. 3, described by the historian Roger Daniels as creating "the closest thing to a police state ever seen in the United States," applied curfew and travel regulations to Nikkei in Military Area No. 1 and all other prohibited areas.[39] Public Proclamation No. 4 froze all Nikkei in Military Area No. 1 as of midnight March 29. Civilian Exclusion Order No. 1 began a systematic program of exile and incarceration on March 24 by ordering the removal of the Bainbridge Island Nikkei. Karl Bendetsen, director of the WCCA, oversaw this move.

Eisenhower, the WRA's reluctant director, initially hoped to resettle many, if not most, of the Nikkei from the camps quickly. A meeting in Salt Lake City with governors from ten western states on April 7, however, dashed these plans. The western governors refused to cooperate with a program of quick resettlement, forcing Eisenhower instead to establish semipermanent concentration camps.

The military completed evacuation of Military Area No. 1 by June 7 and of Military Area No. 2 by August 7. The inmates were first moved to what were euphemistically termed *assembly centers*, temporary WCCA camps, and then to relocation centers under WRA control. The WCCA's jurisdiction over Nikkei ended on November 3 when the last assembly center inmates arrived at the WRA camp in Jerome, Arkansas.[40]

The committee's April 1942 agenda and actions in the face of increasing military restrictions provided the basic strategy for student resettlement throughout the war. Actively working with Nikkei students, the committee's representatives learned of which students were interested in continuing their studies and of their financial situations. The representatives also attempted to arrange ways for students to receive credit for their interrupted studies. In addition, the committee initially approached foundations, churches, and the government (through the WRA and the commissioner of education) and later schools, YMCAs and YWCAs, and students in an attempt to raise the necessary funds for students to continue their college educations. The committee also investigated possibilities for jobs providing room and board in receiving communities. Additionally, Conard and his colleagues wanted to create sympathy for and understanding of the Nikkei situation in colleges and communities where resettled students would later arrive. A final objective was to serve as a clearinghouse for student resettlement information to prevent any duplication of effort.[41] As the obstacles facing student resettlement were better understood and it became clear that student resettlement would not be completed quickly (and certainly not by the opening of the fall 1942 term for the vast majority of the students), the committee began to collect more extensive data pertaining to potential students. In addition to desire and financial need, the academic records of students were investigated in case only limited numbers be able to leave the camps.[42]

Besides creating a basic strategy for future student resettlement efforts, the committee developed practical tactics that were later adopted by the council. It urged those interested in its program to coordinate the activities of local groups and to get the student resettlement questionnaire filled out even if the local college would not accept Nikkei students. The committee suggested that local colleges and communities be informed about exile and incarceration and argued that facts, not speaking simply from sentiment, would most effectively clear the way to student resettlement. The awarding of scholarships and fellowships to Nikkei students was suggested because the Nikkei community's funds had been largely frozen by the government. Donations to the World Student Service Fund (WSSF), an organization dedicated to aiding students and professors victimized by war, were encouraged as one means of contributing to scholarships for Nikkei. Finally, the committee suggested meeting the students as they arrived at the train station so "that they feel . . . welcome at first, when they are lonely and unaccustomed to their new home. It is also important . . . to continue friendship after the first days and weeks."[43]

Work on this ambitious agenda did not begin until April 1, when Conard set out to coordinate the activities of the various groups involved in student resettlement. This formidable job required coordinating the activities of such diverse groups as the Japanese American Citizens League (JACL), the Japanese YMCA, the Buddhist Churches of America, the Student YMCAs and YWCAs, the NICC, the WSSF, International Student Services, and others. Conard also had to work especially closely with three important groups: the students, the colleges, and the government.

Two weeks after active student resettlement efforts began, Conard reported that his "office has been used a great deal as an information center for inquiring Japanese students in this area. This takes a considerable amount of time, as each interview is likely to require about ten minutes. The spiritual value of showing interest well justifies the time, however, quite aside from the actual help given."[44]

The Pacific Northwest office pioneered the use of student questionnaires to facilitate placement. However, Conard noted that even the use of this helpful tool did not provide the full picture of the needs for student resettlement because they did not reach graduating high school seniors. "Our program," the executive secretary argued, "must include these persons also."[45]

The committee resettled its first four students, two of them graduating high school seniors, at Iowa's Grinnell College, a private school with a strong reputation for social work. The college happily cooperated, viewing accepting Nikkei as an act of service during a time of crisis. Conveniently, Conard's uncle, Henry Conard, served as dean of faculty there. Barbara Takahashi and Akiko Hosoi, ranked first and fifth in their class at Roosevelt High School in Los Angeles, had arrived with William Kiyasu from the University of California and Hisaji Sakai of San Francisco by May 9. They were met by a contingent of Grinnell administrators and students. Henry Conard wrote his nephew that the students had been received in a "most cordial [manner]. I could even say there is great enthusiasm. We all expect to settle down to the routine of life as soon as possible."

Grinnell admitted fifteen Nikkei students during the war. Although many Grinnell students welcomed the resettled students, the Nikkei had mixed memories of their college years. Takahashi appreciated Grinnell's spirit but almost left after her junior year. She stayed to graduate, however, because other resettled students had left, and she "didn't think it would be nice since [Grinnell had been] so nice." Another resettled student struggled to fit in at Grinnell. Although he praised the "goodness and charity" of Grinnell, he felt "almost but not quite, a part of the College family."[46]

Approximately 75 Nikkei students were placed, if not yet resettled, by early May. Robert W. O'Brien was especially successful in early student resettlement efforts. With his help both before and after the creation of the committee, 58 of the 458 Nisei students at his university had transferred prior to being evacuated.[47] While the efforts of the University of California in lobbying the federal government to create a program of student resettlement were important, O'Brien's efforts were immediately meaningful: he and his colleagues produced concrete results in the present instead of abstract hopes for the future.

In working with colleges and universities, Conard stressed the importance of clear and open communication. He informed the West Coast colleges of his organization with a form letter that explained the confusing situation that confronted Nikkei students. The letter implied federal support for his program by reporting that "government officials are keenly anxious to do what they can to make it possible for these future leaders to carry on their education. Various plans [including establishing colleges in the camps, extension courses, and student resettlement] have been developed and are being considered."[48]

The committee also began to communicate with colleges located outside the West Coast in an attempt to ensure that these schools would accept Nikkei transfers. Representatives also attended various conferences, including the State Department Conference of Advisors of Foreign Students in April 1942.[49] O'Brien attended the State Department meeting and raised the issue of Nisei student resettlement. Although Nisei were not foreigners, the participants worried about the effect of discrimination in the United States on Latin America as well as its potential use in Axis propaganda. The group agreed that exile and incarceration had been the result of political and economic factors "in a strained racial relationship" as well as military necessity. The session called for a collaborative program that avoided concentrating too many Nisei students in too few colleges.[50]

Dick Mills reported in mid-April that "[m]ost" Midwestern colleges had responded favorably to appeals to help Nikkei students. However, some college administrators wanted a statement certifying an individual student's loyalty before they would accept Nikkei. Mills pointed out the difficulty raised by this request: usually a person's loyalty was not questioned until that person's actions suggested disloyalty. At best, Mills observed, an agency might certify "normal behavior" but never "inner convictions."

Mills realized that college participation was only one part of the battle, however; community attitudes in college locales had to be considered, too. These attitudes presented a difficult problem, especially because some communities were "constantly agitated by the press with stories designed to excite."[51] The committee published newsletters to present information and to urge coordination in combating negative attitudes.

Conard hoped that other groups working in student resettlement, including the Western College Association, the University of California, administrators at several eastern colleges working through the AFSC, and various eastern organizations working to raise money, would approve the committee's program for student resettlement. He believed that the plans presented by these groups generally fit well within his organization's more inclusive program. Conard envisioned the AFSC, church groups, and the Student Christian Movement eventually replacing the committee in the job of preparing community and college attitudes for the arrival of Nikkei students.[52]

A working relationship with the government also had to be established.

Conard did not approach the WRA until April 24 because he wanted to have an organization in place with a unified plan before presenting Eisenhower's agency with a program. Then he wrote Lester Ade of the WRA to apprise him of the committee and its activities and to showcase it as the logical choice to oversee student resettlement.[53]

As the grassroots movement to resettle students gained momentum, appeals for help continued to be made to the government. Mike Masaoka of the JACL had asked Milton Eisenhower for a program of student resettlement in an April 6 letter. He stressed the importance of federal aid to the students. Such a program, Masaoka argued, would boost Nikkei morale and prepare the ethnic community for its future in the United States after the war.[54]

President Sproul of the University of California also asserted himself in April, at the urging of Taylor and perhaps Deutsch, by forwarding a plan for student resettlement first to Representative John H. Tolan, a Democrat from California and chair of the United States House Select Committee Investigating National Defense Migration, and then to President Roosevelt and Vice President Henry A. Wallace.[55] Sproul did not challenge exile and incarceration but pointed out that the program required great sacrifices on the part of loyal Nikkei. Although they had demonstrated almost "universal goodwill" in cooperating, Sproul argued, Nikkei "would not be human if there was not some sense of injustice and resentment in the hearts of those who know they are loyal to the United States and to Democracy."

Nikkei students, Sproul suggested, constituted an important group among the evacuees because they represented the future leaders of their community. A program of student resettlement would reinforce the loyalty of the students and convince them "of the justice of the democracy in which they live."[56] Sproul argued that the "problem" of Nikkei students could best be met by a generous program that granted "[f]ederal scholarships for all collegiate grade students subject to evacuation orders who are desirous of continuing their educations." A committee of college and university representatives, Sproul suggested, should administer this program.

Sproul estimated the total cost of such a program at more than one million dollars annually, a worthwhile investment, he believed, in "the future welfare of the American Nation. . . . Respect and love for democracy cannot be inculcated by depriving citizens of their rights and privileges without compensation, regardless of abstract or concrete justifications which may exist in the public mind." Representative Tolan was so impressed with Sproul's proposal that he publicly endorsed the Berkeley president to chair such an agency if one were formed.[57]

Public officials had begun to discuss student resettlement by this time. On

April 4, a meeting called by Geoffrey May, the assistant director of Defense Health and Welfare, was held. Representatives of the Office of Education and the Social Security Board attended. May pointed out two key obstacles to student resettlement: providing sufficient surveillance of the students (to protect, he argued, both the students and the public interest) and locating private employment opportunities. He did not envision the government providing much, if any, financial aid to evacuated students. May noted that his office might be able to provide some funding for transportation, but even this limited assistance would be available only to citizens. Dr. Fred Kelly, chief of the Division of Higher Education of the Office of Education, believed that most college communities would be receptive if proper financial and other arrangements were made.[58]

The WCCA had also taken an interest in student resettlement, after a joint planning meeting with the WRA on April 11. Lieutenant Colonel William F. Boekel questioned which students should be allowed to transfer. He noted that students already permitted to resettle had been required to furnish basic biographical data (such as their name, age, and sex) as well as evidence that a college requested their presence (as opposed to merely agreeing to accept the student), that they were financially self-sufficient, and that the local community did not object to the student's presence there. Boekel wondered if additional restrictions ought to be placed on students. In particular, he asked if student resettlement should be limited to juniors, seniors, and perhaps good junior-college students who demonstrated a "tempermental [sic] fitness for specialized or vocational work." Whatever the decision, Boekel argued that the military and the WRA needed to jointly establish "controlling principles . . . for release of students with exceptional qualifications."[59]

The Student Relocation Council

Planning at the national level for government-sanctioned student resettlement quickly overtook the Student Relocation Committee's program and moved rapidly toward the creation of a quasi-governmental organization. The new body, called the National Japanese American Student Relocation Council, co-opted the committee, but not without conflict and turmoil.

By the end of April, Eisenhower, aware of the pleas from Taylor, Coffey, Masaoka, Sproul, and Conard to help Nikkei students, had begun working to establish a government-sanctioned student resettlement organization. He discussed the matter with members of Congress, college officials, and others to determine the best approach "in the face of possible widespread public misunderstanding."[60] Eisenhower's search for someone to lead a student resettlement organization proved frustrating, as he found himself caught between American Council on Education president George F. Zook and U.S. Commissioner of Education John Studebaker. Zook had written Eisenhower in early April to extend his organization's help in dealing with Nikkei students, offering to undertake the formation of a student resettlement committee and envisioning Sproul as its chair. Studebaker preferred Haverford President Felix Morely as the chair of the proposed committee. Apparently Eisenhower approached Zook with an offer to chair the government-approved effort; Zook declined but did express a willingness to serve on such a committee.[61]

Eisenhower eventually turned to a third candidate, Clarence Pickett, to head the student committee. Pickett had risen to prominence as a Quaker in 1919 when he became secretary of the American Young Friends Movement. After studying at Harvard, Pickett became a professor of biblical literature at Earlham College in 1923. He served as executive secretary of the AFSC between 1929 and 1950, directing its programs on relief and reconstruction, peace education, and race relations. He had personal ties to Roosevelt, to whom he reported about his trips to Europe in the 1930s, and Eleanor Roosevelt, who had accompanied him on a tour of West Virginia coal-mining villages in 1933.[62] Eisenhower chose Pickett, he explained in early May to John Provinse, chief of the WRA's Community Management Division, "after encountering a hopeless bureaucracy in the region of the Office of Education and the American Council on Education."[63]

The AFSC was a logical choice to head the new organization. Pickett had been apprised of the West Coast situation through reports from a number of Quakers on the scene including Conard. Some AFSC workers, such as Conard and Bodine, had been involved in student resettlement from its earliest stages. In addition, the AFSC had begun to act in April through the efforts of Morely, President John W. Nason of Swarthmore College, and Dr. Frank Aydelotte of the Institute of Advanced Studies at Princeton. Although these Quakers had not formulated specific plans, Cary hoped that forthcoming actions would "ameliorate for the future."[64]

As this small effort progressed in the East, the AFSC remained cautious. Cary urged delaying the contacting of colleges until questions about funding and government attitudes toward the release of students were answered. The AFSC knew about Professor Taylor's proposal, and Pickett agreed that the government, if possible, should award scholarships. The Quakers were also cognizant of the need to coordinate eastern and western committees already working on student relocation. As it became more involved in the debate about who should head the WRA-sanctioned student relocation agency, the AFSC leadership viewed Haverford's Morely as the ideal chair, believing that Sproul would not want the job.[65] Although it was likely correct in assessing Sproul, working with an eastern Quaker probably also appealed to the AFSC.

Eisenhower wrote Pickett that the AFSC could "make a significant contribution to the program of the [WRA]" and officially asked it to assume the work of student resettlement on May 5. Noting that no higher education would take place in the camps and the government would not undertake such a program itself, Eisenhower asked Pickett to establish a committee that would formulate a program for student resettlement and then oversee its implementation. He pledged government help in the process of student selection and certification as well as in the payment of transportation costs. Pickett's committee would cultivate receptiveness in college communities and raise nonfederal funds to support the resettled students.[66]

Eisenhower elaborated on his vision for the student resettlement program in a letter to Sproul the next day. He believed that most of the initiative and effort would have to come from private sources. The WRA might pay travel costs for students lacking financial resources, but Eisenhower stressed the need for the program to rest on private efforts. To do otherwise, he feared, would result in the program's defeat "in the face of misunderstanding and near-hostility." Eisenhower identified three parts to the program: working to create receptive attitudes in the communities students went to, finding sources of financial aid, and selecting and certifying students. Eisenhower believed student resettlement to be of greater significance than the small number involved might suggest. "If we can succeed in what we are setting out to do here," he explained, "it may signal the beginning of a new public attitude and the breaking down of restraints. Immediately it will be encouraging to all evacuees loyal to this country who until now have experienced only a restraining hand."[67]

Pickett's May 15 acceptance letter suggests the tightrope that the AFSC walked in balancing its disapproval of government actions with its desire to aid Nikkei.[68] Thanking the government for its efforts "to carry out the relocation of Japanese with due sense of regard for their welfare and eventual prosperity," Pickett hoped that student resettlement would help alleviate some Nikkei distress, prepare them "for useful membership in the American community [and] atone for the violence that has been done to the constitutional rights of American citizens." Although uncompromising about the evils of mass incarceration, the AFSC toned down this message while cooperating with the WRA. Pickett made a broad commitment to student relocation, promising that the AFSC would "go as far in it as funds and opportunities for study permit."[69]

The AFSC had begun to plan for student resettlement before Pickett accepted the job from Eisenhower, selecting Robbins W. Barstow, president of the Hartford Theological Seminary, to lead their effort.[70] The AFSC, in consultation with Eisenhower, wanted to help high school graduates and college students. It also hoped, as did the WRA, that many students who availed themselves of the program would acquire skills that were needed within the Nikkei community.[71] Pickett was also aware of what he regarded as hasty efforts to place Nikkei students in colleges away from the West Coast and worried that a number had been sent to communities "where the preparation was inadequate and have had to be sent away."[72] In April, six students had been resettled to Moscow, Idaho, but then refused admission at the University of Idaho when townspeople protested. The situation became so tense that the sheriff placed two female Nikkei students in jail under protective custody. One wrote from jail: "I feel very young and lost for once in my life. . . . The jailer was talking to someone over the telephone, and said a mob will come to lynch us tonight. . . . I'm scared." The students were eventually transferred to another state in an incident dubbed "The Retreat from Moscow."[73]

A program of student resettlement promised important social gains from the Quakers' point of view, but they were also aware that it faced considerable opposition. Pickett knew that many Americans believed Nikkei to be untrustworthy. Although Eisenhower had eased congressional objections, public sentiment would clearly be an obstacle to the AFSC's new program. The AFSC discussed plans to visit state governors and the American Legion to help remedy this problem.

The American Legion, in fact, became a tenacious opponent of student resettlement. "Certain 'patriotic' organizations that pose as chief defenders of the American way have piously mouthed the phrase while flagrantly violating its spirit," Galen Fisher observed. "This is especially true of the California American Legion, the Native Sons of the Golden West, the Eagles, and the Americanism Educational League." Prior to exile and incarceration, the California American Legion and the Native Sons had filed law suits to disenfranchise Nikkei, although the American Legion had withdrawn its suit after the Native Sons' case floundered. Still, the American Legion demanded that all Nikkei soldiers be discharged and that the military maintain control over the concentration camps. In Portland, Oregon, local legionnaires organized to prevent members of the Fellowship of Reconciliation from cleaning up a Nikkei graveyard marred by vandals. The commander of the Portland Legion Post No. 1 explained that "the legion is not going to stand for this. It's a bunch of monkey business."[74]

Despite such resistance, the AFSC approached its new task with optimism, in part because of its belief in Eisenhower's "genuine conviction" that student relocation should occur through a single channel. The director's promises to help the program by certifying students prior to release and paying transportation costs also encouraged the AFSC. The AFSC planned to meet the financial obstacles to student resettlement by appealing to a variety of organizations, including schools, church organizations, business organizations involved with Japan before the war, and foundations. The cautious AFSC estimate of the amount needed totaled only $250,000, less than one-quarter of Sproul's projection.[75]

Conard and others on his committee had concerns about the AFSC's assumption of leadership in student resettlement. They feared that the momentum created by the Student Relocation Committee would be lost as the AFSC began to organize its own program. "I know," Conard wrote to Cary, "my committee would be emphatic in saying that we have no ambitions for our own institutional immortality. If the job can be done by some one else, we have no ambition to continue work. . . . [I]f we can take a particular and small share in the task, that is also fine. But we are interested in knowing how we do fit into the new picture."[76] Although the AFSC explained that the creation of a single channel for resettlement would rationalize the process, committee members were uncertain about the future of student resettlement.

Despite apprehension about the transfer of leadership, the Student Relocation Committee supported the AFSC's efforts. Seeming to accept Cary's apology for not providing more information on developing plans, most West Coast activists generally ignored the negative to focus on the positive aspects of the AFSC's arrival. Conard expressed his excitement at the AFSC's participation: "Thee can well imagine," he wrote to Cary, "my own delight at having this important work placed in the hands of a group like ours."[77] Marian Reith, a YWCA representative and a leader in the southern California office, indicated a similar and widespread desire to cooperate. The West Coast committee also supported AFSC leadership in student relocation work.[78]

Committee members believed that the inclusion of the prestigious AFSC promised to open access to the government and to help raise money. The newcomers might not have much experience with students, but they were part of a widely respected organization and they brought much needed financial connections, especially with various foundations and institutions that seemed to be promising sources of funding. The AFSC drew support from West Coast student resettlement workers by making fund-raising a priority. Since Conard and his committee had adopted Sproul's estimate of a one million dollar need, the inclusion of the AFSC, despite its lower estimate of the total need, provided hope that at least some of the necessary money might be raised.[79]

The AFSC strove to establish a working relationship with student resettlement workers. W. O. Mendenhall, president of Whittier College and a member of the West Coast committee, wrote Cary and suggested that the Student Relocation Committee's data on students, the Western College Association's list of colleges, and the AFSC's contacts with Eisenhower might be combined to further student resettlement. Although Cary and the AFSC did not commit to any organizational framework at this point, they included Conard in the planning process.[80]

Despite his willingness to embrace AFSC participation, Conard warned that it must not alienate other groups already involved in student resettlement. He pointed out that some of these groups would question the AFSC working with college students when others clearly had more experience. Cary acknowledged this advice, writing, "we do not have any wide knowledge of the problems in the college world and it is our intention to coopt others who do."[81]

The AFSC immediately attempted, with uneven success, to foster cooperation with a wide range of groups, especially West Coast organizations. Tensions became so serious in some cases, especially with leaders of the Student Christian Association who thought that Conard had been overlooked as the logical leader of the AFSC effort in student resettlement, that Barstow offered to resign on May 16 "if this little friction about our taking over is really going to hinder the work. . . . I am greatly embarrassed to find myself in the middle of a squabble."[82] Although the AFSC stressed its desire to create an organization that allowed groups to work within the framework established by the WRA, this attitude did not mollify everybody.[83]

The AFSC was aware of any number of issues, many already much discussed, that needed attention: managing public opinion, financing the program, establishing policies and procedures, and determining the requirements for a student to be granted release from the camps. It found its already-complex planning complicated by the hastily assembled WRA staff that forwarded additional proposals. Lucy Adams, regional education director for the WRA, proposed establishing college education in the camps themselves, especially for students in the first two years of school, despite Eisenhower's statement to Pickett on May 5 that camps would not provide higher education. She presented the now-familiar argument that such a program was essential because college students represented the future leaders of the ethnic community. Adams forwarded her proposal to Eisenhower on

May 22, noting that some West Coast faculty supported it and warning that Deutsch had remarked that the government did not seem overly interested in student resettlement and had even suggested "that a good many of the college people felt that the government was merely giving a hearing to clamorous college presidents and committees."[84] Adams urged her superiors to present her plan in conjunction with a plan to resettle students. Provinse shared Adams's plan with Pickett but argued that, among other things, it would serve to intensify the isolation of Nikkei.[85]

In late April, California Governor Culbert E. Olson had sent President Roosevelt a letter, which may have been written by Sproul, that noted the problems faced by Nikkei students. Eisenhower later credited Olson's letter with helping the President gain "an insight to the human problem that, had it come in February rather than May, might have prompted him to decide against mass evacuation."[86] Roger Daniels has argued, however, that Eisenhower misread the president. He points out that Roosevelt urged Stimson to "be as reasonable as you can" in implementing a program of mass exile and incarceration and then allowed amelioration once it was implemented. Olson's letter provoked debate that lasted about two weeks. According to Deutsch, the presidential adviser Harry Hopkins argued strongly for student resettlement. Students, Roosevelt believed, provided the safest start to moving Nikkei out of the camps. On May 18, 1942, Roosevelt promised opportunities for "qualified American-born Japanese students" to continue their higher education by fall 1942.[87]

The AFSC and the WRA also sought an endorsement from the War Department. Eisenhower explained the program to Assistant Secretary of War John J. McCloy[88] and argued that it would provide an important symbol of "the tolerance of democracy at war" as well as a boost to Nikkei morale.[89] Just three days later, McCloy, with Roosevelt's approval in hand, endorsed "a properly conceived and carefully executed program" of student relocation and reported his pleasure with AFSC involvement. "Anything," he wrote, "that can legitimately be done to compensate loyal citizens of Japanese ancestry for the dislocation to which they have been subjected, by reason of military necessity, has our full approval."[90] As will be seen, however, approval at the top did not quickly translate into cooperation lower in the military hierarchy.

Support for student resettlement came from Eleanor Roosevelt in midMay. The first lady pointed out: "these young [Japanese American] people are Americans and they are being denied an education. As far as we know, they are loyal Americans, but for reasons of safety, they must go from the areas where there might be sabotage or where they might be accused of sabotage rightly or wrongly. But they are still American citizens. . . . We are not asking colleges to take aliens or refugees, but refugees from our own coast to the interior."[91]

Even as these endorsements arrived, tensions mounted as an organizational meeting planned for May 29 in Chicago approached. Concerned about the AFSC's lack of experience with and firsthand knowledge of the student situation, Bodine argued that many West Coast groups believed "that it was more important in some ways that West Coast Administration people like Bob O'Brien who have been working on the problem almost full time for the last three months should be present than that East Coast people be there, because O'Brien can ask Eisenhower questions which grow straight out of experience, whereas the East Coast people can merely express their willingness to take some students in."[92]

Barstow acknowledged that tensions continued to exist between the strident West Coast workers and the more cautious East Coast administrators even after the organizational meeting, noting that some individuals did not think him knowledgeable enough about the West Coast situation as "a mere Connecticut Yankee."[93] Some West Coast student resettlement advocates had begun to view the WRA as the enemy in the battle over student relocation and its broader implications. Bodine, for example, wanted student resettlement to serve as a lever to open the way for broader Nikkei resettlement. He also argued that WRA publications did not support even a modest plan for student resettlement; instead, he believed that the WRA suggested "that the only place for Japanese people these days is behind barbed wire."[94] This combative perspective did not always mesh with the AFSC's cooperative relationship with the WRA.[95]

Invitations to the May 29 meeting at the Stevens Hotel in Chicago were mailed to representatives of church organizations, the YMCA and YWCA, civilian but not military government agencies, the AFSC, and the JACL, despite Eisenhower's previous correspondence with Sproul and McCloy that had suggested that only educators would be invited (for a list of attendees, see appendix 1). Thirty-three men and thirteen women attended. Twenty-seven represented Protestant church organizations, and the AFSC sent eight delegates. Only seven educators attended. Four representatives of the federal government (including one representative from the WRA, one from the Office of Education, and two from the Tolan Committee) also were present. Seven represented other interested organizations. Mike Masaoka of the JACL was the only Nikkei at the meeting.[96]

The May 29 meeting began with the WRA's John Provinse stressing the temporary nature of exile and incarceration and noting the full support of the government and especially the WRA for student relocation. Provinse reiterated Eisenhower's promise to pay transportation costs for the students. Conard then reviewed his committee's survey of the 2,300 students facing evacuation, emphasizing that funds had to be raised and that many students would need part-time employment. He pointed out that students had to be selected and matched with colleges. The loyalty of each student would also have to be certified. Conard emphasized the importance of educating institutions outside of the evacuation zone about exile and incarceration as well as "the obligation America has to these people who have born the brunt of this war measure."[97] Local communities, he added, would have to be prepared for the arrival of Nikkei students. High school graduates were to be given the opportunity to continue their education, too.

Conard reported that while seventy colleges had agreed to cooperate, one hundred had already said they would not. The results of the committee's survey of colleges suggested that the larger universities were less willing to accept Nikkei, a potential problem since these schools were better equipped to train students in popular courses of study such as medicine and engineering. Private colleges, especially those with a religious mission, were more likely to accept Nikkei students because they did not rely on state funding and were less likely to house military research.

Although Provinse, who later mediated between the council and the WRA, was initially surprised at the small number of educators present at the meeting, he quickly realized that "the church, missionary, and charitable student organizations . . . will . . . finance most of the student relocation. Furthermore, it appears we will find among the smaller religious and denominational institutions greater acceptance of the Japanese than seems to be the case among the larger institutions of learning." Provinse praised the WRA's practical reasons for selecting Pickett by observing that "although the Coast universities are interested in a rather paternalistic way in the Japanese students, they are not equipped to furnish funds, and I think would be more concerned with bringing pressure upon the Government to provide all the financing for these students."[98]

The participants decided that students would be selected on several criteria, all components of the ambassador of goodwill persona. Loyalty represented an obvious and primary qualification. Students would also be chosen on the basis of academic achievement and ability to be an "outstanding representative of the Japanese people." The participants viewed both qualities as "equally important in disseminating better attitudes toward the Japanese race."[99]

The topic of student nurses was on the agenda but apparently not discussed because other topics filled the time. However, the new agency assumed the job of placing student nurses as a staff worker was assigned to work exclusively with such students by July 1942.[100]

The new student resettlement organization consisted of two components. The West Coast office, essentially the renamed Student Relocation Committee, had the task of collecting data, selecting the students to be resettled, and securing releases for them. Conard led the West Coast office, which now had to clear its policies through the national office in Philadelphia. The eastern subcommittee would contact colleges, raise funds, and ensure positive receptions for resettled Nikkei students. "The work of interpretation," the digest of points asserted, "must continue. The Japanese student himself should have a part in this, but it shouldn't be over done. He should fit into the community in as natural a way as possible."[101]

A national executive committee, with representatives from the different organizations involved in student resettlement, was also to be established. This committee had responsibility for setting policy and acting as liaison with the government. The AFSC would have an important place on this committee but not "exclusive membership."[102]

Those present at the meeting envisioned funding coming from a number of sources, including the resettled students, the Nikkei community, college scholarships, national community chests, church boards, and student organizations. The AFSC expressed a willingness to administer these funds for groups not wanting to do so on their own.[103]

A "Saturday group" consisting of Barstow, Provinse, the assistant commissioner of education Bess Goodykoontz, O'Brien, Conard, Reith, Masaoka, and Naomi Binford and Marnie Schauffler of the AFSC met on May 30 and decided on a name for the agency, the National Student Relocation Council. The council, the group stressed, should be a vehicle through which "the AFSC cooperates with other already interested groups to get the job done. The Council would consist of all the individuals and organizational representatives who should be pulled in." This decision represented an attempt to mollify groups that resented the selection of the AFSC to head student resettlement. The Saturday group also attempted to allay the uneasiness of West Coast advocates by stressing "that no Service Committee person should state that evacuation was necessary, unavoidable or justified. [Conard and O'Brien] feel that it wasn't . . . and while they avoid the issue wherever possible as it's obviously a 'fait accompli' . . . they feel that most liberal West Coast people do *not* think it was necessary and would feel very badly if AFSC spokesmen gave the impression that it was" [emphasis in original].[104]

The Chicago meeting established a general organizational framework and an agenda for the council, in the process generating a renewed and broadened enthusiasm for student resettlement as well as increased hopes that progress, so slow to that point, would soon result. Student interest in resettlement fueled these hopes further. Despite this optimism, the newly formed council remained aware of many obstacles that would have to be overcome before student resettlement could occur smoothly and in large numbers. These external obstacles, in addition to internal council tensions that continued to simmer despite the Saturday group's attempt to dampen them, would make for a long and often frustrating first summer of student resettlement.

LIVING IN HOPE AND WORKING ON FAITH,
SUMMER 1942

Commencement exercises at the Santa Anita Assembly Center in June 1942 highlighted the incongruent circumstances of the incarcerated students. The ceremony, held in a concentration camp because of the presumed disloyalty of the inmates, began with the national anthem. More than 250 students from thirty-four different colleges, junior colleges, high schools, and junior high schools then received diplomas. The graduates were congratulated "for receiving their diplomas under such trying circumstances" and urged to use their "education for the building of a better world." The *Santa Anita Pacemaker*'s front-page coverage included a cartoon of a Nikkei student on a boat using his diploma as a sail to catch the wind and move forward.[1] By this time, the council had begun to establish a presence in the camps that provided hope for the educational future of the Nikkei.

Lillian Ota, at the Tanforan Assembly Center, did not wait for the council to offer help; instead, the Berkeley junior began approaching colleges independently and contacting people who might be able to help her resettle.[2] After securing admission to Wellesley College with a full scholarship, the honor student wrote the University of California provost Monroe Deutsch, the Student Relocation Committee executive secretary Joseph Conard, and the YWCA general secretary Leila Anderson in May 1942 for advice on how to get out of camp.

Despite her initiative, Ota remained in camp and unsure of her future in early July. After Conard worked to secure her release and smoothed out financial concerns, the WCCA issued a travel permit on August 21, and Ota arrived at college before the end of the month. She wrote to thank Conard and described Wellesley as "a beautiful place [where] everyone is so friendly and intent on making me feel at home. And the people on the train were very nice too."[3] Ota recalled one unpleasant episode in which a student accused Nikkei of sabotage and espionage. Ota wrote: "[I] argued against the misconception in the best way I could, but didn't finish my spiel as I had to return to my dormitory before lockout time. Later I sent her a copy of the *Pacific Citizen*. She then acknowledged she had been wrong."[4]

The council viewed Ota, who went on to earn a doctoral degree from Yale, as an ambassador of goodwill whose success would promote its program to the wider American public, college officials, and Nikkei students and their parents.[5] Frank Inouye, a resettled student who returned to Heart Mountain to work for the council in summer 1944, cited Ota as one example of the resettled students who had "been the first to take advantage of any method allowing escape into the stream of life outside. . . . Like Julius Caesar in Gaul, the [Nisei] went, they saw, and they conquered."[6]

Students lacking Ota's academic brilliance were not necessarily disqualified as ambassadors of goodwill. Although a University of California administrator described George Tamaki's grades as "inferior compared to the average of students of his own race or of others in the University," other factors made Tamaki an attractive candidate to the council.[7] His grades had improved, providing evidence of his ability to succeed academically. Perhaps more importantly, Tamaki received praise for his ability to both lead and work cooperatively. "Of all the Japanese American students I have known," Reverend Arthur W. Felkley wrote, "he is one of the best to mingle with other students. . . . He is quite refined [and] the type of student we should release to eastern and midwestern colleges. He has abilities as a mixer and as a student. He has polish and good sense." After Reverend W. Carl Nugent, one of Tamaki's references, made contact with J. J. Braun, the general secretary of the Board of National Missions of the Evangelical and Reformed Church, and received assurances of financial aid should it be needed, Tamaki obtained a travel permit in early September and arrived at Heidelberg College in Tiffin, Ohio, on September 17, 1942. Upon his arrival, Tamaki was greeted by Dr. Clarence E. Josephson, the president of Heidelberg, and two students. "The school is swell," he reported to Conard, "and the students are extra swell." Tamaki quickly decided, however, that Heidelberg did not meet his needs for more specialized training and contacted the council about alternatives. He decided on Boston University, and the council initiated a new application process for him. He was in Boston by September 1943.[8]

While the successful migrations of students like Ota and Tamaki added to the optimism that had been generated by the Chicago meeting, a variety of difficulties kept the pace of student resettlement slow in summer 1942. Internally, the council had to organize and finance its work. Different tactical notions held by the council's East and West Coast offices also had to be reconciled. Externally, struggles with the WCCA, the WRA, and the War Department to create a process for student relocation resulted in slow progress. Faced with limited time, funds, and openings, the council focused its efforts on students, like Ota, who would excel as ambassadors of goodwill and open the way for additional students to resettle in the future. The council resettled 360 students by the fall 1942 semester.[9] This meant that many students, although eager to leave, had to remain in the camps. Until internal and external obstacles were overcome, the council, in the words of its national director Robbins W. Barstow, would "continue to live in hope and work on faith."[10]

Tensions in Organizing and Financing the Council

The Chicago meeting had created offices for the council that were three thousand miles apart. Although Barstow was nominally the national director, his limited vision of his responsibilities enabled the westerners to work largely on their own, which, in turn, encouraged Conard and his colleagues to develop a sense of independence.[11] This independence, in conjunction with both a nascent spirit of crusading to right a wrong and an office atmosphere based on the Friendly Way of conferencing and prayerful meditation at the beginning of each day, at times conflicted with the more pragmatic and cooperative approach of the East Coast office. Rapid turnover at the top plagued the council and reinforced this sense of West Coast independence.[12] Executive turnover combined with other factors to produce inherent conflict that never entirely disappeared.

Exhaustion exacerbated these tensions. Trudy King's[13] account of a day in the West Coast office reveals the all-consuming nature of the work: "One wakes up dreaming that he has dictated letters all night to students with complicated names and with numerous problems. None have enough money or if they do they have no college to go to." Following a morning staff conference, King corresponded with the government, colleges, and students, and the occasional unscheduled visitor was the only break from piles of paperwork. Although King ends her account at five o'clock, many on the staff, King included, often worked late into the night.[14] Howard K. Beale described workdays that rivaled King's; his typical day included working from eight o'clock in the morning until seven or eight o'clock at night, "taking a couple of hours out for a leisurely dinner and a walk or a ride on the funny little cable cars, and then working another two or three hours before late bedtime."[15]

King suggested the consequences of exhaustion: "When people are tired,

39

when they work late hours and their nerves are on edge, one realizes anew the difficulty of personality problems."[16] Although the crusading spirit of the office helped King and others endure exhaustion, the combination of these two factors exacerbated confrontations between the West Coast office and government agencies as well as within the council.

Barstow's report on his trip to the West Coast in mid-June suggests his awareness of the delicate state of relations between the eastern and western offices. In addition to conferring with WCCA and WRA officials, Barstow went out of his way to talk with many "active members of the West Coast staff." He approvingly noted "a common feeling of urgency" that resulted from personal contacts with the students. In addition to implying his shared sense of urgency, a point on which Barstow's caution often brought criticism from the West Coast office, he expressly praised its staffers for handling enormous amounts of paperwork, creating an efficient filing system, and deftly handling the difficult job of maintaining contacts with the government.[17]

Barstow's report to the Executive Committee in early August, however, probably treated the military more gently than the West Coast office wished. "We are trying to be generous and fair in our judgments," Barstow noted, "and must acknowledge that the War Department has such a stupendous undertaking on its hands to help win the war that the educational plans of a few hundred young people of Japanese ancestry [sic] seems comparatively inconsequential." West Coast workers likely disagreed with Barstow's willingness to excuse the military's lethargy and his use of the word inconsequential, even as modified. Furthermore, his support for the WRA, which he described as attempting in all ways to expedite student resettlement, did not fit with the West Coast experiences, where the cautious approach of the WRA in imitating WCCA policies and urging caution had been found limiting. Barstow's defensive declaration that "[i]t has not all been passive waiting" probably reflected his awareness that some people on the West Coast thought that it had in fact been so.[18]

Conard's letter to Barstow dated July 31 suggested palpable tensions within the council. Conard described the East Coast office's attempts to secure a list of approved colleges as "failures."[19] Barstow, responding, apologized to Conard for delays in student placements, fixing blame on the army's and navy's "exceedingly cautious . . . policies" and "so very meticulous . . . interdepartmental conferences and clearances."[20] Barstow's excuses received little sympathy from the West Coast office.

King expressed the frustrations of the West Coast office to Marnie Schauffler, an associate secretary of the AFSC, in mid-August. "Before I start," King conceded, "I'll tell you that I fully realize that one of the problems in work in the field is that the field office always thinks that the main office does not understand it and that the main office feels the same way about the field but at present I am just about to explode." King criticized Barstow for naively expecting unlikely progress. She railed against Barstow's predilection for slowing the council's work because the fall term would soon begin and the military moved slowly. "No matter what he says," King promised, "I'll be in here fighting tooth and nail to get the necessary things and none of us will slow down."

Barstow's cautious approach to raising funds also upset King. "Barstow thinks in terms of something small," King argued, "and does not seem to grasp that we are dealing with [two thousand] students and their future and this will not taper off in a fortnight." Furthermore, reports indicated that Barstow had raised only $40,000 for scholarships, obviously well short of the Executive Committee's relatively modest goal of $300,000 (westerners wanted at least $500,000). King also believed Barstow had failed to take full advantage of churches' offers. Barstow had accepted $10,000 from the American Baptist Home Mission Society (ABHMS), but John Thomas, the secretary for the Department of Cities, told King that the ABHMS was willing to give more. "John is helping us in every way possible and this Baptist grant has cheered us," King observed, "but why wasn't Barstow on the ball and why didn't he get the larger sum?"

King expressed the depth of her worry, emphasizing that "this is not just the feeling of tonight, but it has been growing. . . . [T]his is a major concern of mine for what Barstow is up to." Bodine's handwritten note at the end of King's letter demonstrated that King's feelings were not isolated. "It is our feeling," he wrote, "that all in all the AFSC has flopped pretty badly in this student job."[21]

Despite east–west tensions, the departments of the council began to function. The records department received questionnaires and then requested transcripts and references. The questionnaires showed that 90 percent of the students applying in summer and fall 1942 wanted to continue their education immediately, while 10 percent desired to continue their studies at some time in the future. Of the applicants, 23 percent were high school students, 87 percent of whom had earned either A or B averages. Undergraduates, half of whom had maintained a B average or better in college, represented 67 percent of the applicants. More than 50 percent of the undergraduates had completed fewer than two full years of college. Graduate students constituted 10 percent of the group. Male applicants outnumbered female applicants by two to one. Of the applicants, 72 percent were Christians (69 percent Protestant, 3 percent Catholic), 17 percent were Buddhists, and 11 percent listed no religious affiliation. The medical sciences, engineering, and general science were popular and much sought after courses of study. The applications suggested that about 75 percent of all the students would need financial aid.[22]

Once student data was assembled, a committee of college deans and registrars analyzed the information and ranked students by "scholastic and all-around abilities." Conard recommended a system for ranking students on the basis of transcripts and letters of reference. After "preliminary sifting" placed students with A and B averages as well as students with C averages who could pay their own way or who had extenuating circumstances in a pool to be ranked, two referees, usually West Coast college registrars or administrators, independently examined each file. A third reviewer settled cases about which the first two disagreed. Interviews were to be held only when necessary to make an accurate rating. Conard admitted that no plan for rating could be "really adequate and certainly that our's is not" but hoped that the regional offices would use it.[23]

The system employed by the council rated students in two areas: scholarship, which Gary Okihiro has noted "was reduced to grade-point average," and ambassadorship, defined as "the sum-total of all the elements that enter into personality and adaptability and general promise where not related to scholastic ability." Conard stressed the ability to make a good initial impression and "to wear well over a period of time" as well as maturity, self-reliance, and adaptability in the latter category. The composite score weighted scholarship more heavily than personality.[24]

Referees noted several problems with this system. Personality evaluations were particularly difficult to score. One referee estimated that one-fourth of her cases would require interviews. However, the West Coast steering committee had reluctantly decided by mid-August that interviews would not be held because too little time remained before the fall term opened. Furthermore, since letters of reference were frequently inadequate, the steering committee decided to rate top-ranking students (defined as those with a 2.5 or higher grade-point average out of 3) without waiting for the letters to arrive.[25]

The placement department then suggested colleges to students and recommended students to colleges. Students ranked highest by the records department received priority, but any student who had named a specific school to attend was helped. After students were accepted, the financial aid department worked to raise any money necessary. The department first looked to scholarships and part-time employment opportunities and then to outside donors if necessary. The leave department negotiated an indefinite leave first with the WCCA and then with the WRA after a student had been accepted and helped financially.[26]

The council also faced serious fund-raising problems. Denied federal funds, except for promised but undelivered travel aid, the council scrambled to finance its program with grants and donations from private sources. The national chair John W. Nason and Barstow cautiously argued that "it [was] very unwise to make any extensive appeals for funds . . . so long as we [were] being held up by the restrictions of the War Department and [were] uncertain whether we would be able to relocate more than a handful of students." Only in mid-October 1942 did Nason and Barstow feel sufficiently confident that larger numbers of students could be relocated and thus start sustained efforts to raise funds.[27]

The council had separate budgets for administrative and scholarship expenditures. The AFSC as well as other private individuals and organizations made contributions for the council's operating costs. A $10,000 grant from the Carnegie Corporation provided the council with early outside funding. Even with aid from such sources, however, finding sufficient funds to cover administrative costs remained a pressing problem.[28]

The council also remained very much aware of Elizabeth F. Johnson's warning that it would be "tragic" if monetary shortfalls were to keep students in the camps.[29] Conard warned that only $40,000 of an estimated need of $500,000 or more had been raised as of September 1. Although the Executive Committee estimated that only $300,000 would be needed after college scholarships and part-time employment opportunities were taken advantage of, it acknowledged that the council had raised only one-third of this reduced amount by mid-October.

The council relied heavily on churches to finance student resettlement, and many churches did provide support. Most Christian leaders and denominations responded to the government's decision for exile and incarceration with moderation, sensing racism and arguing that the Constitution should be upheld but sympathetic enough to the army's national security concerns to press only for a "humane" exile. After incarceration, most denominations tried to put a human face on the Nikkei experience and to help ameliorate their situation.[30]

Some church boards, in fact, initiated contact with the council. The Baptist John Thomas wrote the council on June 2, 1942, to report that the ABHMS could provide $5,000–$6,000 in scholarship aid and to promise additional funds if necessary. Thomas also shared the names of Baptist colleges that wanted to cooperate. "I hope that, despite all the discouragements with which you are confronted," Thomas wrote to Barstow, "you will feel able to carry on."[31] The Jewish Peace Fellowship also approached the council about contributing to its program, but the fellowship's limited budget ultimately did not allow it to contribute as an organization to the council.[32] The Foreign Missionary Society of the United Brethren in Christ wrote for information after seeing an article by Barstow in *Christian Century*.[33]

In midsummer, the council, noting its "deep regret that we have not been able to make greater progress with government agencies," asked the various churches how much money would be available so that it could begin working to place students "of superior scholarship and outstanding personality."[34] Responses to the council's pleas for scholarship aid were positive for the most part, although some church boards, especially those of smaller denominations such as the United Brethren in Christ, already had funds committed to other Nikkei projects—such as the Federal Council of Churches' Committee on Japanese Relocation and the opening of hostels—and reported that they could not support the council financially despite their approval of its program. Other mission boards, such as that of the Methodist Church, responded positively but slowly. Finally, some church boards, such as that of the Presbyterian Church, quickly established detailed processes for distributing money.[35]

Although the council recognized that most mission boards would look to help members of their own denomination first, it urged the churches not to "limit our Christian helpfulness too rigidly."[36] Responses to this appeal were mixed. The Japanese American Student Relocation Committee of the Methodist Church met in December 1942 and decided to aid Nikkei students but to make the primary focus Methodist students seeking to enter Methodist schools. Next to receive consideration would be Methodist students attending non-Methodist schools. If funds remained, Buddhist students would be aided as "a way of showing Christian attitude toward these Japanese students at this time."[37] The Presbyterians, in contrast, proved more responsive to pleas for generosity across denominational lines, providing funds to twenty-three Presbyterian and fifteen non-Presbyterian students, including Buddhists, in the fall and winter of 1942–43.[38]

The council also urged church boards to encourage their denominational colleges to accept resettled students, to provide scholarships and other forms of financial aid, and to arrange warm welcomes. The Brethren Service Committee responded, as did many others, by making contacts with its denominational colleges and arranging for scholarships. The Presbyterian Church also contacted its denominational schools but reported that, despite a desire to help, few would be able to provide financial aid.[39]

The council had accumulated scholarship funds totaling $20,500 from the church boards by mid-August, including $10,000 from the Presbyterian Church, $5,000 from the Baptist Church, $2,500 from the Evangelical and Reformed Church, $1,000 from the United Brethren Church, $1,000 from the Lutheran Church, and $1,000 from the Episcopalian Church.[40] By late January, this figure had been supplemented by new donors and increased donations from previous contributors. Still, the total amount available from church boards for scholarships had grown to only $29,000 by February.[41]

The council also relied heavily on the WSSF for scholarship support, especially because it provided aid "on an international, interracial, non-sectarian, non-political basis." The WSSF promoted student resettlement by noting that a donation of $200 would "make it possible for a relocated Japanese-American or refugee student to go to an American college."[42] A report by Wilmina Rowland, Administrative Secretary of the WSSF, also publicized the students' situation. In addition to noting government approval of student resettlement, Rowland played to a familiar council theme in praising Nikkei students as ambassadors of goodwill who would, in the words of a resettled student, "help give to my schoolmates a better understanding of the American-Japanese Nisei."[43]

Rowland had promised WSSF aid at the Chicago meeting and later pledged $10,000 for the fiscal year starting September 1. This amount would be available, she warned, only if the WSSF reached its overall fund-raising goal of $300,000. If not, the WSSF would contribute only a proportionate amount of its pledge. Furthermore, most of the WSSF money would not become available until the second semester, since most campus fund-raising efforts did not occur until then. By October, Rowland could assure the council that the full $10,000 would be available; however, she reiterated that the WSSF coffers would be empty until contributions began to arrive from the campuses.

Establishing a Process for Student Relocation

The council also had to develop a working relationship with government authorities. In particular, it needed to negotiate agreements with the WCCA, the WRA, and the War Department that established a process for student resettlement. The different philosophies of student relocation that existed within the council complicated these negotiations.

While the West Coast office's uncompromising actions sometimes raised tensions between the council and the government, the East Coast office's cautious and pragmatic approach fostered an amicable relationship. Although the intransigence of both civilian and military agencies occasionally irritated even the cooperative eastern office, the conservative, by-the-book approach of the easterners, in combination with the pressing of the West Coast office, eventually succeeded in formalizing a process for student resettlement. These negotiations produced results too late to allow many fall-term placements, but they did open the possibility for future progress.

As long as students continued to reside in assembly centers through fall 1942, the army, and especially Karl Bendetsen, presented an imposing barrier to resettlement.[44] The military, in essence, wanted to hold the students hostage, not so much to protect national security as to provide some immunity to criticism. The WCCA allowed council representatives to distribute questionnaires and interview students in its camps, but only under strict supervision. The council was permitted only one meeting in each camp to organize a Nikkei committee to distribute its questionnaires. After this meeting, council representatives were not allowed into the camps except to interview prospective students, and then only in isolation with a guard present.[45]

The council had entered into the Nineteen-Point Agreement with the WCCA for student interviews in assembly centers. The fourth point stated that "[i]ndividuals or committees of the National Student Relocation Council will make no release to the press or public in any manner, except through the Public Relations Branch of the [WCCA]."[46] Conard accepted the agreement on June 21 without qualification, essentially giving up the council's First Amendment rights. Although the WCCA clearly meant to enforce strictly all points of the agreement, the Philadelphia office, apparently unaware of the military's sensitivity, printed a buff leaflet titled "Japanese Student Relocation" without first clearing it with the WCCA.[47]

The buff leaflet described exile and incarceration as "an indiscriminate ban" on all Japanese Americans, both citizens and aliens alike. "Under the pressure of war emergency measures," the leaflet continued, "their basic civil rights have been put in jeopardy and—most serious of all—their faith in American justice and the ideals of democracy has suffered a shock, in some cases beyond remedy." The leaflet pointed out that Nikkei college students were native-born citizens raised on "American ideals" who wanted to serve the war effort and to assimilate further. Student resettlement, it argued, "represented a test of our devotion to the ideals of social justice and freedom."[48]

While both offices agreed with the message of the leaflet, their different perspectives resulted in divergent responses when the WCCA banned distribution of the leaflet in its camps and notified the council that any release of it would constitute a violation of good faith. Bendetsen bluntly warned that strict adherence to the Nineteen-Point Agreement was "necessary to [the] continued execution of the program you propose."⁴⁹ John C. Baker, the director of information for the WRA, echoed the WCCA's assessment of the buff leaflet, describing it as "a violent emotional appeal, shouting about the wrongs that are being committed, rights and privileges being taken away, grave injustices being done, etc., etc." Baker observed that "[e]vidently the tendency of the Committee [sic] is to get out of bounds as fast and as far as possible." He cautiously advised that WRA "policy . . . should be consistent with that of the WCCA for our own protection. The attitude of the Student Relocation Council is such that if no check is put on it they will make our job of public relations much more difficult."⁵⁰

A Major Beasley, an army public relations officer, presented the WCCA's position in a meeting with Homer Morris, a faculty member at Earlham and member of the AFSC, and Bodine on July 4. Although Beasley admitted, according to Bodine's account of the meeting, that the buff leaflet had the facts correct, he argued that "The inference is wrong. . . . I have an objection to your organization attempting to discredit the Army, the Secretary of War, and the President of the United States in connection with the evacuation of the Japanese."⁵¹

The WCCA wanted the council to withdraw the offending pamphlet from circulation and replace it with a WCCA-approved version. The cautious Executive Committee agreed and quickly presented a revised pamphlet to the WCCA and WRA. The new buff leaflet maintained the title but little else of the first, eliminating its predecessor's stress on civil rights for a vague discussion of the "hardship" that war created, even for "the innocent." The new leaflet also praised the WRA for creating "an approximation of normal life" in the camps.⁵²

Although Barstow occasionally referred to the WCCA's decision as censorship, he and the Executive Committee quietly acceded to WCCA demands because they understood the need to accommodate the military in order for student resettlement to continue. The West Coast workers considered the larger picture less often, however, and their agitation would not be muted. Morris and Bodine heatedly contested the banning of the original buff leaflet, not Barstow or the Executive Committee. While both offices viewed exile and incarceration as a grievous injustice, only the West Coast office vigorously protested the banning of the buff leaflet.⁵³

This controversy inhibited the council's public relations efforts. Conard reported in mid-July, "[w]e still have not lived down the buff leaflet," and Clare Brown Harris, an administrative assistant for the Southern California Student Relocation Council, warned in August that even a "minor departure [from the agreement with the WCCA] might endanger our work inestimably."[54] Barstow agreed and advised a cautious approach to public relations. The council, in fact, produced no more public relations materials until army custody ceased on November 3, 1942. Bendetsen attempted to reinforce this quiescent attitude when asked by Robert G. Sproul if the terms of the Nineteen-Point Agreement applied to WRA camps. He admitted that they did not, but he suggested, "public discussion of plans and accomplishments of your committee's work should be kept to a minimum. This feeling is based on the possibility that unfavorable public reaction might develop."[55] The chastened council, in part agreeing that publicity might backfire and increase opposition, restrained their public relations efforts for a time.[56]

A letter from Bendetsen shows the depth of the WCCA's distrust of the council. "I told you the other day," Bendetsen wrote on August 3, "that we do not trust a good many of the representatives of the National Student Relocation Council; and we don't. I told you that they were trying to mix student relocation with their own views of social reform; and they are." Bendetsen's lengthy epistle listed various reasons for his dislike of the council. The AFSC student resettlement advocates had alienated Bendetsen from the start by insisting that exile and incarceration were based on political motivations. Pickett's failure to invite any military agency to the Chicago meeting also rankled Bendetsen. "It may have no significance," Bendetsen observed in suggesting the contrary, "but . . . no invitation was extended to the War Department [for the May 29 organizational meeting]." The council's occasional violations of the Nineteen-Point Agreement also upset Bendetsen. He cited the buff leaflet and a mass meeting at the Tulare Assembly Center as examples of such breaches.

Bendetsen concluded that "from the beginning there existed [among the AFSC and other groups] the idea of discrediting the whole evacuation program" as well as "something even more sinister—the discrediting of the Army itself." The AFSC had supported the curfew violator Gordon Hirabayashi; criticized conditions in WCCA camps; and attempted to circulate "American Refugees," a Fellowship of Reconciliation pamphlet that labeled mass evacuation "fascist," in the camps. Bendetsen connected the council, with its close ties to the AFSC, to this attempt to undermine the army's programs. "Quite true," Bendetsen concluded, "there are many good men on the advisory committee of the National Student Relocation Council. But, need it be remembered that this would not be the first time in history when, to accomplish one purpose, men of good office were enlisted to stand guard over a quite different purpose."[57]

The WCCA's opposition to student relocation resulted in strict leave regulations. The WCCA did not grant travel permits until the student or the council provided it with evidence of acceptance at a school; sufficient financial resources to pay for travel, one year's maintenance, and tuition; community acceptance expressed in a letter from a local public official; and clearance of the college in question by the War Department and the navy. The WCCA refused to issue permits for schools deemed important to the war effort. In addition, record checks by G-2 and the San Francisco office of the FBI, another source of frustratingly long delays, were held prior to granting a permit. About one hundred students secured travel permits from assembly centers before the WRA assumed custody in early November.

As the assembly centers closed, the WCCA continued to attempt to limit Nikkei resettlement. Bendetsen fought the return of students to colleges in the WDC area despite Colonel Ralph H. Tate's notion that students be allowed to attend schools not located in Military Area No. 1 or the parts of Military Area No. 2 in California. William A. Boekel worried that the WRA might fail to rehabilitate Nikkei and argued that the WCCA ought to make sure that WRA plans did not "impinge upon military security . . . because it is not at all unlikely that there may be opportunities for the renewal of espionage and sabotage practices between the Japanese who are on work leave and those who are at large as voluntary evacuees or permanent residents. It is entirely possible that sabotage and espionage arrangements which were temporarily disrupted in evacuated areas may again be resumed under these new conditions."[58] Despite the fact that Boekel's concerns were based on false assumptions of espionage and sabotage prior to exile and incarceration, DeWitt echoed these concerns in criticizing the WRA's desire to release Nikkei quickly and argued that the problem required more careful consideration. Advocating careful study of the evacuees before release, DeWitt suggested that "it would be unfortunate in the highest degree if because of the turn of future events it became necessary to gather them up again, once released."[59]

While the WCCA clearly opposed rapid resettlement, both the council and the WRA wanted quick placements in summer 1942. "It is obvious," Bodine observed, "that if we . . . can secure [students'] immediate release and travel permits, morale throughout the centers (and in the offices of the National Student Relocation Council!) will be considerably enhanced."[60] The WRA viewed student resettlement as the least risky manner of introducing a broader program of resettlement. The students could pioneer resettlement best, the WRA's John Provinse argued, because they were native-born citizens, American educated, and more likely to support American ideals "than most of the skilled and semi-skilled peoples we will attempt to place outside the centers on our employment program."[61]

The WRA developed a process for release slowly and changed it often in its early months, making it impossible for many students to resettle for fall. Bottlenecks in processing paperwork in Washington also slowed the process. The WRA smoothed out the process by the end of 1942–43, and from this point clearance procedures usually ran smoothly. The student dossier submitted for a WRA leave included evidence of acceptance at a college, adequate financial resources, and community acceptance. The dossiers at first went to the WRA's San Francisco office, which then authorized leaves after record checks. In December 1942, the responsibility for issuing leaves shifted to Washington, D.C., in an attempt to centralize this procedure.[62]

The council repeatedly clashed with the WRA about its original offer to pay transportation costs. Despite Eisenhower's initial promise to provide such funds and the fact that Nikkei departing on work leave received such aid, the WRA balked at providing travel aid to students in 1942 for a number of reasons. The WRA did not want to contradict WCCA policy, which flatly refused such payments. Fear of adverse public reaction to the use of public funds for student resettlement also motivated the WRA's change of heart. Finally, the WRA budget did not contain a specific item for travel costs. Although it had been informed by the acting solicitor Lewis A. Sigler that it had the authority to pay students' travel costs, the WRA reneged on its promise. Nason temporarily surrendered on October 8, 1942, writing Provise that it was "unnecessary to go into the matter any further."[63]

The WRA, in fact, began to pay transportation expenses for students only in January 1945. The council reacted joyfully to the news of the long-awaited fulfillment of Eisenhower's promise. "SPECIAL RELEASE!! GREAT NEWS!! HOLD ON TO YOUR HAT!!" Elizabeth Emlen wrote Bodine, "Travel grants for students have finally gone through." Emlen also wrote a more restrained letter to Provise, thanking him for his "very real cooperation in this matter," choosing to ignore the belated nature of the travel aid.[64]

Having established procedures for acquiring student releases in WCCA and WRA camps, the council also negotiated a process for clearing colleges with the War Department. The convoluted procedure created by the War Department required a school to accept Nikkei before being submitted for clearance. The army and navy then had to clear the college before the student was released. This clearance process initially functioned very slowly. Navy intelligence announced on June 21, 1942, that Nikkei would not be allowed to enter schools with classified research programs or naval ROTC units. An early army requirement stated that colleges within twenty-five miles of important power installations, defense industries, or railroad terminals could not enroll Nikkei from the camps. Most schools cleared under such policies were isolated and often poorly equipped. By late June, the army had cleared only one-fourth of the colleges submitted by the council. Barstow remained hopeful even in the face of these disheartening results, expressing his disappointment but noting that Provinse encouraged him to believe that more colleges would be cleared soon.[65] The West Coast office lacked Barstow's patience. Conard wrote that, although it was not displeased with the WRA, his office anxiously waited for colleges to be cleared. Conard also pointed out (with perhaps more than a little impatience at his eastern colleagues) that this job belonged to the eastern office.[66]

Delays caused by the slow clearance of colleges became so serious and frustrating that even the cautious eastern council leaders eventually decided that dramatic action was needed.[67] The council even discussed the option of withdrawing its services if the deadlock could not be broken. Provinse counseled patience, however, and the council never advanced this option beyond preliminary discussion.[68]

The West Coast office was particularly upset at the lack of progress during the first summer of student resettlement, which prompted Schauffler to explain "why the pressure of liberal opinion cannot be brought to bear effectively upon the log jam in Washington." She noted that Nason, Pickett, Provinse, and Myer believed that the army had the upper hand but "could be worked with, even if tediously, if it is 'gentled'—[the WRA and the council's eastern leaders believe] that there is liberal opinion there as elsewhere which can be fortified against the reactionary elements." Too much pressure applied too quickly might lead the army to close down student resettlement, a decision the council would be powerless to fight.[69]

On July 22, Frank Aydelotte, Nason, Barstow, and Cary met at Aydelotte's home because "it had become apparent that radical action must be taken if Japanese American students are to be relocated in any numbers in time for the fall term." The group decided to arrange a meeting with John J. McCloy but limited their "radical action" to doing so only after the WRA had approved this plan.[70]

On July 29, Eisenhower, Provinse, Myer, Barstow, Nason, and Aydelotte met with McCloy and Colonel Tate. Barstow was impressed with McCloy's admission that red tape had limited the student resettlement program. He believed that concrete gains had been made at the meeting and that, although McCloy and Tate had not been "on the ball" to this point, they would now work more expeditiously on student resettlement.[71] Marnie Schauffler, reporting to the West Coast office, described Barstow meeting "all the great" men and getting "them as steamed up as he was. . . . The whole thing is simply swell and I am tickled skinny. Hurray for our side and our Bobby!"[72]

The optimism generated by the meeting with McCloy proved short-lived, however, because student resettlement continued to move slowly. Barstow complained of embarrassment, noting that students could resettle faster by not working through the council. By mid-August, Barstow, "drooping with disappointment," apologetically observed to Conard that "[e]vidently official Washington knows nothing of common English words, and it would even appear that solemn promises are principally useful as techniques for dismissing persistent seekers after justice and generosity, not to mention such trivialities as simplicity and speed."[73] Although telephone calls, meetings, and telegrams all elicited promises of progress in the near future that had still not materialized, Barstow continued to favor cooperation and gradual placement of a few hundred hand-selected "ambassadors of goodwill" to allow more students to relocate in the future.[74] The WRA sided with the military, and Oleta Dunbar, the administrative assistant for the WRA's Community Management Division, rebuked the council for the occasional submission of a college that was unfamiliar with the council's program despite an agreement that this would not be done.[75]

Only 53 of 149 colleges had been approved as of August 2. Barstow's cautious approach began to pay dividends in mid-August, however, as more colleges were cleared, although most clearances came too late for fall placements. By September 2, 111 colleges had received approval. This progress likely made the cautious eastern office even more accepting of Provinse's much-repeated warning "that impatience and pressure on our part can do us a good deal of harm. Right now the Army is in such a mood that it might easily say 'a plague upon you' and cut us off where we stand or even cut back some."[76]

The council's struggles to negotiate a resettlement process at times adversely affected its relations with colleges. Antioch College in Yellow Springs, Ohio, for example, actively sought Nikkei in summer 1942. The campus equal-rights committee requested information, and the college's questionnaire indicated a strong desire to cooperate. The college also offered two full scholarships for resettled students. Despite Antioch's welcoming attitude, B. H. Pillard, the dean of students, wrote in September to express his confusion and disappointment. The college, he noted, had worked to improve local attitudes and repeatedly expressed a desire to cooperate, yet it still had no Nikkei students. Pillard suggested that perhaps the council had acted too slowly in asking the government to clear Antioch.

Conard addressed Pillard's concerns in a long letter dated September 23.

Offering his personal apology, Conard explained the council's difficulty in securing government approval of colleges. He noted that the West Coast office had been informed—repeatedly and falsely—that a list of cleared colleges would soon appear. Conard also fixed some blame on the Philadelphia office, which had placed too much faith in government assurances. When the government had decided suddenly in August that it would not clear a college until a student had been accepted by it, Conard explained, the council had decided not to recommend students to colleges not yet cleared, hoping to place as many students as possible for the fall. Since Antioch had not yet been approved, students were not directed to it. Some schools had been approved, Conard noted disapprovingly, because students had disregarded government policy in contacting unapproved colleges.

The confusion created by the policy change actually benefited Antioch, Conard explained, because the council had submitted it for clearance when it wrongly believed that the college had officially accepted a Nikkei. Thus, the college was now cleared. The student in question, Mary Tanaka, had since arrived. Pillard happily reported that she had missed only four days of classes and described her as "charming."[77] Pillard also noted that one of the scholarships originally offered still remained available. The council responded to Antioch's eagerness, and the college reached its "saturation point" by March 1943. Antioch maintained a quota of six Nikkei through 1945.[78]

The council also ran into conflict with the WRA and the War Department in late summer because of the West Coast office's attempt to resettle as many students as quickly as possible by defining *Kibei,* in the traditional sense of the word, as Nisei who had spent significant time studying in Japan. McCloy had informed Myer, however, that *Kibei,* defined by the War Department as Nisei who had spent any time in Japan, were not eligible for resettlement. West Coast workers, arguing that no official definition of *Kibei* existed, decided that they "should merely present to the governmental authorities the cases of a few individual and very worthy students who *might* be considered Kibei but whom we feel should *not* be considered Kibei" (emphasis in original).[79]

Although the WRA lobbied the War Department for a more limited definition of *Kibei,* it tended to support the War Department's definition when dealing with the council. Thus, WRA administrators could write McCloy on November 5 to argue that the War Department's definition was "unfair," and they could write Howard K. Beale on November 13 to complain that the council was violating McCloy's regulations by submitting the names of students who had been to Japan.[80]

Beale pushed the issue with the WRA in late November, writing a lengthy letter to dispute the strict definition of *Kibei*. The new West Coast director argued that, according to the popular definition of the term, brief visits to Japan did not make a Nisei a *Kibei*. The accepted definition of *Kibei* in the Japanese language and on the West Coast, Beale continued, was Nisei who had spent all or a large portion of their schooling in Japan. He urged the adoption of this understanding of the term. Beale continued the argument a few days later, reporting that the War Department's "concept of 'kibei' has thrown another monkey-wrench into our machinery of a very serious sort."[81] *Kibei*, according to the government's definition, made up 25 percent of the original applicants to the council.[82]

Although the relationship between the council and the WRA was often one of collegiality, Myer's agency at times bowed to the superior clout of the military, valuing expediency and good relations with the military more than its mutual respect with the council. Thus, the WRA, willing to ask the War Department to reconsider its definition of *Kibei* but unwilling to press too hard for changes, continued to ask the council to adhere to the War Department definition. In response, Beale continued to contest the issue, asking on December 9 why student relocation should have to depend on the War Department to make distinctions between Nisei who visited for a few months and *Kibei* "in the generally recognized sense?"[83] Beale's persistence paid important dividends when some Nisei who had visited Japan were cleared for student resettlement in late November.[84] However, the tensions created by the West Coast office's tactics carried into the future.

Faced with this complicated and fluid situation, the council placed only one student, Harvey Itano, before July 25, 1942. Itano, the 1942 academic gold medalist at the University of California, had missed graduation ceremonies because, as Robert Gordon Sproul euphemistically noted in his commencement address, "his country has called him elsewhere."[85] The straight-A premedical student left Tule Lake on July 4 by special order of Myer, who had assumed leadership of the WRA on June 17. He resettled at Washington University in St. Louis as a medical student. Itano received a $275 scholarship from the Presbyterian Board of National Missions to help meet his expenses.[86]

Itano recalled that when he arrived at Washington University, "a man from the police department came to my school. He asked me the names of my friends in this city, my parents' names and addresses, the year of their entrance into this country, their attitude toward the war, and my feelings about the war." Itano later had trouble finding an internship at Midwestern and eastern hospitals. After months of rejections, he received an internship at the City of Detroit Receiving Hospital in July 1945.[87]

The floodgates did not open with Itano's success, however. Two months later, only 29 students had resettled. These numbers were especially disappointing in light of the questionnaires filed by 2,034 interested students and the council's repeated setbacks in trying to sort out the complications offered by the WCCA, the WRA, and the War Department. In September, King reported that 72 students, 49 male and 23 female, had been resettled.[88]

Despite slow progress, Provinse evaluated the council's program positively in late September 1942, praising its important resettlement efforts as "the guinea pig on which tests were made and precedents established."[89] The WRA Director Dillon S. Myer also applauded the council's efforts as a "pilot experience [in] pioneering the relocation program. The reception accorded these students in outside communities and the standing that many of them have achieved have done much to stimulate interest in our broader relocation efforts."[90]

The Council, Colleges, and Nikkei Students

While the council dealt with internal tensions and external complications, it also had to communicate with colleges and students to promote its program. Opposition to Nikkei resettlement and delays in creating a student relocation process made this task more difficult. As a result, the council met with mixed results in both endeavors.

The council mailed questionnaires to colleges in order to determine their willingness to cooperate. The questionnaires collected data on the courses of study available and denominational affiliation, if any; sought information about costs, scholarships, and work opportunities; and investigated the receptiveness of the student body, the faculty, and the local community to Nikkei. Once a process for resettlement had been established, positive responses were relatively easy to handle; negative responses proved more troublesome.

The council replied to positive responses with a form letter thanking schools and promising to inform them "in the near future . . . as to the conditions under which it will be possible for [resettled] students to attend [the] school." The council also reported that it planned to place those with "the highest ratings both academically and personally."[91]

Some colleges did not return the questionnaire, indicating an unwillingness to cooperate or indecisiveness. The council pursued nonresponsive colleges with a form letter generously suggesting that perhaps the questionnaire had been "mislaid during the vacation period."[92] The council noted that it hoped to place additional students in the winter and spring. Evansville College explained its failure to return the questionnaire by noting that vague "local conditions" prevented the acceptance of Nikkei. Ashland was willing to reconsider its nonresponsive position and agreed to accept applications in summer 1943. However, it also ultimately decided not to accept Nikkei "because of local conditions." Defiance, in contrast, never returned a questionnaire but had decided by April 1943 that it would accept Japanese Americans.[93]

Other colleges expressed an unwillingness to accept Nikkei. Princeton explained that, "by good reasoning," it was "not willing to receive American-born Japanese students even though they may be in good standing and not under suspicion."[94] Some cited school conditions in denying the council's request for help. The dean of Notre Dame College in South Euclid, Ohio, for example, reported that her school was full and had a long waiting list. Sister Mary Kostka, the acting president of the College of Chestnut Hill in Pennsylvania, replied that, while her school "in Christian charity [would] like to help," the small size of the college's dormitories and campus encouraged intimate contact. She suggested that Nikkei would feel more comfortable in larger institutions with scattered residential facilities. While the council replied that smaller schools actually promoted a healthy interaction between Nikkei and other students, which would help avoid "misunderstanding due to the general attitude of Caucasians toward people of Japanese extraction," it did not push any further.[95]

Local conditions provided another rationale for noncooperation. Evansville, after "soul searching" on the part of the administration, the faculty, and friends of the school, reported that "local conditions" in the community made the admission of Nikkei inadvisable. The presence of military research on campus convinced other colleges to refuse Japanese Americans. The Massachusetts Institute of Technology, for example, sympathized with the council's program but decided to accept no Nikkei for the duration. The University of Chicago also cited military research in its decision not to accept Japanese Americans. Hiram cited local conditions, although of a different kind, in refusing to cooperate. Although President Paul H. Fall expressed his personal eagerness to accept Nikkei, he reported that Hiram was located within seven miles of "the largest shell loading plant in the world—the Ravenna Ordnance Plant" and that the plant's commanding officer had advised him that "the presence of Japanese students [at Hiram] would be regarded as a hazard to the plant." Thus, the president concluded, it would be "unwise and unsafe" to admit Nikkei so long as the United States was at war with Japan. He did offer his best wishes for the council's "splendid work." Indiana University also decided not to cooperate "in view of the present uncertain military status of the southern Indiana geographical zone." The council did not push either Evansville or Hiram to change their policies, although not because it accepted either excuse. In fact, the council often fought the excuses of community sentiments and military regulations. More likely, the council devoted its limited time and resources to opening the larger and more prestigious schools desired by Nikkei students.[96]

The University of Pittsburgh's refusal to cooperate because of a nearby munitions plant was self-contradictory. Although the university admitted students without discrimination as to race or color, it informed the council, it would not admit Nikkei. How was it, a dean wondered, that students of Japanese ancestry could be permitted to go to college during the war? He reinforced the university's position with an additional list of excuses for noncooperation: the college had been told that the Pittsburgh area was not open to Nikkei, it had no vacancies, and it expected no vacancies for fall 1943. Despite an interest in student resettlement expressed by the local YMCA and Grace Browning, an associate professor of public welfare, the council did not press beyond noting that few communities had proven hostile to Nikkei. "As an American citizen," Hibbard wrote, "it is a matter of pride to me that there are very few communities in the United States where [community hostility is] known to exist."[97]

Pikeville College president A. A. Page turned down E. Fay Campbell's request that the Presbyterian school enroll Nikkei. Page first stressed that most Pikeville, Kentucky, residents had never seen a person of Japanese origin and that anti-Japanese sentiment was high. While sympathetic to the council's program and confident of a positive reception on campus, Page feared the reaction of the wider community. Page later wrote Barstow "after prayerful consideration" and argued that dispersing Nikkei students, especially in schools like his where they would meet prejudice, would not achieve the "most good." He suggested an alternative: "it would be better to set up a college for them and get the very best teachers. . . . I believe in the long run that they would come through the whole crisis and be developed into more wholesome American citizens." Bringing Nikkei students to Pikeville would only add to the resentment exile created by subjecting them to additional prejudice. Ignoring the contradiction in arguing for the segregation of Nikkei to make them a better part of American society, Page argued that "if they were taken as a group, I think there would be less consciousness of being looked upon with antagonism by the people whom they were forced to live with."[98]

Barstow's reply, which did not sway Page, noted the "very delicate and complicated" nature of student resettlement but argued against Page's proposal. Barstow pointed out that most educators agreed that dispersal would make the Nikkei feel less like a "self-conscious minority" than would relocation in large groups. Dispersal thus better promoted assimilation. While Barstow admitted that local sentiments in some communities prevented student resettlement, he argued that most communities, with "a bit of cultivation" if necessary, would accept Nikkei. He hoped that Page would reconsider his position and accept "two or three of these carefully selected young Americans."[99] No resettled students arrived at Piketon via the council during the war.

Colleges that wanted to accept Nikkei students at times also complicated the council's work. President E. H. Wilkins of Oberlin, for example, worked to enroll Nisei before the Student Relocation Committee was formed. He asked Oberlin sophomore Harry Yamiguchi to recommend deserving Nikkei and then asked for University of Washington President Sieg's help in arranging for the students to enroll.[100] As a result of this effort and others, Oberlin reported ten Nikkei already enrolled in its questionnaire.

In August 1942, Barstow expressed unhappiness with Oberlin's actions. He noted reports of community unhappiness and pointedly observed that Oberlin perhaps had not known that the government required prior certification of community receptiveness. The West Coast office had reported, Barstow continued, that Oberlin was an example "of an important case where there have been so many unfavorable reactions by narrow-minded community folk reflected or quoted by public officials . . . that we *cannot* now proceed to relocate students at Oberlin despite the college's favorable attitude" (emphasis in original).[101]

Oberlin disputed this assessment and assured the council of positive reception from the administration, faculty, and student body. Although it could not be responsible for "anything that isolated townspeople say," the college promised to investigate any instances of negative reaction that the council could provide. Oberlin also, at O'Brien's request, had the vice chair of the Oberlin Village council write a letter that argued—in the language in which the council often lectured uncooperative schools—that the Nikkei students were American citizens who should be allowed to live in the Oberlin community.[102] Barstow, sufficiently chastised, wrote in early September of his delight that the situation was "now satisfactory."[103]

An editorial in the Oberlin *News-Tribune* on October 1 prepared the community for the arrival of eleven more Nikkei, stressing that the students were American-born citizens; came with the approval of the military, the FBI, and local authorities; and possessed "excellent records for scholarship, character and citizenship." The editorial argued that all true citizens of

Oberlin wished "for their fellow American citizens an entirely happy and intellectually profitable stay in Oberlin. May their experience here only serve to strengthen their belief, and our belief, in the democratic way of living."[104]

Columbia University also upset the council by acting too boldly in admitting Nikkei students despite the fact that the government prohibited their attendance. The council asked administrators to stop doing so, fearing that it might jeopardize student resettlement in general. Columbia administrators complied but found a loophole in government regulations, telling prospective students, unbeknownst to the council, to apply to a cleared college, attend for a semester or two, and then transfer to Columbia.[105]

While working with colleges, the council also promoted its program in the camps. News of the formation of the council reached the camps quickly, where vague suggestions of student resettlement in camp newspapers were reinforced by visits. For example, Thomas Bodine visited Tule Lake to explain the organization of the council, its role in student relocation, and the War Department's approval of its program. When promised questionnaires arrived late, Bodine apologized. The council, he explained, had confused Bendetsen's "general approval" of the document with army approval. "Such," he lamented, "are the vagaries of Army red tape."[106]

Delays and confusion frustrated some Nikkei who wanted to help with student resettlement. For example, Yamato Ichihashi, the well-known Stanford professor, expressed unhappiness with the deliberate pace of resettlement from camps, which were "altogether unfit for any intellectual pursuits." While incarcerated at Santa Anita, Ichihashi reported, "[visiting council] representatives could give us no definite information as regards the 'movement.' Thus we are forced to work blindly. . . . How am I to function intelligently without necessary information as regards their possible opportunities?"[107]

The council became better known in the camps as its representatives began to visit and its questionnaires circulated. When W. O. Mendenhall visited Santa Anita in early July, he encouraged all students to fill out questionnaires, even if they had already obtained college admission, since travel permits now had to be secured through the council. "In case of doubt," the Whittier president advised, "fill it out." The council also explained that once the East Coast office had identified receptive colleges, students would be matched with appropriate schools.[108]

The meager results achieved by late July did not deter the *Tulean Dispatch* from expressing optimism. Although only one student had resettled as of July 7, the paper reported other encouraging replies and urged students to attend informational meetings about the council. Joanne Russell, secretary of the Portland branch of the council, arrived in Tule Lake in late July and presented an upbeat outlook. "Two students out of so many on the Pacific Coast who have obtained their release is not much," she reported, "but it is better than we recently expected. And indications are for the better." Tom Okuba of the Tule Lake student resettlement organization tempered this hopeful message with a warning: less than one-half of the questionnaires had been returned so far, and if students did not file soon, the possibility of fall enrollments would decrease.[109]

As the council's program became better known, local committees appeared in the camps to promote its efforts. At Tule Lake, a National Student Relocation Council formed to help students pursue resettlement. Manzanar Nisei also became active in promoting student relocation. Poston's inmates created the Japanese Student Committee in order to take charge of local student relocation work.[110]

Dispatch editors continued to believe council assurances that "[t]he program *is* going forward and we are pushing it as rapidly as possible" (emphasis in original).[111] Noticeable progress, however, began only in September, and then still slowly. The *Dispatch* reported nine students leaving for four colleges in four states on September 23, the largest group to leave Tule Lake to that time. As other camp papers reported increasing numbers of students resettling, similar optimism was expressed elsewhere.[112]

The council discovered that, despite its promotional efforts, not all students wanted to resettle. Some college-aged inmates surveyed by the Tanforan *Totalizer,* for example, advised against pursuing a college education. One argued against student resettlement because the current situation was too confused. Another suggested that college wasted four years better spent learning a practical trade. He pointed out that "[a] lot of these [University of California] guys get out and . . . are sad."[113] Other inmates saw little hope for the future. One student, asked by a high school teacher to write an essay on how he was preparing for the future, responded that he had begun "to learn to clean my house, iron my shirt and wash my own clothes, so that I can prepare to be a houseboy when I get out."[114] More constructive reasons for remaining in the camps were also professed: Charles Kikuchi, for example, declined a graduate fellowship at the University of Chicago to study evacuation firsthand.[115]

Despite the council's limited results, other Nikkei students shared an interest in returning to college to become ambassadors of goodwill. The *Totalizer* reported that, in spite of the "present circumstances," the students' faith in college education had "not diminished appreciably." Students saw higher education as a means by which Nikkei could prepare to "enter the mainstream of life." One high school student viewed resettlement as a chance to "strive hard to become and stay Americanized. . . . Then we can become part of the American society, thereby minimizing racial discrimination and prejudice." Another respondent suggested that a college education would allow Nikkei to help develop a better society. A twenty-three-year-old Nikkei argued that education would "develop leaders for the group who will be able to act as ambassadors for us and build up true good will in the larger American public."[116]

These ideas were widely shared. A University of Nebraska Nikkei wrote to thank the council for its help in preventing college students from becoming too cynical. "The freedom you have helped me regain," he continued, "makes me truly ashamed for it is heartrending to think of the 100,000 others who should have the same opportunities I have but are instead being subjected to that environment of mass internment. I hesitate to predict the effect of this type of living on them."[117]

In addition to wanting to avoid wasting time and potential, prospective students also viewed education as important for the future of Japanese America. "It will be our work," Jack Ozaki wrote, "not only to create a good impression but to gird ourselves for the day when this terrible war is over and the inevitable depression follows. Then we shall help our people maintain the American way of life with hope 'and malice toward none.'" A University of California graduate wanted to continue her studies in social services to help address the "many problems which will need to be solved [after the war]." Masao Sugiyama hoped, "[a college education will] strengthen my beliefs in America to the point where I will be able to sway the defeatists to my point of view."[118]

Prospective students in summer 1942 also viewed themselves as Japanese American representatives to the larger American public, an attitude that later contributed to the "model minority" stereotype. A high school junior at Tanforan argued that resettlement presented Nikkei with "[t]he task of winning the future for American-Japanese. . . . We will gain our foothold in new fields of life with hope of winning our future after the war." A senior echoed this theme: "[W]e should always be preparing for our future life in Caucasian society."[119] In conjunction with the process of student resettlement established by the end of summer 1942, the students' desire to pursue higher education suggested that the coming academic year would be a productive one. The future looked promising and inspired high council hopes for real progress after an often-frustrating summer.

3

IN "FREE AMERICA,"
FALL 1942–SUMMER 1943

"I am feeling like Cinderella," Chiya Veronica Asado wrote from Western College in Oxford, Ohio, "and I am hoping that this shall not be a spirit that will wear off in time."[1] Aided by a $295 scholarship from the Presbyterian Church and a job at Western, she had come to Ohio in February 1943 expecting some prejudice. She noted a happy surprise: "not . . . one person . . . seemed to have any resentment against Americans of Japanese ancestry." Asado believed that many of the students had expected her to struggle with the English language, to dress in kimonos, or to bring "a few odd-looking objects [or mannerisms]." Some even seemed disappointed, she observed, that she had permed hair. Others invited her to their rooms to look at their Japanese possessions. Despite these stereotyped expectations, Asado felt warmly received. The local YWCA invited her to visit. The students also welcomed her; Asado attended ten parties in her first week at Western and "came back with many more friends than I expected to make."

Asado hoped to be a "good ambassador." At a Wesley Foundation Banquet in February, students from Thailand, China, France, and Chile were asked to talk about their countries. Asado was asked to speak about Japan. She spoke about California instead, explaining that she was not Japanese and had never been to Japan. "The group were very glad," she reported, "that I said that."

Three years later, Asado felt that she had "profited tremendously as a result of evacuation . . . I have received an education, and gained experiences that I would probably have enjoyed only vicariously through friends." Although, as Asado admitted, not all Nikkei shared such a positive evaluation of exile and incarceration, other resettled students appreciated the opportunity to escape to school in 1942–43. As a Nikkei student at Springfield College in Massachusetts exulted, "It feels grand to be in 'free' America."[2]

"Free" America, however, was not uniformly accepting of Nikkei students. Although the pace of student resettlement increased after summer 1942, various obstacles continued to hinder the council's program. Nikkei students continued to encounter resistance to resettlement from the government as well as some colleges and communities. Freedom in 1942–43 remained relative.

Financing the Council

In attempting to help students leave the concentration camps, the council pursued various sources of funding, many of which proved unrewarding. Faced with failed attempts to raise significant funds from individuals or corporations that had previously had business contacts with Japan, Nikkei living in the eastern United States, and the government, the council looked elsewhere for money and scholarships.[3]

Many colleges responded to the council's pleas for help, providing $107,430 in fee remissions, scholarships, and work opportunities by early 1943.[4] This aid, however, did not meet the program's needs, and the council pursued additional support from the WSSF, which responded by doubling its pledge for 1942–43 to $20,000. Pressured by the council for desperately needed money for the fall semester, the executive secretary Wilmina Rowland urged chapters to return their donations as soon as possible. Robert O'Brien attended a WSSF meeting in January to present the council's case and secured $5,000 immediately and a promise of more aid for 1943–44. He also received bad news; only a total of $14,000 would be available for 1942–43.[5]

Individuals provided additional funds, often earmarked for specific students. The council encouraged students to write their benefactors to establish a personal connection that might lead to additional funding later. Individuals looking for domestic servants sometimes contacted the council and it used these offers to aid students if possible. The council also urged students to look for summer work.[6]

Local groups raised scholarships for Nikkei. John Chittum, a professor of chemistry at the College of Wooster and the president of the local Council of Churches, offered a $250 scholarship at Wooster raised by a local group interested in promoting interracial understanding. After Bob Ishida successfully resettled with the group's aid in September 1942, it offered to support additional students. Elizabeth Emlen wrote Ishida to thank him for being an "ambassador." The college Nikkei, she reported, were doing a "real job of interpretation."[7]

The council also relied heavily on church mission boards, writing letters of recommendation that stressed academic ability as well as personal qualities such as character, adaptability, poise, and trustworthiness. Whenever possible, the council also described students as "true" Christians. Many church groups explained, as the Board of Missions of the Presbyterian Church did in September 1943, that the award "represent[ed] . . . the genuine interest of our church for your continued development and effective Christian service."[8]

Scholarship aid also came from the camps. The Nikkei at the Utah camp, Topaz, organized a successful scholarship fund drive in 1943. Fumi Manabe Hayashi recalled that it was "close to impossible to go to school" from the camp without a scholarship.[9] Designed to provide financial aid "to needy and superior students of the [camp] high school," the Student Scholarship Aid Fund (SSAF) was founded by the education department, the parent-teacher association, the community council, and other interested groups among the inmates. Organizers originally hoped to aid three students per semester but raised money to help many more. The fund grew from $168.79 on May 19 to $3,080.93 by July 20. The SSAF raised money with appeals to individual donors and resettled students as well as dances, concerts, talent shows, movies, an auction of "rustic furniture" made by the industrial arts department, and a tag sale.[10] A similar fund at the camp at Tule Lake, California, exceeded $1,000 by August 25, 1943.[11]

Foundations provided essential support for the administrative budget. The Carnegie Corporation granted an additional $10,000 to the council in January 1943. The Columbia Foundation in San Francisco also contributed $15,000 over a ten-month period to the council.[12] Despite these contributions, the administrative budget became an urgent problem in early 1943. O'Brien worried that the council might become too dependent on the AFSC for funding and feared the results of any one denomination or group assuming control of the council. Bodine also feared that relations with the various denominations would be damaged if the perception of the council as an AFSC project persisted. For example, Bodine wrote, "I do hope we can make [the WSSF] feel that the AFSC isn't hogging the show."[13] Bodine also worried that exclusive AFSC sponsorship of student resettlement might tie Nikkei too closely to the pacifist movement.[14]

The chair John Nason shared these concerns, noting "that while the council has stressed its distinctiveness from the A.F.S.C. almost to the point of embarrassment, it is the A.F.S.C. which has supplied us directly or indirectly with all of our administrative funds. That is an uneasy arrangement which neither Clarence Pickett or I relish." He saw two potential solutions to this problem: relying exclusively on the AFSC for administrative funds or asking the church boards to undertake administrative funding for the council.[15]

The council faced a direct choice in late January 1943 when the AFSC offered to assume administrative responsibility for the council by making it a section of the service committee. The council's Executive Committee decided to investigate the possibility of operating "on a wider cooperative basis."[16] Pleased with the positive responses received from the church boards and feeling less pressure because of the Columbia Foundation's grant, the Executive Committee decided to pursue ecumenical funding instead of exclusive AFSC sponsorship, estimating that $1,500 per month divided among sixteen denominations would allow the council to continue operations. The council wrote to church boards already involved with its program to suggest that each contribute toward the needed $1,500 per month in proportion to the number of potential students of that denomination. It did not ask for money from churches that said they could not or would not pay, and, to make up for the missing funds, it asked the AFSC and other groups that had proved generous in the past to pay more. By February 11, the council had acquired or was close to acquiring administrative funding from eleven denominations as well as the national YMCA and YWCA.[17]

Debating the Council's Future

The council director Robbins W. Barstow envisioned, even as financial concerns loomed and the American Legion clamored for military control of the camps and the prohibition of Nikkei resettlement, at least a scaled-down program for the council after September 1. "The first phases of the problem which brought this Council into being," Barstow observed on August 25, "are now reasonably well in hand." With student data analyzed and a process for student resettlement beginning to function, Barstow believed that four tasks remained: continuing placements, exploring additional opportunities for student resettlement, securing additional scholarship funds, and possibly developing field contacts through personal visits. Returning to the Hartford Theological Seminary, Barstow offered to serve part-time after September 1 if the council wanted only a "nominal director." He argued that the council must decide if it would move "slowly in the light of developing experience, or try to press our campaign of placement more intensively in all respects." The tone of Barstow's report and his actions as director suggest that he preferred the former alternative.[18]

Congressional criticisms complicated the council's discussions. In May, after a press release on student resettlement, a congressional committee had met with the then director of the WRA, Milton Eisenhower, and "attacked him severely. . . . The point of their objection was that the only safe thing to do was to have every Japanese behind a fence, that there are some good ones, but you can't tell the good ones from the bad ones."[19] In the fall, Representative Alfred J. Elliot—a Democrat, rancher, and newspaper editor from central California—wrote U.S. Attorney General Francis Biddle to express his constituents' concern "that the Japanese youth are to be furnished with college and university education, while our own boys are being taken out of these same institutions to serve their country."[20] This argument, echoed by the Democratic West Virginia Senator Harley M. Kilgore, blamed the victim—the government, after all, refused to draft Nikkei. The West Virginia State Federation of Labor also protested to Kilgore, arguing that if "our boys" were being taken out of college to fight, an "enemy race" should not be granted the privilege of higher education.[21]

The WRA responded by emphasizing the voluntary nature of the council's efforts and defending its program as a private effort promoted by "responsible educators and public-spirited citizens." Dillon S. Myer argued that the draft should be applied to Nikkei, thus freeing resettled students from the onus of shirking their duty to their country. He applauded the creation of a volunteer all-Nisei military unit on January 28, 1943 and believed that some Nikkei were likely to drop out of college to serve. He suggested that those not obligated to military service, however, ought to be educated to avoid wasting human resources. Myer declared that "[i]t has not been the policy of the WRA to regard this citizen group . . . as enemies of this country any more than the children of German and Italian nationals" and paradoxically that, even though this was the case, the WRA took "every reasonable precaution . . . to insure that the internal security of the country [was] not jeopardized."[22]

The council responded similarly, stressing the native-born citizenship and the Americanism of the Nisei. It pointed to FBI investigations of each student and the excellent records compiled by the Nikkei to defend its program. Scholarship funds, the council noted in combating the common misconception that the government funded its program, came from Christian organizations. The council also framed its program as a counter to Japanese claims that the current war was a race war. Nikkei would make important contributions to the United States after the war, the council argued; thus, their loyalty must not be undermined. The council also shared the story of an inmate who had decided not to resettle to college after being accepted for enlistment in the segregated Nisei military unit.[23]

Internal debates about the council's future, even as it defended its program from outside attacks, climaxed when Howard K. Beale arrived in San Francisco with both enthusiasm and optimism to assume control of the West

Coast office in mid-October 1942. Beale replaced Joseph Conard, who had resigned to finish his master's degree work at the University of California before going to work for the AFSC in San Francisco. The forty-three-year-old professor of history on leave from the University of North Carolina had volunteered his time to a cause that resonated with him, both personally and professionally.[24] Beale had drawn praise for smoothing the transition between the departure of Barstow and the arrival of O'Brien to assume the position of national director. Marnie Schauffler, an AFSC member with past experience and a deep interest in student resettlement, praised Beale's intimate knowledge of many of the groups involved in student resettlement, including students, college administrators, federal agencies, and government personalities. "He combines, I think," Schauffler observed, "wisdom and maturity with drive and administrative capacity."[25] In addition to these qualities, Beale wanted to move to the West Coast office. He had written Bodine in early October to express impatience with the administration of the Philadelphia office and an appreciation for the fact that the West Coast office did "a good share of the work and that we [in the East] are doing the less important end of it here."[26]

Beale also had a clearly defined agenda: the reorganization of the West Coast office to increase its efficiency. Before assuming his new post, Beale discussed "the 'problem' of this office" with a number of council officials and then read all of the relevant correspondence.[27] Thus prepared, Beale immediately began to implement extensive reforms, which he described in an eight-page letter to Nason that detailed the administrative changes he had made to deal "with the problems of reorganization of this Office with a staff and budget that will permit it to function at all."[28]

Beale thought the first four weeks of his tenure satisfying and effective. However, his attempts to rationalize office work quickly sowed seeds of distrust and revolt among the staff. Ken Stevens of the finance department and Joe Goodman, who handled some liaison work with the WRA as well as the office's finances, chafed under his assertive leadership. Beale also quickly came into conflict with Virginia Scardigli and her placement department. In particular, Scardigli was unhappy with Beale's tendency to micromanage and thought that he frequently infringed on her department's bureaucratic turf.[29] This unhappiness triggered a staff mutiny against Beale.

The displeasure with Beale became apparent when he and King left to visit students in Manzanar, California, while Bodine, a stabilizing force, was out of the office ill. Provided this opportunity, those unhappy with the current situation organized themselves in opposition to Beale. The end result was a staff meeting at which the director recalled, "[I] heard myself pulled to pieces. . . . But for an hour and a half I listened to these petty little people who had spent much of their time for six weeks, while I worked like a slave, gossiping behind my back, reading my letters, whispering to each other that I was giving orders whenever I made a suggestion. . . . If all of this had come from big people, people with background and experience, people who have done things, it would not be so difficult to take."[30] Beale was so affected by this meeting that he offered to resign in a letter to Nason dated December 4. Before sending the letter, though, Bodine convinced him to add a note suggesting that his letter and the resignation it contained should be treated "as what will be fact if something cannot be changed in the situation and not as fait accompli."[31]

The situation did not improve, however. O'Brien traveled from Philadelphia to calm tensions but only exacerbated the situation by firing Goodman, which led to a strike by the placement department. Beale and Bodine responded by trying to make do with the remaining staff while requesting additional help from the East Coast office. Margaret Jones was immediately dispatched to the West Coast office, and Beale was promised that Schauffler would arrive later.

Bodine, however, began a series of individual interviews—based on the office's Friendly Way, which emphasized conferencing and prayerful work—with the staff, unbeknownst to Beale. Although Beale admitted that Bodine had canvassed the office "with the best of intent and a really lovely spirit," the end result was, in Beale's own words, "one of the worst shocks I have ever known." Staff members used Bodine's interviews to convince him that it would be better for Beale to leave than to have placement set back. Faced with this situation, Beale resigned after only two months as director.[32]

The mutiny superficially seems to have been motivated by personality conflicts. Beale later argued that "certain personality problems . . . would be the one insuperable problem. . . . [A] spirit of pettiness and jealousy in this office will defeat anyone who tries to run it until it is eliminated."[33] Bodine, the erstwhile ally of Beale, described Beale as driven, resourceful, and fearless. The former director also had contacts as well as a willingness to sacrifice himself for the cause. However, Bodine also attributed Beale's failure on the West Coast to personality flaws—Beale's own flaws. Beale was tactless, unable to delegate responsibility to equals, and impatient. Bodine also believed, suggesting the heat of the battle just passed, that Beale suffered from a "persecution complex."[34] Nason shared these conclusions, stating after the fact that he "should have been smart enough to realize that [Beale's] history, character, and performance pointed toward a person who works extremely well by himself, but who not only has had very little experience in working with others but is temperamentally not naturally adapted to such work."[35]

To dismiss Beale's resignation as merely the result of personality conflicts, however, misses a deeper source of tension that existed within the council. The West Coast revolt developed from two fundamentally different approaches to student resettlement, centered in the East and West Coast offices, that were never completely reconciled. Although Beale's rhetoric represented an exaggerated picture of the qualities of the easterners, the Beale affair illuminates these different approaches to student resettlement.

The first characteristic of the philosophical division between the two offices centered in the approach preferred by each in combating what was universally perceived within the council as the unmitigated wrong of exile and incarceration. The westerners had developed a crusading mentality and believed that the wrongs of evacuation had to be righted as quickly as possible by any means necessary. The professionally established easterners, in contrast, tended toward a more pragmatic view. They also wanted to right a wrong, but they preferred to do so by cooperating with military and civilian agencies.

Beale's arrival on the West Coast highlighted the different approaches. West Coast staffers irritated Beale with their willingness to skirt the rules if doing so, in their minds, furthered the cause of student resettlement. The director warned that this strategy ignored "the fact that eventually disregard of rules will catch up with us."

Beale complained, despite his tireless efforts to negotiate a more limited definition of *Kibei* with the War Department, about the office's earlier attempt to employ its own definition of *Kibei* instead of abiding by the government's incorrect interpretation of the term. The War Department's response to this attempted subterfuge, Beale pointed out, was an increased reluctance to abandon its very narrow interpretation of the word. This reluctance, in turn, now held up some of the best students in the camps. Had the issue been negotiated openly and in good faith, Beale argued, this unfortunate situation could have been avoided. Instead, the zeal of the crusaders in looking for short-term solutions had created long-term problems.

The split between easterners and westerners spilled over into debates about the proper relationship between the council and students. Beale wanted to discourage resettled students from transferring to another college, arguing that this would delay resettlement for students still in the camps. The staffers, however, thought that no restraints should be placed on these students. Once out of the camps, the students should be allowed the freedom to do as they wished.[36] The moral absolutism of the Quakers isolated Beale in the office.

The second characteristic of this philosophical difference involved the relative influence of Quaker thought in the respective offices. Joseph Conard's tenure as director of the West Coast office had established what the staff considered the Friendly Way and the proper spirit for student re-settlement. The staff believed these were integral to its success. Beale represented the easterners' interdenominational approach as well as their belief that Executive Committee decisions were to be implemented, not debated.

Beale's arrival provoked a staff revolt in part because he made conscious attempts to alter the Friendly Way. He derisively labeled the standard procedure of holding staff conferences before any decision could be made a "sort of pseudo-Quakerism."[37] The embattled director attempted to invoke the spirit of Conard to support his reforms by arguing that the former director actually agreed with most of the changes. However, Beale did not fully understand that the method by which the changes were made was just as threatening to the staff as the changes themselves. Unwilling to accept the Friendly Way as established in the office and unable to establish a new "way," Beale first lost the confidence of the staff and then his control over it.[38]

Beale's directorship did more than simply challenge the Friendly Way; it also undermined the Quaker spirit of the office. Trudy King noted that "the essential spirit . . . has gone out of our work here since the new director has arrived." She better appreciated in retrospect "the many intangibles that [Conard] added to our group. The morning meetings for worship which used to be so powerful are now almost farces as our director does not believe in meditation or periods of quiet."[39] Having thus violated both the Friendly Way and spirit of the office, Beale could not remain its director.

A third philosophical difference, which split the office between the professionalism of Beale, which stressed efficiency, and the amateurism of the staffers, which emphasized spirit and a personal approach, contributed to the tension in the office. The practice of professional efficiency as implemented by Beale succeeded in resettling more students; however, the new methods upset the staff. Beale reported to Nason that some workers believed that the number of students resettled was not as important as the spirit in which they were relocated. Beale tended to dismiss such feelings by describing the crusaders as a minority in the office who thought he "had destroyed the whole spirit of the place."[40] In contrast, the staff worried that Beale used the word *cases* to refer to students. The embattled director argued unsuccessfully that he was interested in the students as individuals but that it was not "a sin against the Holy Ghost" to use the word *cases*.[41]

Beale must have been shocked at the accusations leveled against him. He had worked, as had many others, long hours to help students escape to college. He even worked without compensation for the council. Beale felt sympathy for the students he had met at Tule Lake, writing that "[t]heir devotion to America and their bewilderment at the way America is treating them is really pathetic and quite overwhelming." He also praised resettled students, noting that "[a]ll we have to do is to get one of these kids accepted and then he sells himself and his group and our work to the college."[42]

The divergent thought over the merits of professionalism and amateurism did not disappear with the removal of Beale. Margaret Jones had arrived as a result of the placement department strike, and, an eastern professional, she remained in the office after Beale's departure. She urged reforms to professionalize the staff in order to improve efficiency. Bodine, the new West Coast director, argued against Jones, defending the amateurism of his staff. He bluntly wrote to O'Brien, "Margaret is in some ways as difficult as all the other easterners who come out with different ideas about running things. Many of her ideas are good and have been adopted. Others I don't agree with."[43]

Jones had discussed the troubling issue of finances with Clarence Pickett before traveling to the West Coast office. She brought this issue before Bodine and suggested that he draw up a budget for the office's minimum needs. The resulting budget, she reported to Nason, made it apparent "to any one with any professional experience that the Council is over staffed. I believe that fewer capable persons could handle the mechanics of the work with considerable efficiency." She identified the placement department as one area that might function more smoothly. While Jones appreciated the devotion of the staff's "completely selfless workers," she clearly believed that it needed to be made more efficient and cost effective.[44]

Bodine argued strongly against Jones's recommendations, suggesting that "this office is functioning smoothly and effectively at the present" and urging that the office be continued "on an amateur basis."[45] Bodine contended that more rapid work did not necessarily translate into more effective work. He feared that the thoughtful, personal care of amateurs such as Scardigli and Wyman would be lost if their department were turned over to efficiency experts. Bodine also pointed out that bringing in professionals to run the placement department would be expensive and would temporarily slow down student resettlement as the new employees learned the complexities of the work. He was also "not sure they could be assimilated happily into an otherwise amateur staff, trained only in the job." Bodine instead advocated hiring additional amateurs for placement department work, noting with considerable satisfaction that Jones worked even slower than Scardigli. "At any rate," he concluded, "it is essential to decide once and for all whether we are to operate on an amateur or on a professional basis. So far each attempt to mix the two has led to unhappiness and bitterness and hurt the work."[46]

The often-chaotic reign of Beale ended in "tragedy and unhappiness"; however, the causes of the West Coast rebellion paradoxically illustrate the central reason for the council's success.[47] Tensions caused by the two different philosophies that coexisted uneasily within the council were at the heart of the West Coast mutiny, but they also enabled the council to work effectively with a wide variety of groups. On the one hand, the pragmatism of the easterners softened some of the excesses of the westerners and enabled the council to develop working relationships with the WRA and various military agencies. The conservative nature of the pragmatics also disciplined the council to work toward a larger goal incrementally. On the other hand, the spirit of the westerners allowed the council to distance itself in the eyes of Nikkei from the unpopular WRA, endowing it with a legitimacy with the evacuees that the easterners' pragmatism would not have produced. The personalized approach toward student resettlement that typified the council's work also developed from the spirit of the West Coast office. Throughout its history, the energy created in the tension between the pragmatic and crusading philosophies drove the council's policies and actions. Despite the advantages gained by internal divisions, these council debates wasted energy that might have been more constructively applied to student resettlement.

In his last missive from the West Coast, Beale noted that Bodine and Monroe E. Deutsch had separately proposed moving the office to Denver, a move that would allow the office to jettison its troublemakers and to solve its personnel problem by hiring Nikkei secretaries.[48] The San Francisco office had served an important role as a liaison with the WCCA, but it was no longer needed with all exiles now in WRA custody. By January, the council had initiated discussions about the consolidation of council offices. While the conversations focused on limiting costs and increasing efficiency as the main motives for such a move, it is possible that an unspoken reason remained muting internal tensions. The council eventually settled on Philadelphia, a choice that in many ways marked the ascendancy of the council as a fund-raising organization dedicated to cooperating with the government. Despite council efforts, the move caused disappointment for some students when it temporarily delayed their placements.[49]

Soon after the consolidation, internal tensions arose again. On March 18, Woodruff Emlen[50] criticized Carlisle V. Hibbard's leadership.[51] "I . . . feel," Emlen began, "I can speak at least for all of us who worked in the West Coast office in saying that we are deeply disturbed at the apparent lack of confidence between the Committee and the staff." Emlen argued that workers' West Coast experience was too often ignored in council decisions. Critical of many aspects of the council's operations, Emlen suggested that church boards had too much influence and college administrators had too little.[52]

Nason wrote Cary to express anger that Emlen had gone over Hibbard's head without reason. He complained about "the same old immaturity on the part of Bodine, King, Emlen & Co. in their attitudes toward student relocation." Nason did not believe that the Executive Committee should have to listen to the staff examine "practical details of procedure which apparently they like to discuss."[53]

Although the intense confrontation of the Beale affair was not repeated, internal tensions remained. The West Coast office had been eliminated, but the spirit of the office lived on when West Coast personnel moved east. Bodine remained with the council, and his new position as field director kept him out of the office much of the time and provided him with considerable independence. The outspoken and effective King moved east to continue her student resettlement work. Elizabeth Emlen, Woodruff Emlen's wife, also moved to Philadelphia, where she became increasingly influential and, eventually, national director. Assigned to the finance department before becoming national director, Emlen drew on both her experiences with the West Coast office and the practical concerns of fund-raising in adopting an approach to student resettlement that blended the crusading and pragmatic impulses in the council. As a result, she later enjoyed a successful tenure as national director that drew approval from the both groups.[54]

As the council closed its western office, Nason argued that it should not plan an "indefinite existence" and suggested autumn 1944 as a good ending point. Nason envisioned an increasingly limited agenda that included placing students through October. While the council would continue to fulfill its responsibilities to resettled students afterward, Nason stressed that it "must carry on . . . in a way which adjusts in time and money spent to the results produced."[55]

Bodine vigorously protested Nason's suggestions, describing his bewilderment at plans to abandon the council's work. He suggested that the West Coast committee might once again assume responsibility for student resettlement if the council's eastern leadership backed out. Deutsch and Bodine relayed Nason's plan to the West Coast committee on January 27, 1943, and hoped that they would remain interested and active in the work, "realizing its significance not only to the individuals assisted but to our whole national attitude."[56]

Bodine's anxiety peaked in June 1943. Writing that insufficient staff had hindered placements, Bodine appealed to Pickett "to come back into the Student Relocation picture and take the time to look into it thoroughly." He backed his request with a thinly veiled financial threat, noting that he would meet soon with the Columbia Foundation and felt obligated "to share the whole truth . . . as [he saw] it." Praising the amount of work accomplished by the West Coast office despite "all of its sins and troubles," Bodine damned Hibbard with faint praise, describing him as a "splendid" office director who lacked "drive in Washington, New York, and in his correspondence."[57]

While debating its future, the council continued to run into conflict with the government. The FBI director J. Edgar Hoover wrote Myer on December 16 to express concern that the council sought placements for students in part by stating that they had been "cleared" or "checked" by his bureau. The FBI, Hoover explained, had not given a "stamp of approval" to such students; in fact, it "at no time expresse[d] an opinion relative to the loyalty and patriotism of persons." He emphasized that the FBI only furnished information on individuals in its files on request and did "not vouch for the reliability of the information."[58] Myer dispatched a note to the council urging it to correct this problem.[59]

The FBI complained about the same problem in summer 1943. Hibbard issued a reminder to his staff to avoid statements to this effect. He noted the potential negative ramifications of doing so by pointedly observing that "the recent action at Temple [University] limiting enrollment is due to the shock discovery by Temple authorities that the Nisei were not guaranteed by the F.B.I. to be chemically pure."[60]

On June 4, 1943, the Office of the Chief of Naval Operations further complicated the council's program by issuing a list of 91 newly proscribed schools, bringing the total number of such institutions to 150. Although the navy had previously cleared more than one-third of these colleges, it now closed them because the schools held classified research contracts with or administered training programs for the navy, the marine corps, or the coast guard. College administrators reacted with shock. Joseph Holliday, the director of admissions at the University of Cincinnati, found out about his school's placement on the list from a student. Although local army officials assured him that this was only a rumor, Woodruff Emlen confirmed the report. Nikkei at the University of Cincinnati worried about their future, wondering if it would be better to transfer to a cleared college. Holliday scrambled to find answers about financial aid to students already accepted but not yet resettled.[61]

Hibbard described the navy's new list as "a powerful jolt."[62] The council pressed, without success, for students with educational leaves still in the camps and those accepted by a college but without their leaves to be able to attend colleges just added to the list. The council maintained hope that this new obstacle, like previous ones, could be overcome. The new list might be "more than discouraging—it is distressing," King wrote the WRA's Oleta Dunbar, "[b]ut we have not yet given up hope—or at least those of us that have been in this racket for some time as we recall how dank and dismal the picture was last July and August."[63]

Despite sympathizing with the council's consternation and confusion, Myer urged caution, suggesting that until an appeal of the navy's decision was heard, "it [was] not advisable to relocate additional students in the schools listed."[64] Myer wrote a strong letter of protest to Ellis M. Zacharias, acting director of the Office of Naval Intelligence. After thanking him for removing a number of schools from the proscribed list, Myer noted the list's "disturbing" inclusion of many colleges that the navy had previously approved. Some of these institutions, he noted, already had in attendance "several students of Japanese ancestry, [who were] doing excellent work in medicine, engineering, and other critically depleted trades and professions." Myer, always aware of the potential effects of student resettlement on the broader WRA program, expressed concern that extension of the proscribed list would limit resettlement in general and increase the racial discrimination faced by Nikkei. The WRA director also objected to the use of the term Japanese in the heading of the navy's list, arguing that the great majority of resettled students were American citizens.[65]

Zacharias curtly rejected Myer's appeal. Although the navy did not require students already at newly proscribed colleges to leave, Zacharias defended the navy's decision as one based on a "lengthy discussion" designed to maintain American security. He stated that the navy had kept the list as short as possible and that "therefore . . . nothing would be accomplished at this time in requesting reconsideration." Zacharias tried to soften the blow by pointing out that the Navy Department had proscribed only ninety-two of about seven hundred institutions, conveniently ignoring that the new list included many of the colleges offering courses such as physics, chemistry, and engineering, which most interested Nikkei. He also suggested that the students ought to make sacrifices for the war effort and not protest the new list, arguing that "[t]he war has caused similar hardships to other American citizens by uprooting their normal life patterns."[66]

The WRA reported its failed appeal and suggested caution in dealing with the aggravating list. Dunbar warned that "until something is worked out it will be necessary to withhold action in these cases where students have already been accepted at colleges on the Navy list." The WRA essentially endorsed the familiar course of hoping for improvement in the future, noting that "[a]ll of this presents a gloomy picture, but we hope the situation will become brighter soon."[67]

Not content to hope for potential future improvements, the council tried to convince the navy to reconsider. It argued that racial discrimination violated the principles for which the United States fought. The council asserted that blanket refusals were unnecessary since the FBI checked each student before release. Since the students were citizens, the council suggested, their loyalty and integrity should not be challenged. German Americans and Italian Americans, the council noted, were not excluded as students. Significant secret government research projects would be well protected, the council continued, and the successful resettlement of Nikkei students had already occurred "without untoward incident." The council emphasized the navy's inconsistency with respect to Nikkei: some Japanese Americans and even enemy aliens lived near and worked at proscribed schools. In addition, students who had left the West Coast voluntarily before evacuation could enter any college without restriction.[68]

The council pressed its case with the WRA and the navy. Nason expressed his frustration to Provinse in uncharacteristic language and sentiment. "We have decided," he declared, "that the time has come to put up as strong a fight as possible."[69] The council also arranged a meeting, this time with Adlai E. Stevenson, assistant to the Secretary of the Navy, to discuss its grievances. Nason dominated the August 5 meeting, also attended by Hibbard, Edward B. Rooney (a Catholic representative on the council), and the WRA's Tom Holland, forcefully presenting the council's position while urging Stevenson and the navy to reconsider its policy. Holland endorsed Nason's argument.[70]

Stevenson convened a meeting with Provinse, Dunbar, and military representatives one week later to examine "Dr. Nason's appeal from an intra-governmental standpoint." Provinse backed away from Holland's full endorsement of Nason's appeal but agreed that the council's work had been hampered by the new list. The military representatives explained that "a new directive was in the process of clearance whereby students could be permitted to attend schools upon clearance similar to that used in . . . defense plant work." A survey of proscribed schools was also being completed. If the new plan were approved, some schools would be removed from the proscribed list and others (that could not isolate their confidential work) would require students who wanted to attend to be cleared by the Japanese American Joint Board, just as other Nikkei were cleared for defense work. The hourlong meeting concluded with general agreement that the new proposal represented an improvement.[71]

The council, while not entirely displeased with this development, continued to press for action, even pointing out that some schools recently added to the proscribed list seemed unaware of their changed status and continued to admit Nikkei students. The council blatantly stated that it would not stand in the way of such admissions. Hibbard pressed the WRA with both telephone calls and letters, eliciting a promise from Myer, who admitted to having done little, "to dig in at once" on the problem.[72] Hibbard assumed, however, on the basis of Myer's lack of response to letters asking if the council should contact the navy to follow up, that Myer thought it best to "lie low."[73] Thus, the council had to live with the navy's list and slow adjustments to it until the new process became a reality in October 1943.

The Council and the Colleges

The council continued to face resistance from some colleges in 1942–43. One case originated when Dean Lewis Ford of the University of Southern California's dental school refused to release the transcripts of incarcerated students. After repeated and sharp letters to Ford and President Rufus B. von Kleinsmid, the transcripts were finally issued in November. Ford still proved uncooperative, however, and refused to give the students credit, as many West Coast institutions had, for work completed in the spring semester. Beale considered this one last attempt to inflict "a stab to each student."[74]

Colleges outside of the West Coast refused to admit Nikkei students for a variety of familiar reasons during 1942–43. The presence of military training units and housing shortages prompted some schools to bar resettled students. For example, in July 1943, Washington and Jefferson College in Washington, Pennsylvania, requested that it be removed from the list of schools willing to accept Nikkei students. Noting the one thousand soldiers who were training on campus, the college believed "it very unwise to bring relocated students to the campus in the presence of soldiers."[75] The University of Louisville, in part because of concerns that it was located in a defense area, bluntly refused to cooperate in a terse one-sentence letter: "The University of Louisville is not permitted to admit Japanese American students."[76]

Colleges also continued to cite community hostility in refusing to cooperate. President Ralph N. Tirey of the Indiana State Teachers College in Terre Haute refused to accept Nikkei because he feared the college would be "publicly condemned."[77] Tirey apparently "believed in world brotherhood, but . . . was influenced by possible reactions in the community [from groups such as the American Legion]."[78] Goshen College in Indiana chose not to accept Nikkei in March 1943 after an attempt to employ Nikkei at local farms generated protest from the American Legion and other groups. Thiel College in Greenville, Pennsylvania, decided not to enroll Nikkei after "trouble over the race question" at a local replacement depot resulted in one death and numerous injuries.[79]

The council refused to place students in schools lacking accreditation. When Dean O. B. Dabney of the unaccredited Ashland Junior College in Kentucky wrote to express his school's interest, Hibbard explained that the council limited "the placement of students to [schools with] full accreditation [because] many of the students find it desirable to change from one college to another for special courses or in the case of junior colleges to complete their collegiate work."[80] This policy delayed placements at other colleges as they worked to prove their status. For example, Defiance College in Ohio offered to accept Nikkei, but concerns about its accreditation slowed the process. Although the college convinced the council of its accreditation in summer 1943, no Nikkei students attended, perhaps because more prestigious and better-known colleges were open by this time.[81]

The council used various methods to convince recalcitrant colleges to cooperate, writing them to provide information and statistics pertaining to its program. The council also noted Nikkei volunteers in the U.S. military. Council letters of recommendation for students—designed in part to alleviate colleges' fears—focused on academic and personal qualities. High grades were emphasized, and the council described even a B-student as "top-notch." The council emphasized personal qualities, especially an ability to get along with whites, cooperativeness, patriotism, and work ethic. Students were also touted as "very Americanized." Council members occasionally traveled to speak at colleges that had not decided whether to accept Nikkei. Nason, for example, spoke at Goshen College and helped to mute anti-Nikkei sentiments. However, no students ever resettled at Goshen via the council.[82]

The council's efforts, in addition to changing local and international situations, convinced some colleges to change their minds and accept Nikkei. In October 1942, M. C. Herrick, the director of admission at Fenn College in Cleveland, informed the council that his school would not accept Nikkei because they would be "unduly handicapped in attending college in the heart of a very large city."[83] Fenn reversed its decision in July 1943, "in light of the year's developments," and accepted many students via the council.[84]

Miami University in Oxford, Ohio, had returned a dubious questionnaire, citing a Naval Radio School and limited dormitory space. As applications arrived, the university YMCA and YWCA pushed for resettled students; Nikkei students thrived at nearby Western College, and the Miami administration wrote the council for information in early 1943. By June, Miami had accepted six Nikkei students.[85]

Wilmington College, a Quaker college in southern Ohio, had likewise seemed uncertain. The president S. A. Watson feared that local opinion would be unfavorable, noting that "some families had relations at Pearl Harbor and Manila—outside of Friends' group there is considerable anti-everything of this nature."[86] For example, Watson later recalled a sign displayed by a local business during rabbit-hunting season: "No ammunition available except for the Japs."[87]

Aware of local sentiment, Wilmington's board discussed the issue of student resettlement. A few members opposed enrolling any students, and others favored admitting only Nikkei women during a time when "our own boys" were being drafted. Others reminded their colleagues that Nisei were citizens and that they had not sought exclusion from the draft. The board finally decided to enroll two or three female students. Although some community members complained, the college accepted Barbara Hamabe, who apparently stayed for only one year. Later, Alice Sasaki was accepted and awarded a scholarship.

The University of Cincinnati had assessed its local situation carefully before returning its questionnaire, and its president Raymond Walters admitted that he did not know if his school could take Nikkei.[88] He worried that jobs in city stores would probably not be available to Nikkei and that local attitudes would be "unfavorable."[89] The council viewed the University of Cincinnati's questionnaire as a refusal to cooperate. The issue might have rested there if Nikkei students had not applied for admission outside of council channels. Faced with seven applications, Joseph E. Holliday, director of admissions, decided to accept Japanese Americans. The school demonstrated its desire to cooperate by reserving space in the men's dormitory for them and by appointing Robert Bishop of the university's YMCA as the local sponsor. By February 1943, the University of Cincinnati had enrolled six Nikkei. This number rose to twenty-five by October 1943.[90]

The University of Cincinnati's willingness to admit resettled students did not mean that the city was uniformly receptive to Nikkei. Frank Inouye enrolled at the university in 1944. Although Inouye was sensitive to racism, he found Cincinnati a liberating environment and remembered, "at Cincinnati, the burden of feeling constantly under scrutiny as a strange and exotic Oriental specimen that I had endured back on the West Coast, was now disappearing." Inouye remembered Cincinnati as "a city that was very friendly to the Nisei" and often ate at drugstore counters and local greasy spoons with a group of Jewish friends. Apparently, at least a degree of racial acceptance existed in his new hometown.[91]

Still, on a date with a white friend, Inouye found that Cincinnati could be hostile. Riding the streetcar home with his "tall, blond, and blue-eyed date," Inouye noticed many passengers with disapproving looks. He remembers, "[I] sat, petrified, feeling as conspicuous as a butterfly stuck on a specimen board. [My date], unconscious of my discomfort, chatted on and on, but not a word registered in my brain. All I could think was how to escape this predicament. I swore I would never date a white woman as long as I lived." Inouye later recalled that "living in 'America' did not rid me of longheld proscriptions about actually dating white women. Did that make me less American?"[92]

Thomas T. Sugihara found interracial dating a bit more accepted at Kalamazoo College in Michigan. His fellow students understood Sugihara's social desire for companionship. A staff member at the college, however, was less open minded, warning one female student that dating Sugihara would "jeopardiz[e] her future." Sugihara also recalled, "the parents of women I dated at Kalamazoo [and my mother] disapproved of our dating at some level or another."[93]

In contrast, some initially positive responses became refusals. Allegheny College in Meadville, Pennsylvania, initially expressed an interest in accepting ten Nikkei students, describing a receptive community and a desire to cooperate in an "important undertaking."[94] Allegheny, however, refused admission to a Nikkei student in October, offering the excuse that registration had already been completed. When the council inquired whether Nikkei students could enroll for the second term, Paul H. Younger, the director of admissions, replied that, while his school remained sympathetic toward the council's program, a corps of naval cadets on campus taxed the college's accommodations and prevented the admission of Nikkei.

The council pressed Allegheny to reverse its decision by offering to organize living arrangements, but it acquiesced by spring 1943. When the Allegheny Christian Council, inspired by a speech by Oberlin's Kenji Okuda, wrote to express interest, the council advised caution. Hibbard described "strong opposition to bringing any sort of Japanese into the Pittsburgh Area." He also noted pending legislation in Pennsylvania that would deny state funding to colleges that accepted students from the camps. Although such prejudice was "without justification," the council was reluctant to push the issue "in any college which for whatever reason has not received any of these students up to this time." Hibbard suggested a strategy of waiting that proposed, at most, publicity about the council's program "without reference to any plans for local settlement of Japanese."[95]

The desire of individual college administrators to participate provided one key factor in successful student resettlement. Smaller, less prestigious colleges often had to push to get students. For example, Otterbein College in Westerville, Ohio, expressed displeasure in September 1942 that its offer to provide financial aid to resettled students had been ignored. Beale worked to get Otterbein cleared, and by March, five Nikkei students had resettled there.[96]

Colleges in northwestern Ohio responded in different ways to the council's appeal for help. Bowling Green State University, Heidelberg College, and the University of Toledo all expressed an initial willingness to accept Nikkei students. Local opposition to student resettlement and different levels of administrative commitment at each school, however, resulted in divergent outcomes.

Bowling Green decided to accept Nikkei in spring 1942, but it reversed its position in August.[97] Bowling Green president F. J. Prout explained that the federal government had taken over some of the university's accommodations, which created overcrowding problems. This congestion made the acceptance of Nikkei inadvisable. The university registrar also wrote that dormitories were full and suggested applying early for the following academic year. The council followed this advice, but students were rejected for the 1943–44 and 1944–45 school years. While Bowling Green continued to plead overcrowding, the council came to perceive it as "indifferent if not reluctant toward admitting [Nikkei]."[98]

Local opposition may have provided an unspoken reason for Bowling Green's reluctance. Heidelberg, in nearby Tiffin, welcomed Nikkei.[99] "We think we can assimilate four to five students without any trouble," the college reported. "Objections to more than that will come largely from the community in which the college is located, not so much from the college students." College officials were likely wary of local American Legion Post No. 169, which protested student resettlement at its "Remember Pearl Harbor" meeting in 1942. "With so much at stake," a letter by Post No. 169 to the *National Legionnaire* magazine explained, "Americans dare not be too lenient."[100] Aware of local dissent, Heidelberg asked "that the new American Japanese student be of such a kind that he will quickly win the admiration and respect of other students."[101]

Heidelberg filled its quota for the fall term and its president Clarence E. Josephson expressed wonder that the students were not embittered by the shortcomings of American democracy. However, Heidelberg resisted council efforts to increase its quota, reporting in September 1943 that "public opinion in the city of Tiffin severely criticized the College [for enrolling Nikkei]. The feeling against these students was so strong that for the first semester we seldom permitted them to leave campus."[102] The college identified the local American Legion as the center of opposition. Bodine wrote that the council understood the need for the first resettled students to act as "ambassadors of good will in the college community, building up an understanding and sympathy of the student body, the faculty and the citizenry of the locality."[103] Heidelberg later increased its quota to six.

After the University of Toledo filed a welcoming questionnaire, the council forwarded applications to Toledo in November 1942.[104] The council pushed the cautious administration to increase its quota of three through a local contact, the Reverend Doctor Arthur R. Siebens, executive secretary of the Toledo Council of Churches. Siebens believed that Toledo's president had "a broad-gauged view toward the rest of humanity" and made contacts for the council with the Toledo Young People's Federation. After the city council defeated a movement to discourage resettlement in August 1943, the university began to expand its quota and had accepted ten resettled students by June 1945.

Earlham College, a Quaker school under the leadership of an active Quaker president, admitted two Nikkei transfers from Whittier College prior to September 1942 and expressed a willingness to enroll a total of twelve.[105] Earlham's president William C. Dennis preferred that the students be "American-born of unquestioned loyalty" and insisted that each meet the requirements made of all students at Earlham.[106] In addition, Earlham required that resettled students be able to meet all expenses for the first year without aid from the college or part-time work. Dennis viewed helping Nikkei as a "duty" but alerted the council to Earlham's financial difficulties. He wanted, he explained, "to carry the load without paying for the privilege of carrying it."[107]

Dennis, impatient with delays, communicated with military authorities and Nikkei students independently. Barstow praised his initiative in mid-August but warned that he was likely to be referred back to the council since the WRA wanted it to serve as the sole channel for clearance. Dennis replied by explaining, "I am not trying to bypass anything, but I am trying a la [sic] Foch to attack along the line in the hope of getting somewhere before college opens."[108]

Protests erupted as Nikkei students began to arrive in September. The Junior Order of United American Mechanics initiated the uproar by promoting a petition of protest.[109] Richmond's mayor, who had previously expressed approval of Earlham's actions, caved in to popular pressures and denounced student resettlement in late September. The Junior Order argued, "you can't trust a Jap" and "it [is] plenty wrong . . . to spend money on the education of Japanese when there are 'plenty of American boys who are just waiting for a chance to get an education.'"[110] A Richmond resident wrote Dennis, "It gives me unbounded pleasure to add my voice in vigorous protest to the enrollment of Japanese—even though American born—students at Earlham College. If I were an American Japanese today, I would surrender myself for enrollment in a concentration campus [sic] for the duration. . . . I certainly would not have the gall to accept rare privileges of that country under existing circumstances let alone ASK for them. But the Japs seem to be long on gall, and we . . . in Richmond are long on 'goo'—which makes it very nice and cozy for the 'poor' Japs."[111]

Earlham's college newspaper reported that press coverage greatly exceeded the importance of the protest. While an editorial noted that such a reaction might be expected from "former sympathizers of the old Ku Klux Klan" and other uninformed people, it described student resettlement as "Earlham's newest experiment in real democracy." The editorial refuted the claim that Nikkei students deprived others of an opportunity for education, noting that the resettled students paid full tuition and thus allowed for needy students to receive scholarship aid. The editorial stressed that the college remained united: "We stand by our ideals."[112]

Over Christmas break, "a daring but stupid plan" hatched by three resettled students inadvertently helped reverse public opinion. Hank Tanaka, Yoichi Oikawa, and Bill Uyeda decided to live at Bundy Hall, in violation of college rules, because they had nowhere else to go. They snuck in and out of an unlocked basement window and cooked in the biology lab. When Tanaka developed pneumonia, however, his ambulance ride to the hospital exposed the conspirators. President Dennis forgave the students and, Tanaka recalls, "[i]nstead of reprimands, we were flooded with sympathy cards, help calls and food from friends and from some people we didn't know." Press coverage created "a heightened sense of awareness of the unjust treatment of Japanese Americans" and helped smooth the way for the arrival of additional Nikkei.[113] In September 1943, Dennis reported that the attitude among faculty and students was "well nigh perfect" and that most "serious and sensible" people supported the college, too. He noted, however, that the college still had "to be very careful with a certain rather small, doubtless well meaning, but irreconcilable and irresponsible element in the community."[114]

The council also addressed the issue of Nikkei attending black colleges during the 1942–43 academic year. Although both Howard University and Fisk University expressed interest in enrolling Nikkei, the council hesitated, feeling that the issue would further complicate an already snarled procedure. The council remained resistant until Robert W. O'Brien assumed leadership. O'Brien, an active member of the National Association for the Advancement of Colored People, pushed for Nikkei to have the right to go to any college of their choice, including black schools. By October, he convinced Mike Masaoka to reverse his initial opposition, although Masaoka wanted the names of prospective students at black colleges sent to him, Beale explained, to ensure the council "was not sending the sort who would collaborate with negro [sic] student agitators in causing a troubled situation." The council, however, placed no students at either Howard or Fisk after reversing its policy. A Nisei did pursue graduate work at Fisk during the war, but the council did not play a role in the student's move from the University of Chicago. Despite at least one Nikkei's interest in Howard, no Japanese Americans attended the university during the war.[115]

Most colleges established quotas for Nikkei, fearing that too many resettlers might create resistance. The council supported quotas and informed colleges that none would "be expected to accept any large number and that it is probably desirable to disperse them fairly widely."[116] Kay Yamashita also reminded students at Topaz as they resettled that "the primary purpose of student relocation is to disperse youths."[117]

Quotas fit comfortably with WRA plans. Philip Glick, chief counsel for the WRA, expressed hope in a speech delivered in Poston "that, when the war is over, all Postonians will find a new home not bunched in 'Li'l Tokio's' or 'Li'l Osaka's' but scattered through-out the vast country, like other minority groups in the United States."[118] Myer reiterated this message in a speech to the Denson Community Council and block managers. He explained that "the dense congregation of Japanese in vital Coast defense areas" had provided one of the reasons for exile and incarceration. "[T]he ultimate solution of the entire problem," he argued, "lies in getting the people of Japanese descent resettled through-out the nation."[119]

The Council and the Students

As students arrived at colleges, some wrote about their experiences, often describing the trip east in what Gary Okihiro has called "travel account[s]," which depicted "a venture to novel climes and peoples."[120] Yeiz Kato described his four-day journey from the Heart Mountain concentration camp to Cincinnati as "a grand bus ride." All the passengers, including a soldier

84

who "served in Hawaii before and after the incident," were friendly.[121] Ruth Dohi described her train trip to Swarthmore College as "most stimulating and welcome after such a severely restricted life. Also, it was quite soothing in effect; for once, I was a passive spectator outside of the moving scene, instead of being one of the surging multitudes embroiled in the constant churn of camp life." Dohi also described her new surroundings: "[T]he fall leaves were quite lovely . . . and the countryside was most captivating and picturesque to my unaccustomed eye. . . . [T]he staid but energetic atmosphere, the language, the temperament, and the people—all so very interesting and charming. I was very much thrilled to be in the East!"[122]

The dramatically different environment could appear threatening to Nikkei. Some coped by traveling with other students. Others practiced chain migration from concentration camp to college. For example, the small Asbury College in Wilmore, Kentucky, had eleven resettled students by fall 1943. One had come from Granada and another had relocated to North Olmstead, Ohio, before moving to Asbury. The remaining nine resettled directly from Poston to Asbury.[123]

In contrast, Masaye Nakamura felt very much alone on her trip east.[124] A former freshman at the University of California, Los Angeles, Nakamura had reacted to exile and incarceration with disbelief. "I had felt," she later wrote, "up until that time that we were one hundred percent American citizens. I was aghast at the idea that I would not be considered one hundred percent American and that I would have to be looked on as an enemy and lose all my rights as a citizen." Thrilled by the opportunity to resettle as a student, Nakamura left Santa Anita on an army truck surrounded by three armed soldiers. Her trip became even more uncomfortable when she boarded her train:

> All the people were staring at me as I walked in and they were not pleasant stares. I could feel this hate, this feeling of real anger for the fact that I was boarding that car. [The conductor] snatched [my ticket] and with a look of real hate he spit on me. I was so taken aback with his action I could feel the spit rolling down my face. I couldn't even reach up and wipe it off. I felt so humiliated, and ashamed, and dirty. . . . [N]o one spoke up, no one said anything as he went through the car. Everybody was looking at me and I just sat there frozen. I don't know how long it was—throughout the night and half the day. I didn't eat, I didn't move, I just sat there.

Some students wrote the council with stories of warm welcomes. Dohi was met by a Swarthmore dean who "was very anxious to have my adjustment . . . be as pleasantly and easily made as possible." Administrators at the University of Cincinnati helped Yeiz Kato adjust by greeting him and personally explaining his late enrollment to his professors. Haruo Ishimaru, who would complete four years of college in thirty months at Yankton College in South Dakota, while winning "every possible oratorical competition in the state," praised the school's students and faculty for their cooperation and friendliness. George Oda found the College of Wooster "very friendly" and reported himself "gradually returning to the life of before my evacuation." Wilson College in Chambersburg, Pennsylvania, wrote that Helen Harada was making friends and becoming a "satisfactory member of [the] academic community." Despite this receptiveness, the college pressed for a second Nikkei student "as a protection against loneliness."[125]

Resettled students continued to serve as ambassadors of goodwill. They won student government offices at Oberlin, Bard College, Dakota Wesleyan University, and Haverford College. They also participated in extracurricular life by competing in college athletics, acting in school plays, and joining fraternities and sororities.[126] Yoshi Higa explained that time spent in the camps discussing "the problem of assimilation" had been productive: "[M]ost of us going to colleges will now make direct efforts to join various activities instead of acting obstinate and retreating into a nut-shell of our own." Bob Nakata agreed, noting, "[as Nikkei see] the larger America, for the first time, . . . we are creeping out of a shell that we have unconsciously been in."[127]

Sumiko Kanno echoed these sentiments in describing her experiences as a student nurse at the Mayo Clinic. "I think that you will be glad to know," she wrote, "that we are having a grand time, mixing in with all the Caucasian students. They've taken us in their bunch without question, and now we're just one of them. It's a glorious feeling. We work, study and play together." Kanno reported coming "in contact with many types of people. . . . I am very happy to say that not once have I heard any nasty remark or not once have I run into difficulty. . . . If we, in any small way 'break the ice' and prove to them that we are as American as they, I think we are accomplishing something."[128]

The council encouraged resettled students to follow the examples of Higa, Nakata, and Kanno. A form letter noted that "student letters speak unanimously of warm welcomes and real American friendliness. You have sold yourselves triumphantly and more than fulfilled our faith in you. We are proud of you and of the institutions and communities which have welcomed you." The letter closed with advice. "We hope," the council leaders wrote, "you will do all you can to mix with Caucasian students on your campus and not pal around mostly with [Nisei]. Particularly where there are a number of you at one place, avoid segregating yourselves."[129]

Nikkei students had mixed responses to this message; some believed that

86

such a strategy isolated them from their friends and from Japanese culture. Others of the resettled students agreed. One wrote the council to share her fellow Nikkei students' decision "not to travel around in a conspicuous group. This policy just about covers everything we do. In this way we hope to assimilate ourselves with the rest of the 'mob.'"[130]

Students also thanked the council. One student, blocked by the FBI from resettling, wrote that he still held "utmost faith in Democracy with its American Way of Life, largely because of groups like yours."[131] Although the council tried to discourage such thoughts, some students felt that they owed it something. One recounted his father's parting words: "I am old; some day you will hear that I am dying, perhaps while you are in school. Be strong! . . . Make my dying days happy in the knowledge that you are studying and preparing yourself for service. . . . Go and be of service to man!" The student felt a similar obligation to the council and promised, "I will not fail him or you, my friends."[132] Another declared, "Life begins with freedom" and thanked the council for helping "many of us to really live again."[133]

Other students expressed their thanks by lending the council a helping hand. Nao Takasugi had been a junior business major at the University of California, Los Angeles, when Pearl Harbor was attacked. "Here I was," he recalled, "a nineteen-year-old college student full of ambition and ideals. All of that just came crashing down." Incarcerated at Tulare and then at Gila River, Takasugi found "an unexpected opportunity" in student resettlement and left for Temple University in February 1943. After receiving a bachelor's of science in business in 1945, Takasugi earned a master's of business administration at the University of Pennsylvania's Wharton School. While going to school in Philadelphia in 1945, Takasugi also ran the council's placement department.

After struggling to find a job in postwar Philadelphia, Takasugi returned to Oxnard, California, to help his family resettle. He served on city council and as mayor before being elected to the California assembly in 1992. In a 1998 speech he delivered, Takasugi warned that "the phrase *shikata ga nai* [it cannot be helped] must not be the answer to the question of whether tomorrow's children have . . . a full understanding of the Japanese American experience. . . . America must never again fall prey to the temptation to count its citizens by color."[134] Still, Takasugi expressed little bitterness about exile and incarceration, preferring to look to the future and not to dwell on the past. "When I've gone to speak to high-school history classes or civic organizations or church groups, I just tell them what a great country we have," he explained. "You just won't find the opportunity any place [else] for a person who has been ejected to be able to come back and be a mayor of a city or a state representative. In spite of the many mistakes and flaws, it's still the greatest country in the world."[135]

Kenji Okuda, one of the council's most-cited "ambassadors," was admitted to Oberlin in August 1942 but did not arrive until February, because army intelligence was slow to clear him. While waiting, Okuda worked in the education program at Granada. He promoted student resettlement by corresponding with the council and colleges, creating a college council, establishing a catalog library, and collecting college newspapers. Okuda also observed the effects on the inmates as Granada took on "more of a concentration camp atmosphere." He worried that inmates seemed "speechless . . . either in astonishment, or from lack of interest, or from lack of any direction to the voices raised here and there."[136] Okuda suggested letters from resettled students and return visits to the camps to encourage resettlement.

Okuda's three-week trip to Oberlin helped him realize that some people continued to go out of their way to help Nikkei. This, he declared, "isn't the type of America one pictures after reading the newspapers in camp for a year." Okuda argued that experiencing life outside the camps "cannot help but broaden one's perspective, and that's what I need more than anything else." Still, Okuda found it harder to make white friends, perhaps, he mused, because a "defensive mechanism" developed in the camps. He believed that this would change, especially after the four Nisei living on his floor spread out next term.[137]

Okuda became a leader at Oberlin. He was elected student body president in March 1943 and played a role in making Oberlin "the ideal haven for any evacuated student" by helping to form an interracial group "to push forth [the Nikkei's] problems." This group informed local residents "of the evacuation and future possibilities for the Japanese [and] received a sympathetic and friendly response."[138]

Okuda's activism extended beyond campus. Thomas Bodine visited Oberlin in the spring and, in addition to reporting that the resettled students were assimilating and "rapturously happy," noted Okuda's activism. He reported that Oberlin Nikkei had been traveling to speak about exile and incarceration to receptive audiences. The council recommended Okuda as a speaker at colleges where individuals had expressed an interest in student resettlement.[139]

Okuda's message reached the camps, too. Camp newspapers covered his accomplishments, and Okuda visited some of the camps in 1944 and 1945. He expressed concern about Nisei apathy to the camp newspaper after speaking in Rohwer, Arkansas. Okuda encouraged Nisei to ask questions and express opinions, thus demonstrating an "active interest and courage to learn."[140]

While Okuda was an exemplar of student resettlement, some students, of course, did not resettle. The council attempted to follow up with nonresponsive students who had interviewed with Bodine in a form letter stressing that "[w]e have you very much on our hearts and minds here" and asking the students to file the necessary paperwork. King wrote one student, in what Bodine later described as a "typical Trudy King letter," to encourage action. King's letter was laid out like an act in a play: the first scene had the student filing his financial information, the second scene had the council applying for an educational leave, and the third scene had the climactic "happy ending" with the student at college. King's directions to the "leading man" were clear: "Your cue is to get this financial evidence to us without delay, and I mean now, *today*, [n]ot tomorrow. . . . We will be waiting to hear from you" (emphasis in original).[141] Beale wrote to a student, "[w]e at this council feel that it is a great mistake for you not to get back into normal American life, and we feel that going to college is one of the best ways of doing so."[142]

Family responsibilities kept some students in the camps. George Hara explained that his duties as the only son prevented him from resettling. Mabel Sugiyama thanked the council but related "a shock. . . . My mother . . . will not let me leave to go to school!" Draft registration had changed her mother's mind; she now wanted the family to stay together and planned to move them to join her husband in the Immigration and Naturalization Service's internment facility in Lordsburg, New Mexico. Sugiyama, despite expressing surprise, agreed. "If I were a boy," she explained, "this wouldn't matter too much because then my mother would not worry as much but being a girl all alone in the world which is bound to be filled with prejudices and discriminations[;] I feel I would rather stay with my mom."[143]

Sugiyama's comments suggest some of the obstacles, especially the "[p]atriarchal attitudes and sexism" noted by Gary Okihiro, faced by Nikkei women interested in student resettlement.[144] Women were kept from pursuing a college education by factors including monetary constraints (in part because the education of sons was the priority) as well as limited social roles and jobs. However, exile and incarceration paradoxically helped some Japanese American women pursue a college education. Changes in family structure in the camps granted some Nikkei women the confidence and freedom to go to college. Released from many traditional domestic chores and less controlled by fathers whose power had been undermined, some Nisei daughters pushed to continue their education.

Several factors helped women resettle. Some daughters who resettled had mothers who were better educated and more independent than most Nikkei women. One remembered her mother as "a woman ahead of her time," and another described her mother as "the first feminist to cross my path." Supportive fathers also often played an important role. Leslie A. Ito has found that many female students came from families that were financially stable and active in community leadership. Monetary aid received from the council proved essential to facilitating the moves of many Nikkei women. Since the council did not discriminate by gender in allocating grants, women who prior to the war would have missed out on a college education while their families paid for a son's education were freed of such financial constraints.[145]

Mary Tanaka's story suggests the effort and support required for many women to leave the camps. Tanaka was incarcerated with her mother; her brothers had resettled out of the camps and her father was interned at Santa Fe, New Mexico. After finishing high school at Manzanar, Tanaka remained in the camp, despite the urging of her teacher to go to college, to care for her mother. Tanaka so strongly wanted to go to school, however, that she worked feverishly to reunite her parents, gathering data for her father's second hearing to join his family at Manzanar. Noting her zeal, one administrator told Tanaka at the end of the hearing, "Don't worry little girl, you'll be able to attend school." Tanaka's father supported her dreams, too. She later remembered that her "father was really unusual and believed in educating daughters. . . . And there were many people in our block in camp who said 'You're really foolish to spend money on a daughter. Especially for a college education. They'll just get married and the money will be wasted.'"[146]

While women found new opportunities to pursue a college education during the war, men found new obligations that barred them from attending school. Military service prevented some men from student resettlement. Jack Emoto secured acceptance at Phillips University in Oklahoma in spring 1943 but "forfeited all chances for continuing [his] education when [he] volunteered for the Army."[147] George Ogawa believed, "for [some] men to enjoy leisurely education, while others are marching off to war, is unfair and almost inconsistent with the struggle that confronts this nation in this time of grave emergency." He still saw value in the council's program, however, and was "sure that [its] work is producing real citizens out of hyphenated people who are called 'Japs.' . . . [M]ay the students . . . give you just and great satisfaction so that your project will have achieved its noble end."[148]

Other students complicated the council's job by resettling but not enrolling at the college they left to attend. One student gained acceptance at the University of Nebraska, chose not to attend, and later was accepted by the University of Wyoming and the University of Texas. He briefly attended Texas and then left for work in Colorado.[149] Sumiko Mary Okita decided to leave camp for Parsons College in Iowa in spring 1943 but did not enroll. When King wrote to follow up, Okita reported that she had enrolled at Morningside College in Sioux Falls, South Dakota.[150]

To encourage resettlement, council representatives visited the concentration camps. O'Brien visited the camps to emphasize that "[p]rospects are bright for student relocation" and to encourage students, "especially those graduating from high school," to apply for placement.[151] West Coast workers visited camps in February while traveling east when the council's offices were consolidated.[152]

Bodine visited Minidoka in February and credited the success of the council's program "to the cooperation of government and educational authorities and to relocated students who are 'doing a swell job of selling our program.'"[153] In a speech to students, Bodine lauded them for not thinking about college like the dying man in a joke—"Sure, I wants [sic] to go to Heaven, but—thank you—not tonight." Acknowledging delays, Bodine explained that the council and the WRA had done all they could, but that "wheels turn slowly in the . . . Capitol of the United Nations and so we have all just got to be patient." Bodine appealed to high school students to apply and addressed potential barriers to student resettlement. Women need not hesitate to move, he argued, because local sponsors would look out for them. He encouraged men concerned about the draft to get as much education as possible prior to induction. Reports from resettled students about extreme weather, he continued, were often exaggerated. While admitting that finances were a delicate question, he pointed out that resettling in a new community, continuing higher education, making new friends, and getting a good job were the "[b]est investment possible."[154]

Bodine toured the camps as field director into summer. In addition to interviewing students individually, Bodine held group meetings for students, parents, and other interested groups. At Topaz, for example, he met with the student relocation staff, the intercollegiate fellowship, and the scholarship fund committee. While at Poston, Bodine spoke at the adult education department's student relocation forum. Bodine addressed a number of topics, including the reception of Nikkei as well as the proper conduct and responsibilities of resettled Nikkei. He encouraged resettlement with statistics and the success stories. "I like Manzanar students," Bodine told the Manzanar *Free Press* in a message likely repeated elsewhere, "and I hope to find them all in New England when I go back there after the war."[155]

The desire to attend larger colleges impeded student resettlement in some cases, and the council adopted a number of arguments to convince Nikkei of the advantages of smaller schools. While prestigious universities remained closed, small colleges were open and would help clear the way for additional students to resettle.[156] O'Brien praised smaller colleges at which athletic participation and a friendly environment made it easier to make friends. "My own personal conviction," he wrote, "is that one point where all of us have failed has been in the area of encouraging students to attend a smaller school where orientation and assimilation into the community life are often more easily attained."[157] The council continued to promote small colleges even as the larger ones opened, noting that students knew the professors better on smaller campuses and, most importantly, developed relationships with white students.[158]

The council sent releases to the camp newspapers to reinforce Bodine's message, highlighting success stories such as those of Lillian Ota and Kenji Okuda and reporting in summer 1943 that students with reasonably good grades could expect, if necessary, some financial aid. The council also noted that resettled students "[had] almost invariably told a story of good and tremendous happiness at being out and finding friendliness and helpfulness on the outside."[159]

The council also used statistics to encourage resettlement. Of the 2,166 questionnaires on file as of late December 1942, the council noted, 500 had been accepted by a college. Data collection continued for 1,300 students. The remaining 300 questionnaires were either in an earlier stage of processing or had been postponed. The council also pointed out that 200 additional students had expressed interest but had not yet filed a questionnaire.[160]

Momentum continued into the summer. The Tulean *Dispatch* recorded the growing numbers of applications received by the council, which reached 2,751 in March and exceeded 3,000 by August. The newspaper combined impressive statistics in August—1,136 students resettled at 282 colleges in 38 states—with a personalized examination of student resettlement. The council, it noted in a headline, was "[e]ager to [h]elp." The *Dispatch* also emphasized "exuberant letters" that emphasized enthusiastic welcomes for students.[161]

Camp newspapers personalized student resettlement by providing updates on students leaving for college. As stories of neighbors and fellow inmates— real people instead of statistics—appeared, the council's program became a real force in students' lives, not just an abstract source of hope. As newspapers printed longer lists of student departures, others received reassurance that they, too, could resettle to pursue a college education. As the military's list of approved colleges grew from 110 in fall 1942 to 284 by mid-December, camp papers publicized offers made by specific schools to encourage resettlement.[162]

Inmates also encouraged student resettlement. An essay published by the Minidoka *Irrigator* asked Nisei to think about their future and urged them to stop relying on their parents. "After all," Mary Minamoto asked, "is life really worth living if you cannot find a place in it?" She foresaw opportunities for educated Nisei in the future: "Be better than the rest so as to win the gradual but nation-wide acceptance and approval of [Nikkei] as assets to their community and nation."[163]

In mid-November, the *Outpost* had argued that student resettlement could drain "center leadership" and "cultural activities." The newspaper suggested that college was not necessarily "more desirable" than camp life, which could also lead to increased knowledge and understanding. The editorial staff, perhaps reflecting the changing WRA emphasis from community development to resettlement, changed its message by August, however. Lamenting the "emphasis of the youths [on] the recreational side of life" as a result of camp life, the *Outpost* now argued "that educational training of our youth on the outside would reap the [Nisei] greater benefits by giving those with intelligence an opportunity to better themselves."[164]

Letters from resettled students printed in camp newspapers addressed common concerns such as the cost of living and the availability of part-time jobs. Many also mentioned negative aspects of resettlement, including "silly" questions asked by curious and ignorant Americans, unfriendly whites, the awkwardness of starting in a new school, and the unfamiliar cold and snow. Most, however, accentuated positive aspects. Students joined other resettlers, perhaps most importantly, "in praising the 'free air.'"[165]

The Poston *Press Bulletin* focused on positive aspects in its coverage of the controversy at Park College in Parkville, Missouri, where Mayor Herbert A. Dyer, local citizens, and members of the American War Mothers and the American Legion, which had described student resettlement as "a shocking injustice and breach of faith with our own American sons," protested the arrival of resettled students in September 1942. The college decided to let the students stay "because their loyalty is unquestioned." The *Press Bulletin* used a letter from Nisei at Park to reassure inmates that the students had the support of the faculty and students. The newspaper also praised President William Lindsey Young, described as usually soft-spoken, for taking "up the hatchet in behalf of the [Nisei] to a successful conclusion."[166]

The newspaper did not note in any kind of detail, however, the racial tensions in Parkville. When Masaye Nakamura had arrived, President Young warned her not to go downtown by herself because of local "unhappiness." Nakamura, growing restless with her restraints, decided to go to town alone to buy stamps. As she walked through town, she drew unhappy stares, and, eventually, a group of townspeople began to follow her. When the woman at the post office marveled at Nakamura's ability to speak English, the resettled student testily explained, "[o]f course I speak English, that's the only language I know, just like you." President Young was furious with Nakamura, explaining that he felt responsible for her safety, and he grounded her for one month.[167]

The resettled students also recounted their efforts as ambassadors of goodwill. One noted that "[n]aturally, they wonder what we're like and whether we can be trusted. I am 'good willing' them as best I can with some success already."[168] Another reminded students that they would "be a representative of other [Nikkei]. It is your action among the Caucasians which will foretell our future and determine whether or not we will be accepted as one of them. It is you and I who have to cut the path into the American way of life and the democratic way of living. We can be pioneers so that some day . . . we of Japanese extraction may live in a nation which shall have broader understanding and a universal outlook that knows no color or creed . . . It's really a challenge, isn't it?"[169]

The council advised, "[y]ou are ambassadors, paving the way for others, and we hope you will take the responsibility seriously." Bodine stressed student responsibilities: "[e]very Japanese American, whether still on the project, waiting for an educational leave, resettled in college or on an employment leave, is an ambassador of goodwill, paving the way for others along relocation lines."[170]

The potential contributions of resettled students became especially clear through specific examples. Kiyoko Hosoura, a former University of California, Los Angeles, student at Webster College in Missouri, had convinced the college, the *Pioneer* reported, to establish a $250 scholarship, more than one-third of a year's cost, for a Nikkei woman. Hosoura's record at Webster, both as "a very capable student" and as a citizen "very loyal to the principles of American democracy," had encouraged the school to make this offer. The *Pioneer* used Hosoura to demonstrate an important lesson: "[t]he success of student relocation depends greatly upon the conduct and record of those now in school."[171]

Camp newspapers also commented on *Time*'s coverage of resettled students in its June 21, 1943, issue. *Time* reported that "government officials seem relatively calm about most [Nisei]." The magazine cited the all-Nisei army unit currently training and the more than one thousand students resettled as reasons for the government's confidence. Pointing to Okuda "as a typical [Nisei] student," *Time* stressed that he had been "elected primarily on the basis of merit."[172]

94

The council encouraged inmates to support student resettlement and recommended the formation of a committee, either specifically for student resettlement as at Tule Lake or as an active college club as at Manzanar, to coordinate efforts and provide counseling. The council's suggestion of assembling a college catalog library was widely adopted. The council also urged local committees to imitate Poston's work "in preparing the students for being the best sort of ambassadors to the outside world." A ceremony for each resettled student from Poston involved placing a pin at the student's destination on a map. Those still in camp were to look at the pins as symbols of the students' service as Nikkei ambassadors in their new communities. Finally, the council urged that counseling be done by Nikkei "aided and guided by interested members of the Caucasian staff."[173]

Students often created clubs for college-aged people in the camps. Two of the more active student clubs in 1942–43 were in Manzanar and Topaz. The Inter-Collegiate Club of Manzanar, sponsored by the YMCA and YWCA, wanted to aid student resettlement, to build an interest in college, and to promote student fellowship.[174] The Student Association of Topaz, formed at a rally on January 9, 1943, that drew two hundred people, proposed activities such as educational programs, interest groups, special projects, and recreation. The group staged a musical program in May to benefit Topaz's scholarship fund.[175]

The council used student relocation counselors in the camps to oversee resettlement and to urge students to work through the council. Beale warned that one student who wanted to go to Rutgers was not strong enough academically to apply to a college the council had worked hard to open. Counselors also identified potential problems. George Lafabregue at Topaz, for example, reported that Nikkei were congregating in new college locales, especially at the University of Nebraska and Washington University. This, he believed, "is entirely contrary to the intents and purposes of the student relocation program." He noted that Topaz student counselors were writing letters to all their resettled students "pointing out the importance of mingling in the normal life of the college and community."[176]

Conclusion: The First Year

Although Trudy King, reflecting the personalized approach advocated by the council, argued that statistics could not tell the entire story, the council often used statistics to chart its progress. These statistical summaries provide an overview of the council's tumultuous first year, highlighting the problems it faced as well as its eventual, albeit slow, progress in facilitating the movement of students from concentration camp to campus. The hard-won progress achieved by the end of the 1942–43 academic year, however, left many potential students in the camps, unable to pursue higher education. Still, the council looked optimistically to the future. "Student relocation," Howard K. Beale told Rohwer students in early February, "has changed the attitude in regard to Japanese-Americans. That is one of the greatest things accomplished by the [council]."[177]

By the end of the fall 1942 term, more than 800 of the 2,300 Japanese American applicants to the council had been accepted by a college, although fewer than 400 had actually been resettled at 93 different colleges. About 100 additional students had left camps, with council help, on employment leaves.[178] More than 1,000 Nikkei students were attending 175 institutions of higher learning in 37 states by May 1943. The number of resettled students exceeded 1,500 by August (see table 2). Statistical progress, in addition to the "cordial welcome and . . . many honors" received by the resettled students, suggests that the council had managed to overcome external restrictions.[179] The council's success in overcoming student resettlement roadblocks did not end its work, however; it would find a new set of problems in the coming year even as government restrictions eased.

Table 2. Japanese American Students Enrolled in College as of August 10, 1943, by Camp

Camp	Enrolled prior to August 25	Accepted/WouldEnroll for Fall 1943 Term
Minidoka	169	39
Tule Lake	116	19
Poston	114	16
Gila	99	18
Granada	94	19
Topaz	88	20
Heart Mountain	75	15
Rohwer	55	5
Jerome	42	6
Manzanar	38	7
	890	164
Nonevacuee students	632	5

Source: "1,613 Nisei Students Enrolled in Colleges," Granada *Pioneer,* 25 August 1943, 6. The total to be enrolled according to the figures is 1,691, which does not match the number in the headline. The figures, despite this problem, still provide a general idea of student resettlement from each camp.

96

CHANGE AND NEW CHALLENGES IN A
WORLD AT WAR, FALL 1943–SUMMER 1944

"It is very good," Mary Murata wrote Trudy King, "to be out again and enjoy the freedom of walking the streets, riding vehicles, and so many other things which we missed so long." Blocked from resettlement during 1942–43 by school quotas, Murata resettled to St. Mary's School of Nursing in Rochester, Minnesota, in fall 1943. She wrote to thank King and the council, "for all your kind attention and your untiring efforts, and may God bless you all for your wonderful work."[1]

As increasing numbers of inmates resettled to schools for 1943–44, they played a part in transforming college campuses. The 1944 Drew University yearbook, "a chronicle of a year of transition [and] a graphic account of the change wrought on an American college campus by a world at war," took note of these changes. The yearbook presented sketches of Drew students that suggest one significant change: the presence of Nikkei students. The annual recalled Ben Iijima "hurrying across campus to the dining hall, his face glowing with that friendly smile!" The annual also reminisced about "the quiet and efficient" Albert Mineta working in the dining hall, performing chemistry experiments, and serving with the Student Association Treasury.[2]

Later annuals reveal another important change at the Madison, New Jersey, school: decreasing male enrollment led the university to accept its first female students. Sayoko Nakata, a University of California transfer from Topaz, became the first woman to graduate from Drew. The 1945 yearbook praised Nakata for her "friendliness and attractive personality" as well as her academic success. Sumiko Kobayashi, another former Topaz inmate, also resettled to Drew. Kobayashi, the annual observed, "was a combination of petite femininity and efficient leadership. [H]er friendly nature and wide interests should increase her circle of friends."[3]

Kobayashi had followed a long and winding road to Drew.[4] Born in 1923 in Yamato, Florida, a Nikkei agricultural community near Palm Beach, Kobayashi moved with her family in 1925 to Riverdale, an estate near Chicago where her father worked in the greenhouse and cared for the grounds. When the estate was given to the county to become a forest preserve in 1939, the Kobayashi family moved to San Leandro, California, and Sumiko graduated from her new high school in June 1941.

Kobayashi could not afford to go to the University of California that fall, however, and her plans to enter the university were further sidetracked by illness. The government's exile put Berkeley out of the question. Although she and her family felt betrayed by exile and incarceration, Kobayashi recalled, "[m]ost of our friends were Japanese Americans and in those days the mindset was different. You know, everybody worshiped F.D.R. He pulled us out of the Depression. Everybody believed the government could do no wrong." The Kobayashi family was exiled to Tanforan and then incarcerated in Topaz.

Kobayashi received encouragement to resettle from Thomas Bodine and Kay Yamashita, who worked in the Topaz youth department. Yamashita graduated from the University of California just before the bombing of Pearl Harbor and worked in student resettlement before being exiled to Tanforan and then Topaz. Yamashita was active in student resettlement work in Topaz and traveled to Philadelphia in fall 1943 to work in the council's placement department. A Topaz resident remembered Yamashita "as a friend, as a mother confessor, as a cheerleader and as a mover. . . . She escorted me out of camp [bound for Alfred University] amid all the dust and cold and ushered me into an unknown world." The inmate praised Yamashita for "quietly and tirelessly . . . planting the seeds [that changed] the status of the Nisei generation in our society forever. This thin slip of a woman who had the vision, the conviction and the hopes of our success. . . . She was the one who gave us hope, calmed our fears, and showed us the way. In my history book, Kay Yamashita is the patron saint of the Nisei collegians of World War II."[5]

Kobayashi applied to Ohio Wesleyan at the council's suggestion, but the college had filled its quota and denied her admission in June. Kobayashi spent the summer anxiously looking for a school and a job to help support herself after resettlement. As quotas filled, Cornell and Drake also turned her down. Drew accepted Kobayashi in September 1943.

Kobayashi later described her time at Drew as "a pleasant interlude in my life." She recalled a stranger greeting her upon her arrival with "a very friendly hello," a surprising reception to someone "just out of a concentration camp." Kobayashi received a tuition scholarship from Drew and worked for a local family during her first two semesters. Her mother also sent Kobayashi her entire government "wages," sixteen dollars per month, to help with expenses. Kobayashi moved into the dormitory for her last two years at Drew and had no problems with V-12 naval classmates. After finishing her course work in 1946, Kobayashi worked in the registrar's office to pay back a loan from the school. She then moved to be with her family who had resettled in Philadelphia.

Incarcerated students such as Kobayashi took advantage of increasing opportunities and liberalized student resettlement regulations to pursue higher education in 1943–44. Camp high school graduates resettled. Some students who had postponed resettlement now pursued college education. Others who had tried earlier but failed to resettle finally left, too. The council had helped approximately fifteen hundred students resettle in its first fifteen months of work; almost fifteen hundred more would leave the camps for colleges during 1943–44.

Debating the Council's Future

An ongoing debate about the council's own future framed its efforts with colleges and students in 1943 and 1944. This debate, which continued while the council struggled to find a solution to the problem of the navy's proscribed list, climaxed at the second plenary meeting held September 29, 1943, in New York City. One group at the meeting advocated expanding the council's current program. Marian Reith of the YWCA urged the council to expand its role by working on the problem of student lethargy in the camps. Marjorie Elkus of the Columbia Foundation thought that additional financial support for the council might be found "if new plans were developed to further [the promotion of public relations]."

Others at the meeting favored the immediate reduction of the council's program and the eventual cessation of its work. Representatives of the Congregational Church and the Association of American Colleges bluntly suggested "a prompt reduction of the staff and curtailment of operations." Representatives from the JACL and the AFSC viewed family resettlement as the foremost priority and suggested that it would solve the college "problem" as students resettled with their families and were absorbed "in the [new] Community." John Nason also favored reducing council activities, emphasizing financial limitations.[6]

Nason reported the meeting's decision to "curtail our activities and look toward their ultimate cessation" to the WRA director Dillon S. Myer on October 5. Emphasizing that the council had "fulfilled [its] original purpose" and noting difficulties in raising additional funds, Nason argued that it would be best "to look toward a conclusion of our affairs instead of toward a lingering death by financial inanition."[7] Carlisle V. Hibbard, the council director, informed Myer of divided opinion: some favored ending its program, while others wanted to do so only if other agencies could assume its responsibilities.[8]

Nason explained both arguments in a form letter to council members but clearly favored the arguments for closing. The council, he observed, had placed as many students as had been in West Coast colleges prior to the war and most active "cases" would be completed within four months. As the number of students to be resettled decreased, the budget-conscious Nason observed, the cost per student would increase significantly. Finally, financial considerations limited the council's choices: foundation support would soon expire and the "slender support" of the church boards had no assurance of continuation. Nason presented his recommendation but noted that a final decision would not be made until December: "Under the circumstances it appeared to the council wise to look toward a cessation of our activities as a separate organization."[9]

Dissent from the council's decision to close came from various people. Myer observed that follow-up and trouble-shooting work remained. He argued for the continued operation of the council in view of the WRA's larger goal of family resettlement, believing the Nikkei students to be an "effective solvent of race prejudice at a center of influence."[10] Myer reinforced these points in a November 22 letter to Nason, arguing that the council's experience made it best suited to deal with resettled students and recalcitrant colleges. The council's central role in coordinating the work of church boards, camp personnel, and government officials, Myer added, made its continued existence invaluable.[11]

Bodine also opposed the council's decision to cease operations. He believed that the decision resulted from council administrators' wrongly assuming that students had little need for the council. The lack of scholarships, administrative funds, and college openings, he observed, had also influenced the decision. The key problem, however, remained a "[l]ack of vitality in the . . . council's leadership." Believing that the correction of this underlying issue would fix the others, Bodine argued that the council should continue helping camp high school graduates and providing resettled students with advice. He pointed to a unique and important contribution of the council: it helped build morale in the camps as a private agency that treated students as friends and not clients.[12]

Support for continuation of the council also arrived from Nikkei. "What is this story I hear," one resettled student asked, "of the dissolution of the [council]? I do hope unless it is for a very good reason it can continue and bring the happiness I'm enjoying to others and there must be deserving applicants."[13] Yosh Kodama, a relocation adviser and chair of the Heart Mountain Relocation Committee, argued that the council remained necessary, especially because of its social significance for students still "under the influence of the Center environment."[14] Kodama believed that the council's closing would disadvantage hundreds of students: "Without the invaluable assistance of the council, these young people will feel utterly helpless."[15]

As protests against the cessation of council activities mounted, changes in the process of student resettlement also convinced the council to reconsider. The new procedures for clearance discussed by WRA and military officials at the August 12 meeting called by Adlai E. Stevenson finally became official on October 14, 1943, when the Provost Marshal General's Office (PMGO) received responsibility for clearing Nikkei students for attendance at colleges important to the war effort. The new process pleased the council because it allowed for Nikkei attendance at any school in the United States except those located in currently restricted West Coast areas. Unfortunately, from the council's perspective, the new procedure also added yet another level of red tape and its concomitant delays.[16] Despite such disadvantages, this change represented a significant step toward treating Nikkei like most other students.

While Myer expressed his disappointment at the "discriminatory and unnecessary" process of individual investigations, he cautiously chose to accept the new arrangements. Fearing that colleges would find the new paperwork too cumbersome to administer and noting that the PMGO would only clear students after they had been accepted, Myer asked the council to serve as "a central clearing house . . . to handle the initial arrangements."[17] The executive committee agreed to assume this additional responsibility on November 24, 1943, providing it with another reason to continue operations.[18]

The new process closely resembled the clearance procedure used for factories engaged in important war work.[19] Designed to use a Nikkei workforce while protecting against "possible injury or destruction national-defense material, national-defense premises and national-defense utilities," the new plan allowed "no person of Japanese ancestry . . . to attend or be employed by an educational institution important to the war effort until approval for such attendance or employment has been given by The Provost Marshal General."[20] On WRA clearance alone, Nikkei could now attend all colleges not on the proscribed list. Students could also enroll at proscribed colleges after obtaining acceptance and PMGO clearance, allowing students to attend most large schools, which until this point had been strictly off-limits. The council prepared students for the long delays that came with another set of forms, suggesting that "[i]t's just part of the process of fighting a war which all of us everywhere in the country are learning not to complain about. Sure, the student has to fill in a long form in six copies [and] it takes four to six weeks and even longer sometimes. . . . Washington is a very busy place these days; wheels turn slowly. The important thing is that the new procedure does make it possible for students of Japanese ancestry to attend large universities." The council pointed out in July that the PMGO had rejected only thirty-five of the four hundred students accepted by proscribed schools.[21]

The council took advantage of the new procedure, sending a form letter to a selected group of students informing them of the change. Choosing students it thought likely to gain acceptance at proscribed colleges, the council encouraged them to apply, using "Caucasian references" if possible, and not to communicate directly with the schools since the new process was "in its preliminary stages."[22]

The cumbersome yet promising new procedure for proscribed colleges was plagued by delays in its early months because the council had to communicate with the WRA, the PMGO, the camps, and the colleges.[23] The council's cautious approach influenced its communications with colleges. Nason responded to a question from Oberlin's president Ernest Wilkins about how to protest his school's proscribed status by explaining that he could contact the chief of the Japanese American branch, Captain Clarence Harbert; however, Nason stressed that "Harbert is trying very hard to straighten out a difficult situation and that his heart is in the right place." Nason thought Harbert "more liberal and sympathetic" than many military officials and urged Wilkins to keep this in mind.[24]

The council also attempted to take advantage of the new procedure by eliminating colleges from the proscribed list. It mailed letters to proscribed colleges, pointing out that some colleges remained on the list because of confidential research activities in only "one or more buildings or parts on the campus."[25] Harbert was willing, however, to apply restrictions only to those parts of the campus. Thus, the council asked for information and even maps of campuses that detailed classified and nonclassified areas. Hibbard passed college responses on to Harbert.[26] While Hibbard appreciated Harbert's promptness in considering clearing students, Harbert did not always view the council as kindly, complaining to the WRA that the council's letter to colleges complicated his work.[27]

Trudy King argued against the necessity of a proscribed list even while the council coordinated the new PMGO process. She suggested that although certain colleges held contracts with the military, "Japanese Americans on the whole are too conspicuous for espionage." An additional background investigation constituted an unnecessary additional step considering the checks already in place. King noted that the new PMGO process imputed danger to a group with "very low records of delinquency." Furthermore, the disloyal members among the inmates had been identified and "weeded out" by the FBI and the WRA.

The American Civil Liberties Union had employed a similar argument in December 1943, asking Secretary of War Henry Stimson to allow loyal Nikkei (meaning those not segregated in Tule Lake) to attend colleges without restriction. John J. McCloy still did not presume Japanese American innocence even in 1944 and responded in January by noting that while the War Department favored "full participation of loyal persons of Japanese ancestry in the war effort," it could not safely assume "that all persons of Japanese descent not in the Tule Lake center are loyal to the United States." McCloy added, "[s]ometimes it is difficult to satisfy oneself as to their loyalty—more difficult than in the case of the Caucasian who is usually better assimilated in the community. This amounts to discrimination of a sort I suppose but it seems reasonable and not burdensome."[28]

King criticized the arbitrary nature of the new system, wondering who made the seemingly casual decisions to add schools to the list. "We are," she pessimistically concluded, "worse off than before. More colleges are on the list. More will be added. No one seems to have the power to take them off." King complained that the PMGO moved slowly. She pointed out that the new system was based exclusively on race and violated the Constitution and basic principles of American democracy. King presented a drastic solution to the problem: abolish the procedure as "undemocratic, time consuming, and unnecessary." Barring improvements, she advised that the council "drop out of the picture [and] not endorse this discriminatory policy."[29] Despite King's complaints, the new PMGO process represented at least some progress; although it may not have been clear in February 1944, the new process was a transitional step toward the removal of all restrictions on Nikkei students.

The WRA worried that pressing for faster action might backfire and advised the council that follow-up letters would not speed PMGO actions. Hibbard relayed this message to Bodine, noting "some rather sharp letters from Mr. Provinse and Mrs. Dunbar" that criticized the council for writing too many letters and making too many special requests.[30] Provinse reminded

Hibbard's successor, Helga Swan,[31] of the WRA's advice not to flood the PMGO with letters. He pointed out that while Harbert and the PMGO were "thoroughly sympathetic and wherever possible [gave] an individual the benefit of the doubt," too many special requests might harm the current positive relationship.[32] "I have been quite frank with you," Provinse concluded, "since I feel this is a serious matter, and I hope you will give this letter your earnest consideration."[33]

The executive committee, faced with strong opposition to its plan to cease operations and a new role in facilitating the PMGO process, voted to continue operations through 1944 at its November 24, 1943, meeting. Noting a "chorus of objections" to closing the council, Nason acquiesced to continued operations but remained dubious about actively encouraging student applications, suggesting that students still in the camps "have lost their ambition and have developed a defeatist attitude." He also continued to worry that financial limitations might prevent further council actions.[34]

Having decided to continue operations into 1944, the council set its future agenda. Noting that it had fulfilled its original purpose of placing students whose college education had been interrupted by exile and incarceration, the council now turned to focus on interested camp high school graduates. The council continued, however, to resist aiding students interested in trade or vocational schooling, arguing that the WRA and the YMCA had better information on such schools.[35]

The council's proper role in the camps sparked internal debate. Nason pointed out in March 1944 that Bodine advocated "a quite different function [than he imagined]—that of going into the Projects to encourage or cajole or otherwise stimulate young men and women of college age to get out into the mainstream of American life." Clearly believing this job belonged to the WRA, Nason continued to argue that the council's work ought to be "curtailed and eventually eliminated."[36]

Bodine's position received support. Esther Rhoads, while willing to countenance the eventual closing of the council if other groups accepted its work, agreed that it performed an important job by boosting morale in the camps. Walter Balderston, a former student resettlement worker employed by the WRA as supervisor of community activities at Poston, supported an increased role in the camps, too. He argued that the council's efforts freed advisers to do more student counseling and placement. The stability of the council also helped smooth inconsistencies created by rapid turnover in camp personnel. Student interest remained strong at Poston and the council's help with scholarships provided important aid. Finally, Balderston argued that the council played a key role in stimulating students as "an outside non-government agency that is deeply interested in the welfare of our young people." Students would listen to the council because it was an "outsider" and not "suspected of having axes to grind."[37] Similarly, Monroe Deutsch had written previously, "we should encourage those who are qualified to go out." Student resettlement, he believed, provided valuable opportunities and helped "to bridge the situation for their families when they come out."[38]

Myer and Provinse took a position between those of Bodine and Nason. Myer expressed his appreciation for the council's "good work" that meant so much to the students as well as their families and friends. The financial aid and facilitating work of the council, he continued, "has done much to offset the disillusion and frustration resulting from the evacuation. You have also been able to bring directly home to several hundred institutions an awareness and greater appreciation of basic principles and responsibilities."

Myer did not, despite his praise for the council's success in combating disillusion, endorse Bodine's position. He wanted the council to continue operations in light of the WRA's goal of total resettlement. While Myer agreed with Bodine that Nikkei needed encouragement to resettle, he did not see this as a job for the council. "Tom Bodine," Myer remarked, "in his enthusiasm and interest, goes further than is necessary." Instead, he envisioned the council operating on a reduced basis to maintain its friendly contacts with students and colleges.[39] Provinse reinforced Myer's point; he preferred that "already available agencies . . . take care of the work."[40]

The executive committee debated the merits of increasing the council's fieldwork at its May 10, 1944, meeting. Nason had concisely reviewed the terms of the debate in a form letter, noting that "[i]t seems probable . . . that the number of new applications and consequently the number of students relocated, will dwindle considerably . . . unless steps are taken to encourage more of the potential students on the Projects to apply for relocation." He described growing discouragement, apathy, and fear as well as Issei pressure for students "to stay [in the camps] where it is safe" as barriers to student resettlement. Bodine, he noted, had encouraged resettlement while touring the camps, and thus the council had a precedent if it chose to enlarge its program. However, Nason wondered if such an extension would overlap with work already being done by other organizations. He also questioned the likely results in light of the increased costs the council would have to bear.[41]

The council followed the WRA's lead at its meeting on June 15, 1944. While stating that "every effort should be made to encourage students on the Projects to relocate in colleges," the council decided that other groups should have primary responsibility for doing so. The council also noted that it lacked the financial resources to undertake such a project. It decided instead to aid groups already trying to stimulate resettlement.[42]

The Council and the Colleges

As the 1943–44 school year progressed, more schools became willing to accept Nikkei students. The new process of PMGO clearance convinced some of the safety of the council's program. The course of the war in the Pacific made it easier for others to cooperate. Positive propaganda produced by the Office of War Information and the WRA had at least begun to improve popular images of Japanese Americans. The success of earlier placements also broke down barriers. Finally, some colleges became desperate for students as the war went on and looked to the enrollment of Nikkei as a possible solution to declining enrollments.

President K. C. Leebrick of Kent State University had initially replied that he could not cooperate because of local war work in a highly industrialized area.[43] The council did not attempt to place Nikkei at Kent again until May 1943, after a year of successful placements elsewhere, and Leebrick agreed to accept Marion Kobara for the fall. Kent eventually enrolled more Nikkei, in part because of Kobara's success. The registrar reported that Kobara was "doing exceedingly well. She adjusted herself in different groups, is well thought of, and has talked, I judge, about the Japanese to several groups."[44]

Kobara seemed just as pleased, writing that she had met no hostility. Although the college was smaller than others, she praised it as "very friendly and inviting." She noted that local newspapers had covered her enrollment but was happier to report, "in the class rooms I am just one of them receiving just as much attention no more no less from the professors." Residents invited Kobara to their homes and she spent many weekends and vacations with a family in nearby Uniontown. "Many a time when I was in the Tule Lake Project," Kobara wrote, "I would daydream trying to picture how Kent would be. Now when I think it over Kent is what I had dreamed in Tule Lake."[45]

Carrie E. McKnight, the registrar at Muskingum College in New Concord, Ohio, had reported with regret to the council in December 1942 that her school could not cooperate because of local hostility.[46] The council approached the school again that summer, noting successful Nikkei at many Ohio colleges. McKnight relented in August, noting that some community resistance remained but adding that the college could withstand some criticism because "it is the Christian thing for us to do."

Muskingum's reversal quickly drew interested students, among them Kinji

Hiramoto at Rohwer. Hiramoto remembered an idyllic prewar existence in Lodi, California. "When I saw the Waltons have dinner on TV," he recalled, "I was reminded of our happy days before the War when eleven of us would be at the dinner table together." After graduating from high school, Hiramoto found a civil service job with the Quartermaster Corps but was fired after Pearl Harbor. The Hiramoto family was incarcerated first in Stockton and later in Rohwer.[47]

Hiramoto's decision to resettle to college perhaps began to take shape one mid-August evening at Stockton, when he and his friend Frank Ito "watched the outside world through [the] fence . . . at sundown."[48] One week later, however, Hiramoto received a pessimistic letter from the council. After being transferred to Rohwer, Hiramoto resisted the apathy that he sensed creeping into the other inmates' lives; a diary entry on November 1, 1942, pledged to "[m]ake use of time." As the number of people resettling from Rohwer seemed to increase almost monthly, Hiramoto explored two options for escaping camp: work and college. He negotiated with two potential employers without success. Then, on May 20, 1943, his one-year anniversary of incarceration, Hiramoto noted that many of his "friends [had] scattered all over the country now because of relocation." The anniversary and a late-night "bull session" with Ito seem to have convinced Hiramoto to pursue a college education more aggressively. Hiramoto wrote that he was "[g]etting nowhere in camp—might as well go to school or outside employment." Within one week of a friend's return visit from college, Hiramoto was writing to the council and Muskingum College.

The council officially forwarded Hiramoto's application to Muskingum on June 12, 1943. As part of an appeal to assuage Muskingum's apprehensions, Woodruff Emlen noted that Nikkei students had received "fine and happy reception[s]" at many Ohio colleges. Emlen noted Hiramoto's "exceptional record" in high school and provided references attesting to the student's loyalty, intelligence, diligence, and "very high principles." A teacher also praised Hiramoto's "exceptional ability to get along with his fellow man."[49]

During this time, Frank Ito left for Muskingum College. McKnight invited Ito, the first Japanese American to arrive at Muskingum, to her home for dinner. Although she served a simple meal, McKnight reported that Ito "more than once told me that he had not had such a meal for more than a year."[50] Although McKnight seemed oblivious, the environment in which the food was served probably explains the student's comments better than the quality of the food itself.

After hearing positive reports from Ito, Hiramoto finalized his decision to enroll at Muskingum. The next three weeks were a blur, filled with getting his release in order, packing, and saying good-bye to friends. After stopping off in Chicago for a week to visit friends and to watch the Pirates defeat the Cubs by seven to four at Wrigley Field, Hiramoto arrived in New Concord in early September, where he was greeted by Ito and Reverend McMillan, with whose family both students would live. Hiramoto fondly recalled the McMillan family, remembering that they included him in holiday celebrations and made him feel like family.

Hiramoto found life at Muskingum full. Between washing dishes in the dormitory, ironing shirts for Reverend McMillan to earn his board, studying, and joining the Alban club, Hiramoto led a hectic life. He also visited a number of small country churches to speak about exile and incarceration. He recalls no hostile questions or feelings. After one speech, Hiramoto was even invited to lunch. Although the Nikkei at Muskingum spent time together, they also socialized with white students and administrators. At least one discussion on campus about exile and incarceration was contentious, but even this argument resulted in "no hard feelings." By the end of the first semester, McKnight reported that the five Nikkei at Muskingum were doing well.

Hiramoto had "very positive" feelings about Muskingum from the start. He found even top officials at the school to be "very kind and helpful," which eased his anxiety about being "a small town country boy just out of high school, who was away from home for the first time in his life." Hiramoto fondly described the "closeness and general friendliness of the small quiet college town" as well as "fine friendships" with students. The students apparently felt the same way; Hiramoto was tapped to join an honorary club for upperclass students as a sophomore in 1945, perhaps, he speculated, because the students knew he would be leaving soon to help his family resettle from Rohwer to Lodi.

Indiana Technical College also initially refused to cooperate because of local conditions.[51] Its president A. T. Keene regretfully explained that "until the Pearl Harbor incident [the situation of Japanese and Japanese American students at his college] in Fort Wayne [was] satisfactory."[52] Herbert Keno, a WRA relocation officer, convinced Keene to reverse his policy in November 1943 by surveying the local area and finding it to be "favorable toward the relocation of not only students but also other persons of Japanese ancestry."[53] Five Nikkei were attending Indiana Technical College by July 1944.

The council continued to use local contacts in working to open colleges in 1943–44. Letters from individuals and organizations at colleges expressing an interest were pursued, with varying degrees of success.[54] Personal connections aided council efforts at Indiana's Valparaiso University, where Hibbard wrote Dr. Adolph Theodore Esaias Haentzschel to follow up on a positive questionnaire and the acceptance of one Nikkei student. Hibbard explained the council's work to his friend, and Valparaiso eventually accepted another Nikkei.[55]

The Case School of Applied Science proved more difficult.[56] Although it had initially accepted Nikkei, by September 1942, Case began to refuse resettled students, explaining that the rejection of a Nikkei applicant that month had "nothing to do with the fact that he is a Jap." A dean noted that Case had a Nikkei student on campus and that two or three more were coming; it had rejected this student only because he had applied late.[57] The additional Nikkei did not arrive, however, and Case had just one resettled student in March 1943.

Although the reasons for the absence of the additional students mentioned in September 1942 are not clear, Case had obviously reversed its policy and decided not to accept Nikkei. The school offered a series of excuses in rejecting Nikkei applicants: it would only train students who could work in essential or military industries; it would not admit students lacking the necessary funds, especially since the Nikkei student at Case had failed to find a summer job; and the presence of a naval engineering unit on campus made Nikkei attendance unwise. Although these revolving excuses, used once and then discarded, suggested a deeper unwillingness to cooperate, the council continued to push to open Case. Despite such efforts, Case did not agree to accept Nikkei again until the new PMGO process had been created.[58]

While the general trend in 1943–44 was toward a wider willingness to admit Nikkei, some colleges decided not to accept them. DePauw University in Greencastle, Indiana, had already enrolled a Nikkei student and returned a positive questionnaire in September 1942.[59] However, in October, the college reported "running into some difficulty . . . with the local community."[60] Edward E. Bartlett, dean of the university, noted in January 1944 that the Nikkei student had left and that townspeople were strongly opposed to the admission of male Nikkei. He later observed that the American Legion had taken a message of "complete antagonism to minority groups" across the state.[61] Hibbard surrendered, explaining in a brief letter, "Indiana seems to be a center of prejudice against all people of Japanese blood. Earlham College has been able to weather the storm of prejudice but we cannot do better than to leave to people like yourself the question of whether it is wise to introduce fellow American citizens into a community where they will be subjected to persecution and possibly even violence."[62]

Tri-State College in Angola, Indiana, had initiated a survey of students, faculty, and local citizens when Nikkei began to apply soon after Pearl Harbor.[63] While the registrar Raymond T. Roush initially reported that local opposition would delay the enrollment of Nikkei until after the war, he later asked for data on cooperating colleges to help combat local opinion. While Hibbard provided Roush with the information typically disseminated to combat local opposition—voluntary Nikkei military service, participation in the U.S. Cadet Nurses Corps program, citizenship, and assimilation— he did not push to open smaller and less prestigious schools that were not in demand. By this time, plentiful openings made Tri-State less important to the council.[64]

Some colleges strongly resisted council overtures during 1943–44. William H. Vaughn, the president of Morehead State Teachers College in Kentucky, tersely explained, "[w]e hope that you will not send any students of Japanese ancestry to our college. Our people would not welcome them. I fear it could be an unfortunate arrangement."[65] Hibbard thanked Vaughn for his "kind response to our letter" and noted the council's respect for "[the] decision not to receive any American citizens of Japanese ancestry." In addition to the pointed use of the term "citizens," Hibbard stressed that more than two thousand students had been successfully resettled in four hundred colleges in forty-three states with very little local resistance.[66] Vaughn never replied.

Quotas remained a centerpiece of many colleges' policies in 1943–44. Kenyon College in Gambier, Ohio, enrolled four resettled students by May 1944. One had graduated but remained at Kenyon as an assistant instructor in the physics department. The dean of students Robert B. Brown wrote Woodruff Emlen to express his school's pleasure "at the way all of these boys have fitted themselves into the life of the college." He did not want to enroll any more Nikkei, however, because the student body had been reduced to fifty and because "we feel that it would be unwise to accept another Japanese-American student until a little later on when we can know what is to happen to those already here. [If any Nikkei students leave prior to the start of the fall term,] we will be glad to consider taking another."[67]

Other schools struggled to find Nikkei students. Bluffton College had accepted Nikkei briefly but found itself without any by the end of 1942–43.[68] The college offered a full scholarship and the opportunity to earn board to attract another student. The council forwarded a student, whom the college accepted in January 1944 despite an unclear high school transcript. Despite Bluffton's efforts to enroll this student, her mother's illness prevented her arrival. Bluffton continued to seek Nikkei students and had enrolled one by summer 1945.

As it considered closing in fall 1943, the council had learned that the U.S.

Public Health Service had ruled Nikkei eligible for the U.S. Cadet Nurse Corps and decided to make a concerted effort to place students at schools of nursing.[69] The council urged WRA student resettlement counselors to inform students of this possibility and followed up with nonresponsive nursing students. Mabel Kuba, for example, had interviewed with Bodine at Heart Mountain in July 1943 but had not responded to subsequent council inquiries.[70] A form letter reported that since "[t]he work of this Council . . . may be discontinued early in 1944," it hoped to place as many nursing students as possible within the next few weeks. The letter asked interested Nikkei to "[p]lease sit down and write us NOW."[71] Kuba responded at the end of November. Her father, she explained, was ill, and this prevented her from pursuing nurses' training. The council urged Kuba to pursue nursing school after her father recovered. Kuba never responded, however, and apparently never resettled as a student, at least via the council.

The council also sent introductory form letters to schools of nursing that emphasized WRA and War Department approval for the council's program. The letter stressed that Nikkei students—as scholars, soldiers, engineers, and war workers—"are making important contributions to the United States, the country of their birth and education." Already, the letter concluded, almost 1,700 students had been placed in 334 colleges. Many of the Nikkei student nurses, it emphasized, had enrolled in the U.S. Cadet Nurse Corps. Applications for Nikkei students accompanied each letter.[72]

Helen G. McClelland, director of nursing at the Pennsylvania Hospital School of Nursing, responded enthusiastically to the council's appeal. She reported that her school's next class began February 3 and asked if the student included with the letter could make it by then. The council's file on McClelland's school became a thick one, a rarity for nursing schools, although other positive responses arrived. St. Luke's and Children's Medical Center in Philadelphia enrolled a Nikkei student in response to the form letter and asked for another in April 1945. Methodist Hospital in Philadelphia limited its willingness to cooperate to Protestant students but requested immediate action. Methodist's director of nursing Agnes J. Taylor actively cooperated, telephoning Kay Yamashita about an opening in her spring class in November 1944.[73]

Negative responses to the council's appeal, however, outnumbered the positive. A number of nursing schools simply did not respond, indicating an unwillingness to cooperate.[74] Others suggested intransigence with vague excuses. Sister Beatrice St. Louis, director of nurses at Toledo's St. Vincent Hospital, explained that her institution would not accept Nikkei because it was getting other applicants "whom we think should have first consideration."[75]

Others wrote to offer a variety of more-specific excuses. Full classes, some explained, made the acceptance of Nikkei impossible. While crowded classes certainly provided a valid excuse, some schools apparently used this as a pretext. Alice Dorian, director of education at Fairview Park Hospital, initially reported that the spring class was closed. When Hibbard then inquired if Nikkei could be accepted for later classes, Dorian responded with silence.[76]

Other nursing schools, especially those at smaller hospitals, cited local conditions in denying Nikkei enrollment. Martha M. Cunningham, director of nursing at Philadelphia's Northeastern Hospital, wrote, "[t]he work you are doing is excellent and I hope it continues," but she reported that she would have to give local applicants preference because the local community so strongly supported the hospital.[77] Martha C. Peeler, director of nursing at Osteopathic Hospital, wrote that the small size of her institution made it "unwise to take this step under present conditions."[78]

Lulu Ferris, director of White Cross Hospital's School of Nursing, wrote from Columbus, Ohio, that "local conditions" prevented her from cooperating. Although admitting that Nikkei should be accepted, she reported that they would not be because "we cannot control certain international emotions that have flared up in the last few years."[79] Sister M. Leonis, St. Alexis Hospital School of Nursing's director, cited a hostile group of students in her Cleveland-area institution as the reason for noncooperation. Although the protesters were a minority of the student population, she believed it was best to "wait a few months when the subject may not find dissatisfaction."[80]

Elizabeth C. Wivel, superintendent of nurses at Indianapolis City Hospital, focused her rejection on race. Vaguely noting an "unfortunate experience" with a Japanese nurse in the past, Wivel expressed concern about her school's current racial composition. "Since we do have colored students," she reasoned without further explanation, "it would seem best, for the present, not to consider any other racial group."[81]

Some students took advantage of the council's push to resettle at schools of nursing. Fumiye Morita Furuya had been enrolled in the nursing program at the University of California, San Francisco, for almost six months when exiled to Heart Mountain.[82] She enjoyed her time working at the camp hospital but also recalled that the nursing students employed there "were . . . ambitious. We were young, and by hook or crook we finished [nurses'] training."

Furuya postponed her plans for resuming her education when her mother became ill but began looking in earnest in early 1943. Rejected by five schools because quotas were full or Nikkei were not accepted, Furuya left Heart Mountain in spring 1943 to work for a family in Evanston, Illinois.

The council continued to try to place Furuya and finally reported in November that Bellevue in New York had accepted her. Wishing her, in the personalized style of the council, a happy birthday, the council anticipated her reports from New York City.

Other aspiring nursing students were unable to continue their education via the council. Jane Nemoto, interviewed by Bodine in Colorado's Granada camp in May 1943, received a letter from Woodruff Emlen to initiate the placement process.[83] Although the council at times complained about nursing students who were accepted but did not resettle, Emlen forwarded Nemoto's application to Abington Hospital without first asking if she were interested. Nemoto was not accepted, however, and repeated council attempts to place her failed. The council lost track of Nemoto by February 1944, mailing a form letter that asked for an update. The letter noted "a number of possibilities," but warned that her file would become inactive if she did not respond within three weeks. Nemoto did not reply.

While nursing school placements rarely resulted in open conflict, occasional outbreaks of anti-Nikkei sentiments did occur at other colleges. Although lacking the high drama of earlier conflicts at Ohio University, Earlham, and the University of Idaho, local opposition to resettled students occurred sporadically in 1943–44. For example, local antagonism to the election of a Nisei as student body president at Southwestern College in Kansas resulted in his resignation. "Perhaps this was the best and only thing he could have done," a fellow Nikkei student at Southwestern wrote King. "For, these times, public opinion is a very important factor."[84]

Manchester College in Indiana raised a rarely discussed issue in summer 1944 when it asked about job placement for Nikkei graduates. The council noted that job placement was not among its duties and referred Nikkei graduates to their colleges, the WRA, and Christian organizations for help in securing jobs.[85]

Tensions between the council and some colleges continued in 1943–44. Marietta College in Ohio had enthusiastically supported student resettlement and enrolled Mary Ono in January 1943.[86] President D. T. Schoonover believed that Ono would be well received despite reports of "super-patriots, some calling themselves Christians but manifesting a most unchristian attitude," who had caused problems elsewhere. He did not know, he wrote, of any such persons in Marietta.[87]

The Marietta student newspaper reported Ono's successful transition from concentration camp to campus. The article stressed a familiar theme for student ambassadors, noting Ono's "enviable scholastic record." The reporter concluded by pointing out that Ono's roommate, Hilde Unterleitner, had fled Germany a few years earlier. "While their favorite joke concerns 'axis collaboration,'" the reporter humorously reassured readers, "we know there is nothing further from their minds, but rather deep thanks for this splendid American opportunity. This is education at its finest."[88]

Problems arose in October 1943, however, when the dean W. Bay Irvine complained of an unhappy pattern: great interest and a need for haste, a period of silence, and postponed arrival. Irvine pointed out that Marietta "assumed a liability in the opinion of the community" in accepting Nikkei. "If one were to be nasty," he wrote, "he could imagine hearing the 'so-sorry' being repeated in colleges throughout the land."[89]

Bodine reacted angrily to Irvine's message. "This one," he wrote in a note clipped to Irvine's letter but not mailed, "is a lulu—colleges don't understand that these people are *incarcerated* and that getting them out of the camp takes time" (emphasis in original).[90] While Bodine and King rightly pointed out that government regulations and the psychology of incarceration slowed the enrollment of some, neither acknowledged—as Irvine failed to do as well—that prospective Nikkei college students were teenagers just like other teenagers, at times uncertain about their future and prone to changing their minds. Students, regardless of race, sometimes applied to a college and then decided, even after being accepted, not to attend.

Hibbard also wrote Irvine to plead the case of the offending student, George Hata. He had first met Hata's father while working in Manchuria some forty years previously and had met him again at an internment camp in New Mexico. Hibbard tried to help his friend's son go to college, a process complicated by the family members living in Santa Fe, Manzanar, and Chicago. After Irvine agreed to give Hata a second chance, Hibbard wrote Hata. Hibbard did not sugarcoat his message, threatening not to act until the student provided "some definite assurance that you would enter Marietta College and continue as a student there if we again persuaded the college authorities to accept you."[91] Hata, however, apparently stayed only one year. His name appears as a freshman in the 1944–45 college catalog and then disappears from school records. In fact, a glance at future college catalogs suggests that none of the four Nikkei at Marietta stayed through graduation.

As one might expect, such temporary stays were not uncommon. For example, Gary Okihiro has found that only ten of Nebraska Wesleyan's twenty-six wartime Nikkei students finished their degrees at that school.[92] A number of factors contributed to the high "horizontal mobility" of resettled students. Uncertainty led some to enter any available college with plans to move on when possible. The difficulty of obtaining good information about colleges in the camps caused other students to select schools "in a blindfold manner." The quality of a college, family considerations, and financial issues convinced others to transfer. Of one sample of 304 resettled students, 29.3 percent had transferred at least once.[93]

The Council and Camp High School Students

The council faced a challenging job in working with high school students. Although the Topaz camp yearbook encouraged students "to strengthen our conviction that the day shall come when all avenues of opportunities will be open to us," it also admitted that Nikkei youth naturally felt "a dread and bewilderment of the future." The Topaz principal Drayton B. Nuttall encouraged students, "establish without question your place in American life." Even athletic competition became a means to this end: "When our athletic teams venture out to play the neighboring schools, they go out with a purpose. They are out to prove to the schools and the white communities that we are just as good Americans as they. To us, it is not just a matter of who is going to win; it is more important to leave behind a good feeling. Yes our teams' [sic] play clean and hard, not only to beat the opponents, but to demonstrate our worth as American youth."[94]

Despite confusion and fear, Denson High School's *Victoria* (Arkansas) viewed the future rather optimistically, predicting that students would become engineers, lawyers, and professors—all occupations that required higher education. Thomas Sakaguchi's copy of the annual also suggested resettlement aspirations. One friend hoped that if, "in this hard trial of life," they met again, it would "not be in a place such as this." Another wished Sakaguchi the best "when you are out of camp." Bodine signed Sakaguchi's annual, "hoping we'll next meet in New England, the best section of the USA."[95]

Camp organizations also encouraged students to resettle. Topaz inmates continued their successful drive to raise scholarship funds. The Topaz Student Aid Fund Committee raised $3,196 and distributed grants of $100 to thirty-one students in its first year. The chair Sasato Yamate described the scholarship fund as a "big success," less in the amount raised than in "the spirit of encouragement . . . given to [students] that caused them to fight for higher education." He believed that these students would "become a big asset to the Japanese Community by becoming useful members of society. . . . This will be our worthy investment to the future of Japanese in America and to the second and third generations of American Citizens of Japanese Ancestry." Asking for continued support, Yamate emphasized that students *"will go if we give them encouragement and incentive for higher education. They will fight for it if we give them a chance"* (emphasis in original).[96] The council encouraged others to emulate the Topaz effort. Hibbard wrote Kikuye Masuda, secretary of the Poston Student Relocation council, to point out that the amount of funding available would determine the number of students resettled. He noted that workers at the Poston Camouflage Net Factory had donated money to the council and wondered whether Masuda's group would consider starting a scholarship fund. The College Bound Club at Unit I eventually developed a scholarship fund in fall 1944.[97]

By summer 1943, Gila River residents had established a scholarship fund and Heart Mountain inmates were talking about one. Elizabeth Emlen encouraged these efforts and promised that the council would help scholarship recipients meet additional expenses. Emlen emphasized the need for such efforts with WSSF monies quickly running out and the church boards uncommitted for 1944–45.[98]

Students also attempted to raise money for the council in spring 1944. A form letter written by and addressed to resettled students pointed out that "most of us have never taken the opportunity of expressing our gratitude and real concern for the continuation of the program in any concrete or united way." The letter urged students to support a nonpartisan and nonprofit organization that was, it emphasized, not supported by the government, by sending one dollar to help the council work with high school students. The student drive raised $250.75 from 157 students by June.[99]

Bodine's tours helped to maintain close council relationships with students. Students wrote Bodine to thank him for extending himself "out of the line of duty."[100] The appreciation felt by Nikkei, exemplified by one student's mother doing Bodine's laundry for free, partly helps explain why so many Nikkei continue today to view student resettlement as primarily an AFSC project.[101]

Limited in their face-to-face meetings with students, council workers also fostered personal relationships through correspondence. Nikkei in the camps looked forward to the letters. Lilly Fukui, a resettled student at the University of Wyoming, recalled that "[w]aiting for bit of news from Philadelphia [was hard], but we managed to pace the floors to calm our nerves and taxed the patience of our student counselor, Virginia Lynn. . . . Encouraging letters from [friends] and council members are real morale boosters during such hard times. They kind of brace when dark clouds hang heavy."[102]

Nobu Hibino experienced the personal care of council members in a unique way. She worked for the council prior to attending Boston University in fall 1943, and King let Hibino live in her Boston apartment when she left for college in the fall. When the maid showed up to clean on Thursday, Hibino recalled, "I was in heaven then." Hibino's happiness was tempered, however, when the building superintendent reported that while she "didn't mind having you people stay here, . . . the rest of the tenants would like to see you vacate the premises." Hibino called King, who came to Boston that night by train and had the tenants sign a petition stating that they had no objection to Nikkei residents. When the superintendent made the same claim to King, she produced the petition and had the woman fired.[103]

Students responded to the personalized approach of council members with warm letters of thanks and promises to serve as ambassadors of goodwill. "I shall try my utmost," a University of Cincinnati Nikkei wrote Hibbard, "to live up to the faith you and the Council have in me as a student and as an individual. I shall also try to fulfill my obligation to society for the opportunity it is giving me in my pursuit for higher learning."[104] Another, explaining her decision to major in music, wrote that "our acceptance into the American community must germinate from us, from our activities. [W]e must have something to work with, something to show that we too are humans that we too love and appreciate the same things they do. Music was my answer because it knows no creed, no race, no class. It reaches out and touches all and everything."[105]

Occasionally, the personalism of the council failed. Fred W. Ross, a Cleveland WRA official, criticized the council after receiving a letter from Woodruff Emlen that described the "fine reports" the council had received about a Nikkei nursing student. He reported that the student had not been admitted and sarcastically suggested, "[i]n light of this, the fine reports to which you refer could scarcely have reference to [this student]. We trust this information will prove helpful to you."[106]

Hibbard's quick response in explaining the mistake suggests the importance the council invested in its personalized approach. He noted that Emlen was overworked and questioned Ross's reading of Emlen's letter, suggesting that the offending phrase "may have been intended to modify the word hospital which it immediately follows and not the word work which occurs earlier in the sentence." While Ross's reading was "not unnatural," Hibbard suggested that his interpretation better fit the intended meaning. Hibbard also explained that the failure to place the student was not the fault of the council; the New York Board of Regents had found a deficiency in her transcript at the last minute.[107]

The council continued to stress the advantages of small colleges. Bodine's notes for talks included a letter from a student at Michigan's Adrian College, who wrote that, "[a]lthough small colleges like Adrian are relatively unknown, I found that I can fill in a wide gap of things that I missed while I was attending the University of California." At Adrian he had "lost [his] racial consciousness" because he was a part of the student body and treated like everyone else.[108]

Bodine took this message to the camp newspapers, too. As he explained to the Minidoka *Irrigator:*

> One of my pet opinions is that it isn't so much the training you get at college that makes the job, but the contacts that you make on campus. That is why I am so sold on small schools where the Nisei gets a chance to know his professors intimately. Perhaps it will help out in trying to blast the idea that shopwork or secretarial training will land a person a job if you point out that in the post-war period, ordinary everyday secretaries and shop men will be a dime a dozen, but that secretaries with background in medicine, social work, economics, philosophy are the ones who will land jobs. And the man in radio work or auto mechanics who has a year or two of college physics will be the one who is going to be able to compete with hundreds of thousands of discharged defense workers.[109]

With funds limited as always, the council encouraged students to work prior to entering school if possible.[110] Bodine also advised students to resettle on employment leave, which made them eligible for government aid. Giles Zimmerman, chief of the employment division at Poston, had sharply criticized the council for this practice in summer 1943, noting that some resettlers had been labeled "Six-week Japs" because of their short tenures with an employer. Hibbard argued that a student could apply for an employment leave if intending to fulfill work obligations before enrolling and stated that the council would not advise a student to evade the meaning of the employment leave process. Despite Hibbard's assurances, Bodine explained in March 1944 that "nobody [files for an educational leave] if he can help it, since he'd miss out on a travel grant if he did."[111]

The council found its work further complicated by the resumption of the draft for Nikkei—even those still in captivity—on January 20, 1944. The possibility of the draft had concerned the council prior to 1944, however. Uncertainty as to if and when military service would be required of Nikkei had kept many young men in the camps. Myer approved of this, arguing in late 1943 that men should not be placed in colleges in large numbers until Selective Service began to include them. Although he countenanced helping to place any Nikkei classified IV-F, Myer argued that the council should "push the girls[,] especially nurses. Urge the men to go to work."[112] He emphasized this point in a letter to Nason dated November 22, 1943: "Pending the reinstatement of Selective Service [for Nikkei]," Myer declared, "I feel strongly that these boys should seriously consider their responsibilities toward their country, and I doubt whether this group of young men of army age should plan to go to college in war time unless Selective Service is applied to Japanese Americans. I have given this advice to a number of young Nisei who have questioned me."[113]

The council, although it supported the draft for Nikkei in the hope that they would be treated like other Americans, developed a different point of view. Sensing that uncertainty held back some young men from resettlement, the council urged them to face the problem like other Americans and suggested that they get as much education as possible before being drafted, arguing that the experience of campus life, even if abbreviated, was invaluable. If a student started his higher education prior to military service, it pointed out, he would have a place to return to after the war. The council also noted that men drafted out of colleges had a better chance of getting into a special training unit. Noting that some young men hesitated to resettle because of their uncertain draft status, Bodine argued that "[t]he soundest advice is to go right on with what you're doing until the call comes."[114]

The reinstatement of the draft in January 1944 directly affected the council's program. Shigeki Yasutake wrote from Ohio Wesleyan in April 1944: "Three of us [Nisei] are leaving school. Uncle Sam is very generous with his greetings. I am still 4–C [enemy alien] and praying that I will at least finish this semester."[115] The percentage of male students relocated by the council "declined sharply" from the two-to-one ratio of early resettlement. With many men who previously would have gone to college now entering military service, the gender ratio of the twenty-five hundred relocated students currently enrolled in college became balanced by October 1944.[116]

The council continued, however, to offer the same advice as it had prior to January 20, advising those already in school to remain there until drafted and suggesting that students resettle to college prior to being drafted if possible. Kay Yamashita told a nonresponsive student in March 1944 that his academic record and references showed him to be "an outstanding Nisei representative all around." She urged him to look at the long-term picture, even with the uncertainties of the draft. Yamashita argued that those with "specialized or higher education" would be the ones landing jobs after the war. She pointed out that starting college prior to being drafted would make it easier to return to college after service. "You are apparently a top-notch fellow," she wrote, "and I am very anxious to see you get ahead."[117] The council urged all seventeen- and eighteen-year-old males not yet classified I-A to go to college, "before Uncle Sam taps [them] on the shoulder."[118]

Some students began but did not complete the process of getting from concentration camp to campus. Their files begin stories that are unfinished. While some of these students may have managed to pursue higher education on their own, others chose not go to college. Those who did not resettle for college are an important part of the council's history; unfortunately, most have left at best incomplete records.

The council kept a large file of no-records folders (NRF) for Nikkei who did not file questionnaires with it after initial contact. Some students in these files wrote the council for information about its program or a specific school. Bodine interviewed other students in the NRF file. Follow-up letters to both groups of students were mailed; those that did not respond were labeled NRFs.[119]

Nikkei decided against college for a variety of reasons. Some volunteered for the army. King encouraged Masao Yano, one student who had done so, to contact the council if the military rejected him. "So be it reveille or class bells, the bugle or the gong," King wrote, "here's wishing you the best of luck."[120]

Mary Watanabe, after an interview with Bodine, did not file a questionnaire. When William C. Stevenson of the records department wrote to ask for an update, she explained that she had decided against college, at least in the near future. Watanabe planned to resettle in Chicago instead. Stevenson applauded this move, noting that she could always go to college from Chicago at a later date.[121]

Other students felt a need to contribute to society more immediately. Ayako Obano resettled in Cincinnati, but decided not to enroll at the university. She explained that her decision was based on "an oppressive sense of responsibility—a restless desire to do constructive work." She was working in a doctor's office, volunteering at a hospital, and attending evening classes.[122]

Parents continued to influence decisions about college. Some parents would not allow their children to resettle. Saburo Baba wrote Woodruff Emlen that, "[v]ery reluctantly, I fear I must inform you that my chances for relocating outside to college are practically nil. My family have repatriated and they will not hear of my doing anything but repatriate (expatriate in my case) along with them." Baba hoped his parents would allow him to resettle after the family moved to Tule Lake, but he disappeared from council records after this letter.[123] Parents also controlled their children's choices by resettling and insisting that the entire family move with them. These students were not necessarily rejecting a college education; instead, they were forced to operate within constraints established by their parents.[124]

Some students faced additional obstacles because of negative reference letters. Ken Ota applied through the council and one referee praised his loyalty, especially in light of his family's pressure to expatriate. A neighboring farmer, however, described Ota as selfish, careless, and irresponsible. The neighbor's criticisms were clearly based in racism. "Perhaps some people would call this narrow-mindedness—but—do the Japanese have to be educated before going 'home' [to Japan]?" he asked. "That has always been a Japs [*sic*] second desire, the first is money. After-all our boys are taken out of college and many are giving their lives for their country." By January 1944, Ota had moved to Tule Lake with his family. His file ends there.[125]

The council had trouble keeping track of other students. Letters to WRA officials urged that the students use council channels. Woodruff Emlen complained to Helen Amerman, a student counselor at Minidoka, about "one of the more difficult students." Council representatives had written twelve letters to or about the student in three months, but he had failed to follow up with both the University of Wisconsin and the University of Chicago. Emlen's message was clear: the council could not help until the student took the initiative.[126]

Some students continued to place themselves without council help in 1943–44. Yoshie Chida impressed Bodine during her interview at Topaz.[127] He reported that she had "[a]n all-around personality" and an ability to adjust that made her a "most promising" student.[128] The council worked to raise money for Chida and secured admission for her at Webster College. Chida, however, chose not to attend Webster. She instead independently secured acceptance at Indiana's Hanover College, a school recommended to her by a friend at her summer job in Utah. Chida wrote King in October 1943 and described a friendly reception, both on campus and in town. A second letter sent Chida's regards to Yamashita: "I can almost picture Kay and her grin. . . . I can imagine how happy she must be with so many students from Topaz accepted. I was really amazed at the number of my friends, who graduated with me, now attending college or . . . planning to do so in the near future."[129]

The council encouraged camp administrators and personnel to support its program. Hibbard mailed a series of letters introducing Bodine in February 1944 as the field director prepared to embark on another tour of the camps. He reassured the administrators that the council had decided to continue its work through 1944 and would now focus on camp high school graduates. Hibbard also cited statistics to demonstrate the council's progress: 2,500 resettled students in 442 colleges in 44 states, more than $100,000 raised for student aid, and more than 200 Nikkei in nursing schools (with most participating in the U.S. Cadet Nurse Corps). He explained the new PMGO process for clearance and noted that many opportunities existed for 1944 graduates. Bodine followed up with letters detailing his agenda and expressing a desire to live with the inmates while in the camps.[130]

Kay Yamashita sent out a series of newsletters for WRA student resettlement counselors. These allowed the council to update them on changes in procedures, new college openings, and other information. Yamashita modeled a personal relationship with the counselors that she hoped would influence their relationships with students, writing in July 1943, "[w]e've been thinking a mighty lot about you folks and the kind of problems you must be confronting as the hot weather drags on, and your most capable leaders and workers leave the Project for relocation. We realize, in small measure, the kind of counseling you must do, to cope with the growing frustration or lethargy and apathetic spirit of those who are left behind. More Power to You!"

Yamashita also used the newsletters as a forum to disseminate two increasingly important themes. First, the council wanted to encourage all eligible Nikkei to resettle, either for school or for work. Second, Yamashita stressed, "if we are to make the relocation program successful in ideal terms, we cannot overlook the opportunity and necessity of dispersing our college young people throughout a wide area. They *are* our best representatives and we hope they will eventually find opportunities in the areas of their schools" (emphasis in original).[131]

The September 1943 newsletter contrasted what that month had used to mean—"the happy return of students to the stimulating life of the campus"—with its current "grim and serious" nature. Yamashita realized the anxiety of incarcerated students as they waited for letters from both the council and colleges and experienced "the gosh darn awful feeling of utter dependency." She suggested that camp life distorted inmates' views of the world and led to apathy and bitterness.

Yamashita also discussed a letter received by the council. "Your Council," a disgruntled student had written, "hasn't done anything for me and I'm sick of waiting so I'll go on my own then maybe I could rot in camp faster—thanks!" Yamashita stressed that counselors needed to help students understand what was happening outside the camps in order to combat such feelings.

Although she described the unhappy letter as rare, Yamashita acknowledged its importance and spent considerable time explaining why things seemed to move slowly. Yamashita admitted, "[o]ur best doesn't seem to be enough at times," and she explained that it remained difficult to find enough openings to place the number of students interested in technical fields such as engineering, medicine, nursing, pharmacy, and science. The desire of students to attend better schools and certain programs also slowed resettlement.

Students also contributed to the council's perceived slowness. Some failed to answer the council's letters promptly and specifically. Others did not report their arrival or problems that developed. Some failed to see the larger picture in focusing on themselves. Students who applied late complicated things and often could not be immediately placed. Other students created "[t]he worst sort of thing for public relations and future placement of other [inmates]" by failing to attend colleges that accepted them. A key reason for student complaints was their failure "to realize we are also human."[132]

Bodine viewed his primary job in 1943–44 as combating inmate apathy. In June, Bodine explained to Swan that inmates distrusted the government. "Embittered?" he asked. "You guess!" He went on to describe, citing WRA community analysts in support, the inmates as "psychopathic cases . . . in need of mental therapy [who] do NOT act normally." Resettlement, he argued, helped to rehabilitate Nikkei. Bodine explained that he had to say this "because it seems to me so crucially important that those of you in the East who have never been in the camps sense with us who have that this is not the simple, easy problem it appears to be."[133]

Bodine argued that "new hope [for] a better world" had to be built inside the camps: "[W]e have the task somehow of demonstrating to the people *in* Camp the *other* side of America—the sincere, honest, integrous, Christian America" (emphasis in original).[134] While Bodine's focus was usually inside the camps, he, like most of the council, also saw a need to work on the outside. They viewed student resettlement as a way to educate Americans and to make the United States more democratic both during and after the war. With the outside thus improving, Bodine could honestly "try to convince both young people and old that there is a future in America for the [Nisei]. The story of Student Relocation is one of the best arguments in support of the notion that the [Nisei] do have a niche and should go out and fill it."

Bodine could not accomplish this daunting task alone; he had to rely on WRA student resettlement counselors in the camps for help. He was generally pleased with the counselors in 1943–44. Mabel N. Sheldon and Lucille T. Peddy at Gila River performed well with the help of two Nikkei administrative assistants.[135] At Heart Mountain, the students appreciated the hard work of Virginia Lynn. Minidoka's Helen Amerman had "been too busy to do much for [the council]" but was eager to contribute. She received considerable help from Joe Kitigawa and Hana Yamada. Junko Hedani ran student resettlement efficiently at Topaz, where an office devoted solely to that purpose existed.

Although Bodine was not entirely displeased with any of the counselors, some worried him. He observed that Jerome's Minnie Lee Mayhan was viewed as "little more than office clerk" by her principal and superintendent. She wanted to help the council, however, and the situation appeared better in April when her sister, Etta Neal Mayhan, began her job in the relocation office.[136] Poston I's Estelee Hinson was burdened with a heavy teaching load that allowed little time for counseling. Robert Wells in Poston II faced the draft. Martha Hays in Poston III presented a different kind of problem. She was motivated and had formed a College Bound Club but "was sore [at the council] for not sending her more information and material."[137] Rohwer's Opal Albright, despite a "schoolmarm sort of personality," had the students' respect. They did not like her as they did other counselors, but her organization and willingness to help impressed Bodine. At Manzanar, Helen Ely was "[t]erribly overworked" but shared a mutual devotion with the students. The council's once-promising relationship with Tule Lake had deteriorated in the aftermath of segregation. Bodine knew little of Lily Roudabush except that she had been recommended as "a good person."[138]

As Bodine maintained a grueling schedule of camp visits, exhaustion and frustration surfaced. A visit to Tule Lake, now primarily a segregation camp after the "registration crisis," in spring 1944 upset Bodine.[139] Although he talked with many groups and individuals, he reported that "*not one* has come to see me or sign up for an interview" (emphasis in original). Bodine attributed this to the strong forces against resettlement that permeated the camp. He described "overwhelming difficulties about this place," including threats of violence against *inu* ["dogs"] who talked to whites and "Vigilantes" who had tried to break up—without success, he happily reported—a too-American jitterbug party. "There are soldiers everywhere—marching with rifles on the shoulders," he reported. "[T]here are towers throughout the camp, with soldiers with guns sitting up in them and huge searchlights at night." Still, Bodine believed his visit "worthwhile. To spread the story of Student Relocation, to wander naively hither and yon, trusting people and saying 'HI!' to people, . . . to pal around with kids and make them realize that somebody outside cares—that they're not just Japs—unwanted Japs—but swell American kids enthusiastically received by other American College kids—ALL THIS makes my stay here worthwhile."[140]

Bodine's critical report, although intended only for AFSC representatives, resulted in his being recalled to Philadelphia after government officials somehow saw the report. C. Reed Cary lectured Bodine, reminding him that he was in the camps "under sufferance. Your permission to get into the camps will be revoked unless you eat a little 'humble pie' with the people you criticized." Bodine later recalled, "[I] made a trip to Washington and met with some government officials and ate my 'humble pie,' and said that everything wasn't all bad and that I wouldn't write any more reports like that. It was important to keep permission to go into camps to do the job."[141]

Bodine's frustration grew as he continued his tour. After interviewing only thirty-five students at Jerome, Bodine described the camp as "one of the most difficult Centers to work in." The combination of "Arkansas prejudices" and a staff of "political hacks" alienated the Nikkei. The inmates' disdain for "Arkies and Oakies [sic] [as] the dregs of the universe" exacerbated tensions. "Mud—heat—ugliness—despair—the evacuees browbeaten—the Southern Arkansans nasty cracks, the discourtesies—these are my memories," Bodine wrote. "There are even bed bugs in the cottage I'm staying in. [They] are a sort of symbol—to me—of Arkansas."[142]

Bodine's explanation for why people had not treated him like "a damn Yankee" this time damned Jerome with faint praise. "I have carefully avoided making any favorable remarks about evacuees," he explained, "and have steered assiduously away from the negro [sic] problem and have laid low on the pacifist angle—and as a result have got along famously with nearly everybody. . . . It does no good to discuss issues on which there can be no agreement."[143] Bodine could get along in Jerome, in other words, only if he hid his deepest moral beliefs.

Lack of student response in Rohwer, the other Arkansas camp, and Idaho's Minidoka further frustrated Bodine. He was "deeply discouraged" at Rohwer. Constant rain, ankle-deep mud, and ever present mildew, in addition to arriving during final exam week, limited student turnout. Bodine wrote Swan, "the more I think about it . . . I'm still plenty blue. Mebbe [sic] that's because it's still pouring rain. It has rained now for two weeks—and long before that, when I wasn't here." Bodine was equally discouraged at Minidoka. Despite numerous speeches there, "only a limited number of kids came in to interview with me individually." He attributed this to a number of factors: a poorly timed visit that conflicted with new school schedules, cold and stormy weather, and a warehouse strike.[144]

Bodine acknowledged his exhaustion and its effect in a letter to Swan dated June 1. "I guess I must be getting pretty tired," he wrote. "This afternoon, for the first time, I've talked with students who 'riled' me. They made me mad—and though I leaned over backward to do my best for all three of them—I *was* exasperated. And so—it is time I came home. You cannot do this job without tremendous resources of patience and understanding and deep good cheer. You give and give and give. I remember Reed Cary scolding me last year for thinking that I could go on doing this job after I'd been out wandering for two months. This year I've been out over three months now."[145]

Before returning to Philadelphia, Bodine filed a depressing report on Poston and Manzanar. Once the best-organized camp, staff turnover at Poston had resulted in "vagueness and uncertainty of a most debilitating sort." Camps II and III did not have files of college catalogs. The chaos of Poston allowed Bodine to accomplish little during his five-day visit. He also reported that the principal at Manzanar opposed college education for Nikkei, believing they should work instead. Manzanar's director, Ralph P. Merritt, hoped that students would remember his camp as a city that taught "the ideals of American citizenship" and "an experience worth living." The students did not share these sentiments; the yearbook praised Helen Ely for "working continuously in order that we, who are behind barbed-wire fences, can in some way further our education by relocating to some college."[146] Bodine also described a "persecution complex" that made some students hypercritical of all whites, including the council, and that made others too dependent on the council. When students in the latter group did not receive prompt responses from the council, their disappointment was magnified. He also criticized "Hell and Damnation" ministers, who "spill the blood of the Lamb of God all over everybody," for giving churches a bad reputation in the camps.[147] Despite Bodine's depressing message, Manzanar authorities believed his trip a success. They praised Bodine's visit by noting "students have been literally streaming in to see Miss Helen Ely [since his visit]."[148]

In spring 1944, the council decided to combat growing apathy among students by having resettled students visit the camps. Nason supported the proposal, although he did not want the council to finance it, because he believed the returnees "would speak the language of the people to whom they are talking and should . . . be more persuasive than any Caucasians could be."[149]

After gaining WRA approval and raising money to fund the returnee project from church boards, the YMCA and YWCA, the WSSF, and the AFSC, the council wrote project directors to inform them of their plans. Bodine presented the program as an attempt to meet "the apathy, apprehensiveness and misconceptions that are so often a part of relocation center life" with returnees acting "as 'sparkplugs' for student relocation and for relocation in general." He introduced the returnees in each letter and noted that the council hoped that they would talk with 1944 graduates and participate in community activities.[150]

Bodine told the returnees to stress that they represented both the council and the organization sponsoring them. Keeping in mind the importance of appearing independent of the WRA, Bodine reminded each student, the "WRA has no part in your return trip."[151] Bodine encouraged returnees to live with inmates. Meet the camp administrators, he advised, but do not associate too closely with them. The returnees could then perform their job in variety of ways: speaking to students individually, attending social functions, or even just hanging out with the kids. "You will notice," Bodine observed, "that we hope you will stimulate the general relocation program as well as the program of student relocation."[152] To this end, he encouraged returnees to spend time with students not of college caliber—"the dumbies, the toughies, and the loafers" in his words—who needed to be encouraged about the future, too.[153] Above all, Bodine concluded, returnees must realize that they faced a tough job that would produce few tangible results: "DON'T GET DISCOURAGED!!!!"[154]

Bob Sasahara added to Bodine's advice in a letter dated July 28. The Minidoka returnee had shunned publicity at first, fearing, "[it would] create a gap between me and the people in camp. I'm just . . . a college student. I want them to feel that I'm just one of them." To accomplish this, Sasahara downplayed his accomplishments at school. He did not, he explained, want to appear exceptional to a group of people with an "inferiority complex." While the ambassador of goodwill persona in council public relations, it could be a stumbling block in the camps.[155]

In addition to receiving regular reports from the returnees, Bodine asked each to answer a series of questions as he prepared a report on their efforts. Bodine used statistics to prove "the amazingly good job" performed by the 13 students. They had interviewed more that 1,200 people, about three-quarters of whom were students, and had attended 223 meetings. "They spread their stories and ours throughout the eight centers," he concluded. "The impact they made is indicated not only in their own detailed and voluminous weekly reports, but also in the glowing comments that have come to us from WRA officials and from relocated students."[156] The returnees agreed that their efforts had been worthwhile, reporting that inmates often regarded Caucasian efforts to promote student resettlement as propaganda. The returnees, however, "who speak their language, act their ways and know their innermost thoughts, [were able] to give them the extra 'push' on the road to education."

According to statistics compiled by the returnees, there had been 1,850 camp high school graduates, excluding Tule Lake, in 1944. Of those, 55 percent had left the camps, and 24 percent had left for college. Parental objections and financial concerns prevented some from resettling. Return-ees urged the council to counter these by informing the inmates, especially parents, about life on the outside. This would, they hoped, help to dispel rumors. The parents, often pro-education, needed to hear success stories. All they saw in the camps, a returnee observed, were failed students. The council also needed to advertise the financial aid available.

Apathy also kept graduates from resettling. Described by Bodine as *shikata ga nai*—"it can't be helped"—or lose-fight, this attitude created doubts about the future for college-educated Nikkei. Even though one returnee reported that he had pursued Bodine's "toughies, dumbies, and loafers" into latrines, mess halls, and baseball diamonds to talk their "slanguage," Nikkei apathy remained a pressing problem.

Despite reporting this general sense of apathy, "[t]he returnees were surprised to find that the boys and girls in next year's high school senior class are not particularly apathetic or discouraged about their future." About one-third wanted to go to college and another one-third were interested in trade, nursing, or specialty schools. Although some were taking the initiative, Bodine reported, others believed there was little hope for the future.[157]

Bodine's interpretation of the returnees' reports called for continued council activism. While the new PMGO process for clearance and increased college openings had required the council to work longer than some had hoped or wanted, by the end of 1943–44 the council again began to consider slowing its operations. This tendency was reinforced by changes in government policy in fall 1944 that lessened considerably the need for the council.

CLOSING DOWN AND SAYING *SAYONARA,*
1944–46

Nobuko Emoto joyfully wrote a supportive minister in June 1944 that "God must have heard my prayer."[1] Her parents had finally allowed her to leave the Gila River concentration camp for Gettysburg College in Pennsylvania and "now there [was] nothing to do for [her] freedom but wait until August." Emoto planned to major in creative writing to "accomplish something for my people—the Nisei. . . . I must go to college to do what my heart tells me to do."[2]

Emoto had to do more than just wait, however; she had to secure financial aid. Gettysburg provided a $200 scholarship. In addition, the Presbyterian Church awarded a $250 grant that, in combination with a few individual gifts, allowed Emoto to pay for her first year of school. Emoto also worked for her room and board at the home of a Presbyterian minister, Reverend Robert Hunt, and his family.

Dorothy G. Lee, dean of women at Gettysburg, reported on Emoto in June 1945. Although Emoto had enjoyed her room-and-board work, Lee suggested that the Hunt home was too far from campus to allow her "to participate in campus life to a great extent." This condition, in addition to Reverend Hunt becoming a navy chaplain, left Emoto unsettled for 1945–46. Lee praised the student's "creditable scholastic work" under such circumstances but noted, "We are determined that Nobuko must be placed in a dormitory next year. We feel sure her work will then improve scholastically and there will be much greater opportunity for her to become acquainted with a larger number of students. . . . We are eager to have Miss Emoto continue her work at Gettysburg College as we feel the benefits to both Nobuko and the College will be greater as time continues."[3]

William F. Quillian Jr. of Gettysburg's philosophy department also detailed

Emoto's financial difficulties. Reiterating the importance of placing Emoto in a dormitory where both she and the college community would benefit from her "intimate contact with the other students," Quillian estimated a total bill of $900. Emoto had arranged a summer job at the Naval Depot in Mechanicsburg as a typist, but this would only cover her summer expenses. Quillian reported that about $850 had been raised thus far, although "[n]ot all of these sources of income have been assured as yet."[4]

Similar financial concerns dominated the council's work in its last two years. Thomas Bodine lamented this development, noting that correspondence became "less interesting" after Trudy King left the council in April 1944. In addition to the loss of the voluble King, Bodine observed that the letters also became more formal and increasingly focused on raising scholarship money. The council, he believed, reflecting the perspective of an early participant who had once battled unjust government policies, now engaged in less exciting work. It focused, as the context in which it operated was liberalized, on raising money to help Nikkei go to college rather than engaging in its previous struggle to secure, in Bodine's words, "permits to leave camp and travel across country as a 'Jap' during a war with Japan."[5]

The Council Ends Counseling

Students remained interested in resettling after summer 1944. The council's role in student resettlement, however, gradually decreased after that summer, beginning on September 4 when the War Department announced that PMGO approval for Nikkei attendance was no longer necessary, relieving the council of one of its primary jobs. Japanese American students were now to be accepted "on the same basis as any others," and the council wrote colleges to explain, "[a]ll restrictions are now removed . . . save for those [on] West Coast Institutions, where [students] will need the consent of the Western Defense Command."[6]

The council—citing its success, the removal of military restrictions, and financial limitations—sought to further reduce its role by suggesting later in September that the WRA assume responsibility for counseling camp students. Dillon S. Myer, the WRA director, accepted the council's proposal and wrote the chair John Nason to delimit the new division of duties between the council and the WRA. He explained that the WRA would counsel incarcerated students; help them find housing and part-time jobs; and keep the council informed of acceptances, rejections, and other pertinent information. The council would provide information to camp counselors with its weekly information sheet, furnish financial advice and aid to students upon request, assist with difficult cases, and continue its former services to students outside the camps who asked for help.[7]

Nason informed colleges of the new arrangement. While promising continued help should any problems arise, he hoped that Nikkei students would now be able to apply "on very much the same basis as all other citizens of the United States."[8] As the council reduced its work, Bodine urged it not to relinquish all of its duties to the WRA. Pointing out that he continued to be "hounded" by students in the camps who liked the council and its work, Bodine argued that students did not respond similarly to WRA personnel.[9]

The council attempted to ensure a smooth transfer of responsibilities. Elizabeth Emlen wrote to camp counselors, preparing them for new WRA releases on student resettlement and providing reference materials. The council also pressed the WRA to make certain that the camp counselors fulfilled their new duties. Ann Graybill,[10] the council's final director, continued to press the WRA to free up time for counselors to perform their new duties. The WRA also became more involved in student resettlement by ordering its local resettlement personnel to relay any information they had about colleges to the council.[11]

As general resettlement increased, the council and student relocation counselors in the camps exchanged information. The council sent information sheets to update counselors, but, increasingly, information provided by the counselors to the council was more important. Counselors informed the council as they learned of new openings, apprised it of the colleges students were attending, and detailed camp personnel changes relative to student resettlement.[12]

Camp officials described local student resettlement efforts. Minidoka's principal Ray Harker reported that the College Bound Club had painted the library to create "an attractive scene for browsing [college] catalogs." The club held bull sessions on various topics, including race relations, international relations, anthropology, and metaphysics, because Nikkei students had "very little opportunity for such intellectual gymnastics." These sessions, Harker explained, helped students develop the "poise and self confidence" necessary for social situations at colleges. The club also prepared students for resettlement by hosting discussions with visiting resettled students.[13]

Perhaps more importantly, camp counselors provided updates on resettled students. They alerted the council to students, especially men facing the draft, who needed help. These reports demonstrate that many counselors felt a personal connection to students. Mataileen L. Ramsdell of Rohwer wrote about two students at Indiana Tech, reporting, "[w]ith the help you are sending them, I feel certain they can get along all right."[14]

The WRA camp counselors struggled to deal with changes in the process of student resettlement after summer 1944. At Minidoka, the changes and the composition of the incarcerated population required "an individualistic sort of approach to the outstanding boys and girls from very understanding families who could visualize a few steps into the future." The transfer of counseling responsibilities complicated Minidoka's student resettlement efforts, especially since the counselor Helen Amerman had replaced a Nikkei and was viewed with distrust by some inmates as a WRA employee. The administration, viewing student resettlement as "a necessary evil," provided little support. This resulted in students increasingly feeling "confused, frustrated, and aggressive" as well as in incidents of "juvenile delinquency."[15]

The WRA continued to view student resettlement as a valuable component of its larger goal of dispersal. "Already many of the Nisei college students have gone out," a report noted, "scattering in colleges and universities throughout the United States where they have given a good account of themselves. [Many] have relocated in areas of the Middle West and East where they will probably make their permanent homes." While the WRA worried about the Issei, it hoped that the

> regional scattering of Japanese Americans will probably prove to be a definite advantage to their future assimilation in the United States for, with the breaking up of the former "colonies," a closer contact between individual Japanese residents and their new American neighbors is bound to emerge. This offers hope and promise for a better absorption of their descendents into American cultural patterns than was the case for their elders who lived in groups and clung pretty closely to their traditional ways. The evacuation order of 1942, unfortunate as it was, may prove in the long run to be the ill wind that will blow much good along with it.[16]

Other government officials likewise viewed dispersal as the best solution to the Nikkei "problem." In June 1944, President Franklin D. Roosevelt wrote Harold L. Ickes to suggest that changes in the status quo of Japanese Americans be gradual. For the sake of "internal quiet," he proposed discreet determination of how many Nikkei would be acceptable to West Coast localities and "[s]eeking to extend greatly the distribution of other families in many parts of the United States." The president believed that the West Coast would be willing to have some return and that the rest of the country would not be bitter if Nikkei "were distributed—one or two families to each county as a start." Roosevelt returned to this idea at a November 1944 press conference, suggesting that "probably half a dozen or a dozen families could be scattered around [any given county] and worked into the community. . . . And they wouldn't—what's my favorite word—discombobolate—(laughter)—the existing population of these counties very much. After all—what?—75 thousand families scattered all around the United States is not going to upset anybody."[17]

The council favored dispersal as well. Graybill encouraged students to persuade their families to join them in the East. While this advice fit the WRA's broader objectives, the council noted an additional advantage: "We have found . . . that students who have on their own initiative left the camps to go to college have frequently stimulated their parents to relocate and to find more adequate means of financial support than they would have otherwise."[18]

The council's presence continued in the camps after the WRA assumed responsibility for student counseling. Bodine began his final tour of the camps in fall 1944 to help arrange the transfer of college placement responsibilities from the council to the camp counselors. Traveling as a consultant to the WRA, he critiqued the organization of student resettlement efforts at each camp.[19]

Bodine favorably evaluated student resettlement efforts at Heart Mountain, Manzanar, Topaz, Granada, and Rohwer. Most had well-organized operations that included catalog collections and clubs for students interested in college. The vitality of the high school was also important. "While at Topaz," Bodine wrote, "I had the opportunity to address the entire high school. . . . It was a great success. I was particularly impressed by the display of school spirit during the cheer leading and the attention the students paid to me."[20]

The common denominator in Bodine's assessment of successful camp counseling was the people involved. At Heart Mountain, Irene Damme and Chiyo Okano operated a first-rate student resettlement room with catalogs and photographs of students on the walls, Bodine reported.[21] A committee of whites and Nikkei at Manzanar ran the program efficiently. Eleanor Gerard taught and counseled seniors at Topaz, providing opportunities to talk about resettlement in class and after school.[22] Grace Lewis was so well organized at Granada that Bodine made only a brief stop and discovered that many families had resettlement plans centered on students. Mataileen Ramsdell held a less well organized program together at Rohwer.[23]

Bodine registered a split opinion on Gila River and Poston. The Butte Camp at Gila River received high marks. Mabel Sheldon and Dr. Joseph Reagan placed seventy-seven 1944 graduates in the fall. Seventy-one received financial aid through the council, an indicator, Bodine suggested, that counselors followed up with most students. The Canal Camp suffered from a lack of leadership, however. Although Maxine Hagan had, Bodine observed, "the best rapport with the kids of any counselor I know, [s]he seemed to me to be one of those persons . . . who bites off more than they can chew." Hagan's schedule left little time for counseling and resulted in the worst catalog collection of any camp.

A party thrown for Bodine by parents of resettled students provided a highlight of his stay at Gila River. More than thirty attended to express their gratitude to Bodine and the council. After a few awkward speeches, the parents broke the ice by beginning to talk, some through interpreters, about their children. Some mothers even asked Bodine if he could get their children to write home more often.

Bodine praised student resettlement in Poston I, where Estelee Hinson and Ben Sanematsu formed "an ideal team." Hinson's devotion to the cause made Bodine especially optimistic. Martha Hays had created "a splendid set up" at Poston III. She taught only two classes and could "throw her unbounded energy" into the students. Poston II, however, was "one of the most discouraging situations" because the counselor was overburdened teaching six classes.[24]

Bodine found Tule Lake "appalling. [A]ll the worse [sic] in Japanese life and culture are present there and very little of the best. I guess the exposure to much of the worse [sic] side of American life and culture (our race prejudice and inhumanity and stupidity . . .) has brought out the worst side of the Japanese."[25] Although he approved of the counselor Lillie Roudabush, Bodine talked with only twelve students during his stay "and came away profoundly discouraged by the retrogression that has taken place at Tule Lake since last spring." One student reported that he had not resettled because of pressure from his parents and peers. Another tearfully told Bodine he could no longer be seen with him.[26]

Minidoka also disappointed Bodine, who noted its decline from one of the best student resettlement camps to one of the worst in a year's time. Personnel turnover explained this reversal; interest had been overwhelmed by bureaucracy, and the high school struggled "just to keep body and soul together. . . . I don't blame the kids for feeling they are not getting an education in these camp high schools!" A controversy over the building of a school gymnasium and an evacuee strike had antagonized inmates toward anything sponsored by the WRA.

However, Bodine had also created problems for himself at Minidoka. A critical account of the administration by Bodine had fallen into the administrators' hands. They refused to cooperate, lecturing Bodine that the council did not know how to operate through proper channels. Bodine wrote that he was willing to take a scolding and then move on to helping the students, but this never happened. "They had no use for a pipesqueak [sic] like me and showed it," Bodine wrote. "So I do not have much hope for anything coming out of Minidoka."[27]

Further Reductions in Council Activities

As Bodine toured the camps in late 1944, the council continued to scale back its operations. Working with a reduced staff, it encouraged students to place themselves if possible. The council focused on recommending students to church boards for scholarship aid and allocating WSSF scholarship funds as its primary jobs, hoping that Nikkei students would now be treated like all others.

The determination of church boards to reduce donations also pressured the council to limit its program.[28] For example, the Presbyterian Church, which had provided significant financial and moral support for the council in the past, wanted to decrease its contributions. E. Fay Campbell, the council's Presbyterian representative, argued that "Bodine and some of the other younger workers saw this problem somewhat out of perspective."[29]

Bodine strongly opposed the decision to contract the council's functions. He had reluctantly agreed with the decision to have the WRA assume more responsibility, but argued that the council, as a private agency, needed to continue sending a representative to the camps. He observed "increasing discouragement" in the camps, reporting, "[t]here is a greater need than ever before for help from understanding and trusted friends from the outside. . . . They seem so *lost* this year. Many are eager and full of enthusiasm but they don't seem to know how to translate their energy and eagerness into action" (emphasis in original).[30] Elizabeth Emlen addressed Bodine's concerns in assessing the council's future. "The Council," she observed, "has been a symbol of [Nisei's] rebuilt faith in themselves and in their future in this country. I believe one of the most important questions for us to consider at this time is what our part should be in the future in helping to overcome the relocation center psychology [that resulted in apathy, dependence, and lack of confidence]."[31]

The council met on December 15, 1944, to discuss an agenda for 1945. Nason explained that the council would continue to function through 1945 "in spite of [its] eagerness to discontinue its work" in order to facilitate financial aid, to place students residing outside the camps, and to serve as an information clearinghouse. The council adopted a relatively limited agenda that included another student returnee project, noting that the returnees had greater influence than any white visitor in reaching "the parents and the non-college group of young people as well as the prospective students." The council agreed with Nason that the responsibility for job placement for Nikkei college graduates belonged to the colleges.[32]

Public Proclamation No. 21, issued on December 17, 1944, by Major General Henry C. Pratt, acting commander of the WDC, complicated the council's work. This edict, which became effective on January 2, 1945, restored the rights of loyal Nikkei citizens to return to West Coast. Myer, in part because he realized that the thorough dispersal the WRA had hoped for was unlikely, suggested that, "[s]ince the NJASRC came originally from the local effort of a small group on the Pacific Coast, the cycle would be complete when we could see the presently eligible students re-established in schools in the areas from which they came."[33] Soon after the military reopened the West Coast, the WRA's John Provinse wrote the camp directors and urged that student resettlement counseling be coordinated with family plans to return to the coast.[34]

A few students had entered the WDC area prior to 1945 with special permits, once again viewed as pioneers, this time blazing the way for the Nikkei return to the West Coast. Nineteen-year-old Esther Takei's registration at Pasadena Junior College in September 1944 created controversy. Although students, faculty, and administrators at the school strongly supported the enrollment of Takei, opposition from some in the local community resulted, according to Audrie Girdner and Anne Loftis, in "a storm of protest." For weeks a "parade of cars" passed by the home of Hugh Anderson, an officer in Friends of the American Way with whom Takei was staying. Although many residents sent supportive messages, hostile telephone calls and letters convinced Anderson to move Takei and his family out of the house. The conflict over Takei's return climaxed in late September 1944 at a public meeting of the Pasadena chapter of the Committee on American Principles and Fair Play. Myer and others spoke to the gathering and so impressed George Kelley, a vocal leader of the exclusionists, "that he publicly recanted and applied for membership in the Fair Play Committee."[35] The tense situation having calmed down, Takei remained at the junior college.[36]

As a few students began to return to the West Coast, the council discussed its role in this process. Bodine advised against establishing a new West Coast office, believing that volunteers could perform the necessary tasks. Bodine also thought that most seniors preferred to move east where they would find acceptance, integration, housing, and economic opportunities. Bodine worried that high school students in the camps were "less-inclined and less well-equipped to act as ambassadors and pioneers" and urged, "for the sake of sound future attitudes on the Coast, a few—dozen or two—should come to each big campus and 2 or 3 to each small one. (And this might not happen if we don't help it happen)."[37]

The council decided against opening a West Coast office but pledged to extend its services there as far as possible. Bodine's report to the executive committee on February 27, 1945, reinforced this decision. He did not believe that more than fifty students would be returning to West Coast institution for the spring semester. The executive committee also decided to collect data on West Coast colleges and their willingness to accept Nikkei students.[38]

Bodine foresaw a "chaotic and troublous" 1945 as Nikkei returned to the West Coast. He expected little support from most Americans, remarking that "its tough on these folks and I hope people in the East aren't blithely saying—'why, how nice, they can go back to California and the eveil [sic] done to them by evacuation has been removed.' . . . It still burns me to think that the Supreme Court declared the evacuation constitutional—as if it really had been military necessity! One more step downward for all that America—should—stand—for."[39]

Myer estimated that 60 percent of Nikkei would return to their old homes and the WRA opened relocation offices in Seattle, San Francisco, and Los Angeles to meet this anticipated need. The council also helped interested students return to the West Coast, still preferring that the students not cluster. The council agreed with Secretary of the Interior Harold L. Ickes's desire "to continue and intensify the effort to relocate as many of these people as possible in places other than the West Coast area."[40]

The council's staff urged in February 1945 that student requests for advice be met with a form letter "pointing out the long-range advantages of remaining in college, suggesting that they consider bringing their families to the college communities in which they are beginning to feel at home and discouraging concentration in the large cities." The proposed letter, council minutes noted, met the need felt by those present "that the council should do what it could to encourage dispersion of the Japanese Americans."[41]

Despite WRA and council hopes that dispersal would be fairly permanent, more students looked to resettle westward. At Heart Mountain, the majority of students enrolled in colleges east of the former forbidden zone through July 1945, largely because of a "hesitancy to go where they were not sure of their [acceptance]." As more Nikkei resettled on the West Coast with relatively few problems, however, the majority of students were heading west by August 1945.[42]

The WRA, anticipating student interest, compiled information on West Coast colleges in spring 1945. This data was forwarded to camp counselors and local WRA offices. The mixed response to inquiries to West Coast colleges suggests that, even as the war in the Pacific was nearly won, racism continued to influence some opinions.

Business schools did not adopt a uniform admissions policy. Some welcomed Nikkei. The Dyar Shorthand School in Hollywood promised "no discrimination as to race or creed."[43] A secretarial school pledged cooperation "to the best of our ability. Japanese American students will be given every consideration if and when they apply."[44]

Others bluntly refused to cooperate. James G. Bond of the Willis Santa Monica Business College warned that "good business practices" were more important than "personal feelings" and concluded that the question was "dynamite at present."[45] F. D. MacKay, the president of a business college bearing his name, provided catalogs, but explained that his school would not admit Nikkei students for the duration. While he praised "Japanese" students, MacKay noted that "[w]e have enrolled widows for [sic] service men; if you are a woman, I feel that you will understand their reactions at the suggestion that a Japanese student be admitted prior to the ending of the war. . . . I shall be very glad to again open my doors to Japanese students . . . when the war is over, but I do not think it fair or wise to do so now."[46]

Many West Coast colleges readily admitted Nikkei students in 1945. The registrar at Occidental College wrote to explain that the school had enrolled two resettled students during the past academic year. Many schools that had enrolled Japanese Americans prior to the war quickly accepted them again. Others, however, refused to cooperate. Woodbury College in the Los Angeles area, for example, resisted, citing parental requests that resettled students not be admitted and an incident of hostility between two Korean students and discharged veterans in the student body at a school dance. A poll conducted by Woodbury faculty had resulted in students voting 485 to 115 against the admission of Nikkei. The school denied admission to resettled students for the fall 1945 term, weakly citing a dwindling supply of catalogs and capacity enrollment. Perhaps, the registrar noted in pointing to Woodbury's favorable attitude toward Nikkei in the past, openings would occur for the spring semester.[47]

The council continued to slow its operations in spring 1945. In April, Emlen suggested that the council should pull out of student resettlement as soon as possible. She pointed to the danger of both colleges and Nikkei students becoming too dependent on the council. Students, she argued, needed to do more on their own, and the council had already begun to encourage students to take the initiative.[48]

Dwindling financial support also convinced Emlen that the time had come to close operations. Emlen had initiated a $20,000 scholarship drive in early 1945, mailing 242 letters of appeal to raise what she viewed as funds that were necessary for the continuation of the council's program. Emlen noted with frustration and disappointment in May that these efforts had resulted in only eighteen contributions totaling $364.50. "The needs," she wrote the new chair John Thomas, "are increasing, not decreasing as you know. . . . Frankly, we are all up a stump."[49]

By early July, the totals had only climbed to forty-five donors and $965. Emlen worried that if the remaining $19,000 was not raised, many resettled Nikkei would drop out and few high school graduates would leave the camps for college. "If only assistance can be extended for one more year," she wrote, "the majority of these students' families will be on their feet again so that additional scholarship aid will not be necessary."[50]

Emlen wrote Nason with obvious relief on August 1, her last day as director of the council, to report that the scholarship outlook had brightened considerably. The council had gathered $3,000 in individual contributions. The Hattie M. Strong Foundation had donated an additional $10,000 and Carnegie Corporation and WSSF donations seemed likely.[51] Although Emlen expected to reach her fund-raising goal, the difficulty in securing funds provided the council with another reason for closing.

The council again postponed terminating its operations in September 1945, however, and voted to continue working until June 1946 in order to help resettled students and to meet increased needs for help as the camps closed. Nason, no longer the chair but still a council member, suggested that no other agency could carry on the work of student resettlement as cheaply and efficiently. The executive committee set June 30, 1946, as the closing date. The council focused on referring needy students to church boards or other agencies and on preparing a historical report on its activities.[52]

The council scrambled to meet its self-imposed deadline, reviewing 528 students it had helped, contacting 262 of these to advise them of its closing, and awarding 34 students additional scholarships. In May the council began to refer most remaining students to their respective church boards. Nine boards had promised to continue to aid students helped in the past, and several agreed to accept new applications. The council did not meet its closing deadline; Dorothy Yamauchi worked into July, concluding council operations, completing its records, and responding to late mail.[53]

As the council and the WRA moved toward terminating their operations, each scheduled for June 30, 1946, they exchanged mutual congratulations. Myer described the WRA's experience with the council as "an extremely rewarding one."[54] He also praised the council's "effective and intelligent job."[55] Myer had earlier noted what certainly remained a key reason for his pleasure with the council's work: "We are all aware that the successful student relocation program has been of great value to the ultimate relocation goals of the Authority, as well as to the future life and adjustment of the student group itself."[56]

John Thomas expressed to Myer the council's "appreciation for the sympathetic understanding and unusual cooperation which you have given us. . . . You never gave the impression of simply doing the job for which you were paid. On the contrary, you always expressed an interest in the evacuees as human beings who were going through a difficult experience. I was impressed by your courage, insight and vision."[57]

The mutual congratulations exchanged between the council and the WRA in the summer of 1946 conveniently ignored past tensions. Clearly, the council, and especially its West Coast office, had on occasion pressed harder with the military than the WRA would have preferred. Certainly, the council at times had found the caution of the WRA stifling and frustrating. Despite these difficulties, the two organizations had managed to forge an amicable and largely cooperative relationship.

The Council and Colleges

Colleges outside the West Coast continued to open to Nikkei after fall 1944. So many, in fact, accepted Nikkei by 1946 that some schools struggled to find students. However, some colleges continued to resist cooperating with the council. Some never enrolled Nikkei students while others closed certain programs to them.

The University of Cincinnati had begun to accept resettled students in fall 1942 and enrolled large numbers quickly.[58] The university's engineering program, however, remained officially closed to Nikkei. The council became aware of this in April 1943, when King wrote Joseph Holliday, the director of admissions, about reports that Nikkei could not enroll in physics and chemistry classes. Holliday denied these reports but noted that the College of Engineering and Commerce's co-op system required it to refuse Nikkei enrollment because of the difficulties in placing them in local industries, especially because Cincinnati was "a center for the machine tool industry, and practically every factory of this type is engaged in defense work."[59]

The council accepted Holliday's excuse, at least temporarily. King described the university's policy in a May 5 letter to Holliday as "very farsighted" in light of potential problems. However, she hoped that, as time passed and Nikkei students excelled socially and academically, "wider fields [would] be open to them."[60]

Although one Nikkei student was admitted to the College of Engineering and Commerce and placed in a co-op job in fall 1943, the university's general policy remained to deny Nikkei admissions. Elizabeth Emlen took up the issue again in November 1944 through Kate and Arthur Brinton, who ran a Cincinnati hostel for resettlers. She explained that although few Nikkei wanted to co-op at the University of Cincinnati, "we always hate to see a restriction go unchallenged."[61] Emlen also wrote Harry E. Titus, a Cincinnati WRA relocation officer, and Reverend Nelson Burroughs, the chair of the Cincinnati Citizens Committee on Relocation, to pursue the issue. Louise Fletemeyer, an associate relocation officer in Cincinnati, discussed the co-op program with university officials and reported that the school had encountered difficulties in placing all foreign students, not just Nikkei. A Chinese student had faced "a great deal of difficulty" in finding a co-op job, and a Polish student had, too, until he changed his last name. Fletemeyer also noted that a few Nikkei were currently enrolled in the engineering program.[62]

Emlen's multipronged attack did not result in a clear-cut victory. The root of the problem lay with individual administrators and labor organizations at local plants that did not want Nikkei students. Emlen knew that at least some Nikkei had entered the program and seemed to accept that the council might not be able to go any further than this informal arrangement; she dropped her effort in January 1945.

Other colleges refused to cooperate. Some refusals came from schools that had previously expressed a desire to admit Nikkei.[63] Lebanon Valley College, in Annville, Pennsylvania, had initially returned a receptive questionnaire.[64] No students had arrived by late 1944, however, when the United Brethren Church offered a $200 scholarship that the college pledged to supplement, if necessary. Lebanon Valley College, however, abruptly reversed its decision in June 1945. A male student "who was born in Japan," the president explained, had been "socializing with some of our girls." These actions had discredited the college in its small community, he continued, because a Japanese male and a white female could not be seen together often without "arousing comments and indignation, especially when there [was] considerable affection displayed."[65] The council, faced with the obvious racism of Annville and the college president, decided that it "shouldn't bother any longer trying to place Nisei into this school."[66]

Susquehanna College in Selinsgrove, Pennsylvania, had cautiously pursued student resettlement in late 1942, announcing its willingness to cooperate if the military approved and if resettled students could finance their studies.[67]

The president G. Morris Smith rejected a Nikkei applicant in early 1945, explaining that "local sentiment" opposed the acceptance of Nikkei; although he, the faculty, and the student body wanted resettled students on campus, "the prejudice of local environment is a difficult thing to overcome."[68]

While the wartime context and the need for college cooperation had previously mitigated council responses to unreceptive schools, by summer 1945 the council could be more critical. "It is hard to believe," Emlen lectured Susquehanna, "that a board of trustees still is unwilling to take these Americans of Japanese ancestry in view of the splendid record they have made overseas and in view of the fact that almost every other accredited college and university in this country has opened its doors to these young people."[69]

Other colleges resisted council pleas into 1946. Geneva College in Beaver Falls, Pennsylvania, had rejected council overtures in 1942, explaining that, while it would be happy to accept Nikkei "in ordinary times," it could not admit them in fall 1942 because "they might be subjected to embarrassments and annoyances in spite of our efforts to protect [them]. Besides, this being a vital defense area, we would be subjected to criticism by the citizens of our town."[70] The college remained resistant in 1946, refusing the council's request for college bulletins, which, it explained, were needed for returning veterans. Despite its initial promise in 1942, Nikkei were apparently not welcome at Geneva College, even "in ordinary times."

The council also faced potential conflict with cooperating colleges when Nikkei students were accepted but did not enroll. Juniata College in Huntingdon, Pennsylvania, responded positively in summer 1942 and expressed disappointment that no students arrived for the fall term.[71] When the council applied for a student in early 1943, however, the college rejected him, citing local opposition. College officials worked to calm local fears and again expressed a willingness to enroll resettled students in 1944.

The college accepted Shizu Katase, but he did not enroll. Kay Yamashita wrote to defuse possible conflict by explaining the reasons for Katase's actions: his parents had changed their minds and did not want him to go, he lacked the necessary funds and faced uncertain arrangements in Huntingdon, and "the Pennsylvania area was absolutely strange to him." Small towns such as Huntingdon that offered limited job opportunities especially exacerbated financial problems.[72]

Western Reserve University in Cleveland had returned a receptive but worried questionnaire.[73] The vice president W. G. Simon wrote in June 1942 that the university would be glad to accept Nikkei, but he seemed dubious about doing so. "In general," he explained, "we believe that these Japanese students would be happier in universities located in small towns rather than one located in a big city. There are practically no Japanese in Cleveland and a Japanese student here would feel constantly conspicuous. We do sympathize with them in their embarrassment in these terrible times and will do everything to make a student coming here comfortable; and I should try to help in their adjustment in present conditions."[74]

The university, citing unfriendly public opinion, had decided to bar resettled students by October 1942. Howard Beale pressed the school to reconsider, writing the president W. G. Leutner to point out the importance of his institution as "one of our good universities." He also noted, "we have had universally happy experiences between our Japanese-American students and the rest of the student body. . . . Once our students have arrived, they are charming, intelligent people thoroughly devoted to America." The council forwarded government approval for Nikkei students to enroll and encouraged Leutner to work with local religious leaders to prepare a positive community reception.[75]

The school's policy on the admission of Nikkei did not change until Reverend Sunji Forrest Nishi of the Cleveland Church Federation decided to reopen the issue in July 1944. Although he noted that some Nikkei by then had been accepted at Western Reserve via Cleveland College, Nishi wanted to place students directly. Swan advised him to exert "outside pressure" on the school.[76] Nishi took the story to the *Cleveland Press* and reported success after an article ran on September 14, 1944, under the headline "Japs Born in U.S. Barred from Reserve Classes." Negotiations had been fruitless, he noted, until "the story was released in the local press[;] we [then] had action within three days."[77]

The University of Pennsylvania, which had furnished naval intelligence with information on its Japanese American students prior to Pearl Harbor, decided not to accept Nikkei in summer 1942 after discussing the matter with Lieutenant General Hugh A. Drum, who was Lieutenant General John L. DeWitt's East Coast counterpart.[78] President Thomas S. Gates reported that Drum advised "against the bringing into this area . . . as students any aliens because of the possibility of their having to leave the area."[79] Despite student interest at the university and the presence of the junior-class president Naomi Nakano, a Nikkei born and raised in Pennsylvania, the university so firmly resisted accepting Nikkei that Beale suspected that officials had asked the government to take their institution off the list of approved colleges. Greg Robinson suggests numerous reasons for the university's decision, including confusion about government policies, eagerness to support the military, cautious bureaucracy, ignorance of Nikkei, a desire to avoid trouble, and racism.

Gates continued to pursue a general policy of noncooperation, although the biracial daughter of a professor in the university's linguistics department was allowed to enroll in graduate school, until Nakano graduated and applied to the university's graduate school. The school denied her admission. Nakano's story, which highlighted the university's discriminatory policy, received considerable attention in the press. Nakano, a University of Pennsylvania graduate whose father was a distinguished alumnus as well, had been active on campus and had also toured East Coast colleges to encourage the admission of Nikkei from the camps. She expressed "great disappointment at not being allowed to continue graduate study at the university where I spent four very pleasant years. The principle of discrimination upsets me very much. This is the first time—the only time—it has touched me."[80] Press coverage seems to have convinced Gates to reverse his decision.

The university's belated acceptance of Nakano, however, did not provide the breakthrough that the council anticipated. Nakano had already committed to attend Bryn Mawr, although she would later return with her master's degree to become the first female instructor of sociology at the Wharton School. The University of Pennsylvania had changed its policy on the surface, but Bodine complained in February 1945 that it "has placed so many barriers in the way of [Nisei] that no one has actually been successful in enrolling [as a full-time student]."[81]

The racial tensions associated with student resettlement continue to resonate today. After an article on Nakano by Greg Robinson ran in the *Pennsylvania Gazette*, one Wharton alumnus wrote to complain about Robinson's "galling . . . use of the phrase 'anti-Japanese hysteria sweeping the United States.'" The writer continued,

> Well, when half of your fleet is on the bottom and your outmanned and outgunned soldiers are being captured and beheaded with Samurai swords, you might get a little nervous about some of those folks living in L.A., too. How would authorities know for certain whether or not Miss Nakano was an agent for Japan? Because she didn't wear a rising-sun flag on her sweater? How would you be certain that a navy carrier with 3,500 personnel aboard slipping out of Philadelphia wasn't being observed by an Axis agent? Isn't 20–20 hindsight great? . . . This war was not Kosovo; this was a struggle to save the world from two fiendish militaristic regimes and, while some steps were taken that in this day and age seem unpalatable, they were taken and it's done with.

This rhetoric mirrored many arguments used against student resettlement during the war. However, subsequent issues of the *Pennsylvania Gazette* contained strong criticisms of this letter.[82]

Ohio State University decided not to accept resettled students in early summer 1942 after brief consideration.[83] The university examiner Bland L. Stradley explained that the school would not admit them because it lacked navy clearance. Stradley became a primary obstacle to Nikkei admission, and Ohio State remained closed to resettled students until fall 1944.

Everett L. Dakan, a WRA relocation officer in Columbus with connections to Ohio State's Department of Poultry Husbandry, wrote Carlisle Hibbard in November 1943 for an explanation of why Ohio State remained closed to Nikkei: "Maybe I am stupid; if so, it is time I got wise!"[84] When AFT Local 438 inquired about Ohio State's status in April 1944, the council, perhaps sensing a groundswell of local interest, forwarded applications. Stradley continued to reject Nikkei, however, citing the presence of confidential research and military units on campus.

Dakan presented the council with a ground-level account of the situation in 1944. "I am not too hopeful," he surmised. "It is my belief that we are being given the run around and that there are reasons which do not appear on the surface for the evasion which comes from the University administration." Dakan urged the council to continue working on Ohio State, at least until there was "a straight out and out denial or acceptance."[85]

Dakan sensed an opportunity when Stradley rejected a Nikkei graduate school applicant in June 1944 by citing only the student's average grades to explain his decision. Dakan advised continued pressure: "Keep applications coming. Ohio State University, I am sure, is weakening. Get us applications of boys and girls with good grades, with good records above reproach. There are so many people in this town working on this that you must not fail us in Philadelphia."[86]

Ohio State finally accepted Nikkei students in August 1944. This policy reversal resulted in part from local pressure. The appointment of Ronald B. Thompson as registrar and university examiner, replacing Stradley, who became vice president, also prompted change. Thompson came to Ohio State from the University of Utah, which had accepted more than one hundred resettled students.[87]

The WRA relocation officer Carl L. Spicer recommended that the council advise students to correspond directly with Thompson, whose arrival had "considerably quickened the process in acceptance of applications and the enrollment of students."[88] Spicer also advised the council that, in publicizing Ohio State's new policy, it should not discuss the old policies of Stradley. Any such references, he warned, would gain nothing for the council and potential students.[89]

Nao Takasugi of the placement department agreed to ignore Stradley in publicity that pertained to Ohio State's change of heart. He explained that the council believed that Spicer and "the Columbus office of the [WRA] as well as Ronald B. Thompson have done a marvelous job bringing about the present excellent relations with Ohio State University and we certainly do not wish to disturb these conditions in any way."[90] The council's success here highlighted its work at its finest, coordinating the efforts of diverse local individuals and groups as well as local government agencies to open a recalcitrant school.

Cracking Penn State University required the council to exercise similar patience and skill in orchestrating diverse groups.[91] D. Ned Linegar of the Penn State Christian Association had written Pickett in July 1942 to report that his group was "working to develop a favorable administrative policy at Penn State."[92] The council shared information with Linegar, but school trustees decided before the end of summer that the university would not admit Nikkei for the duration.

Although Penn State refused to admit Nikkei, citing a request by Third Corps Area Army officials, local contacts with Dr. R. Adams Dutcher, a professor of agriculture and biological chemistry, and the Penn State Christian Association encouraged the council to continue working on the school. Beale wrote Dutcher in late September to advise him that the commanding officer of the Third Corps Area had no authority to speak on the issue of Nisei students. He understood the predicament faced by reluctant university officials because of the unwieldy process of student resettlement: schools wanted to be cleared before accepting Nikkei, but the government would not clear schools until they accepted Nikkei. Beale was "very anxious to open up the situation" and urged Dutcher to get a questionnaire returned.[93]

The council pressed Penn State in spring 1943. Elizabeth Johnson, assistant to the council director, wrote President Ralph D. Hetzel to point out that colleges that had received Nikkei were pleased with the results for both the resettled students and the student body. Johnson listed some of the participating colleges and reported that Christian Associations often supported student resettlement, although she did not reveal the council's contact with Penn State's association. The council also remained in touch with the Christian Association and the World Friendship Commission at Penn State. Hetzel refused to cooperate, however. In late April, he wrote Hibbard to explain that the university had given student resettlement "full and sympathetic consideration" but that, at the time, it was not in the best interests of Nikkei or Penn State for resettled students to arrive.[94]

C. L. White, a Harrisburg relocation officer, pursued Penn State in fall

1943. He found many college officials and employees supportive of student resettlement and reported that the administration "seemed not at all opposed to the idea of accepting [resettled students]." The administration, however, faced overcrowding problems that caused it to turn down qualified in-state students.[95]

The council acted on White's research in March 1944, writing Hetzel to inform him of the local WRA report and to reveal its contact with Penn State's Christian Association and the World Friendship Commission. The council also forwarded Nikkei applications. Hetzel issued a blunt rejection, citing general trustee opposition.

In July 1944, Penn State offered a new excuse for continuing to deny admission to Nikkei, explaining that the school accepted only a limited number of out-of-state students. So many Nikkei had applied in 1942, however, that the school had decided to take none to avoid complicating its admissions policies. Bodine urged action and suggested that Mary Gorai, a "thoroughly attractive girl" who would be an "excellent opener of a new school," be used as "a guinea pig."[96]

When Penn State still proved recalcitrant, Emlen contacted H. Leon Yager, a Philadelphia relocation officer, and explained that Penn State had turned down Gorai by citing lack of dormitory space. She added, however, that it had long been clear "that [the] institution [had] been unwilling to accept Japanese Americans."[97] Emlen continued to write Yager, encouraging him and wishing him "the best of luck on 'cracking' Penn State."[98] She also wrote to keep him apprised of new information. Emlen relayed, for example, a report suggesting that Penn State's reluctance was "primarily political." Hetzel, she explained, would likely accept Nikkei if the university's funding were not dependent on the state legislature. He feared, in particular, the American Legion's influence on that body.[99] Although the university examiner continued to cite lack of living space and limits on out-of-state students, Howard E. Mather of the Pittsburgh relocation officer reported that the policy rested on "fear of campus tensions and misunderstandings."[100]

Hetzel finally relented in October 1945, explaining that "[t]he circumstances on which the decision . . . was based no longer exist. [T]he same policy which governs other applicants will apply to students of Japanese ancestry."[101] The WRA thanked Hetzel for his decision and hoped "that there [would] be a representation of this element in our citizenry, so that you and your student body may meet them and come to know them, and so that they may become acquainted with students throughout the state and nation. . . . A multiplication of such experience all over the country is certainly an exercise and strengthening of democracy."[102] Snyder enclosed

Hetzel's capitulation and his reply in a brief note to Graybill that summarized the three-year struggle to open Penn State: "The enclosed copy of a letter from Dr. R. D. Hetzel . . . and my reply winds up this long-winded matter. They are suitable for framing."[103]

Indiana University also opened its doors to Nikkei only slowly, returning the Student Relocation Committee's questionnaire in May 1942 with a flat refusal to cooperate because Bloomington was located in a defense area.[104] University officials had actually discussed other, and blatantly racist, reasons for rejecting Nikkei applicants at the May 9, 1942, board of trustees meeting. Faced with four formal applications from Japanese Americans, President Herman B. Wells raised the issue of student resettlement. Three board members strongly opposed accepting Nikkei. Judge Ora L. Wildermuth, the board's chair, succinctly explained his opposition: "as I see it, there is a difference in Japs and Germans or Italians—they are Aryans and can be assimilated but the Japs can't—they are different racially. I can't believe that any Jap, no matter where he is born, is anything but Japanese." The board voted to reject even Nisei natives of Indiana. President Wells supported the decision, worrying that increasing numbers of casualties in the Pacific War might result in "disturbances on the campus," especially with a naval unit arriving.[105] This decision disappointed Beale, who perceived the university as a "bigger and on the whole better" institution.[106]

A. L. Kohlmeier of the office of the vice president and dean of faculties reiterated Indiana's position, echoing President Wells in explaining that, since the university provided military training, "it would appear obvious that bringing some of these Japanese American students on to our campus would present us with a problem. . . . Needless to say, we are in most hearty accord with your noble effort. . . . If, before the close of this academic year, we see any favorable opportunity to assist you in the placing of some of these students, we will at once get in touch with you."[107] Indiana maintained its policy through spring 1944. By summer 1945, it had enrolled one Nikkei.

As larger schools such as Ohio State and Penn State began to open to Nikkei after summer 1944, smaller schools at times struggled to find Nikkei. Berea College in Kentucky, a school with a long radical history, had accepted two stranded Hawaiian students who had been attending a conference of Christian students at Ohio's Miami University on December 7, 1941, and, after considerable debate within the community, had cooperated with the council and admitted Nikkei students early in the war, enrolling five Nikkei by July 1943.[108] Berea maintained a quota of five, despite occasional council requests to increase it. By summer 1945, however, the college was seeking additional Nikkei applicants. Although it had positive experiences with resettled students, applications were declining.

The Council's Role in the Concentration Camps

The council maintained an indirect presence in the camps during its final years, despite the WRA's assumption of student-counseling responsibilities. Emlen encouraged camp scholarship funds, especially in light of the slow release of WSSF money. Bodine praised such scholarship campaigns for promoting the council's work, stimulating students, and increasing "parent participation in the student relocation program."[109] Bodine used his visits to promote scholarship drives. He talked with various Nikkei leaders in Granada in February 1945, and, within two weeks, a student scholarship fund was organized. The Granada committee based awards on grade point average, personality, extracurricular activities, and academic honors. The committee established $50 as the maximum award and promised to recommend recipients to the council for additional aid.[110]

Inmates at Poston also belatedly established a scholarship fund. The College Bound Club, organized in October 1944, took the lead and set a goal of $2,000. The counselor Estelee Hinson had high hopes for the project. She wrote Emlen in January 1945 to recommend that the council focus on aiding Poston students who had already resettled since they were not eligible for help from the new fund. The current class, Hinson believed, would not need much outside help.[111]

Camp artists contributed to the Poston fund in February 1945, selling watercolor paintings and donating the profits to help resettle students. John W. Powell, the chief of the community management division, authorized the sale and urged organizers to act quickly to take advantage of the staff's interest. The sale raised $125.50. After $80 was paid to the artists to cover their costs, the remainder was distributed among the scholarship funds of the three Poston camps.[112]

The Poston I scholarship committee met in May 1945 to determine policies for awarding scholarships. It decided that students who applied would receive a $75 scholarship after presenting proof of acceptance. Any money refunded or not used would be divided and distributed on an equal basis to recipients still in college. The committee required a B average for eligibility, but agreed to waive this "in the case of a student who has rendered unusual service to the College Bound Club as a member."[113]

The council also decided to repeat its returnee project in summer 1945.

Although modeled on the 1944 program, the new effort had important differences. The council provided returnees with student resettlement information and encouraged them to participate in camp life. Significantly, it also prepared them to discuss wider resettlement issues with visits to local WRA offices and hostels as well as talks with resettlers.[114]

Placement director Nao Takasugi wrote the camp counselors to explain the new focus of the returnees. He explained that the council had selected students who could talk with both young and old inmates. Poston I counselor Estelee Hinson applauded the 1945 project. She could help students once their parents consented to their resettlement, but believed returnees more effective in securing permission. She also suggested a particular student because many in the community—both parents and students—had confidence in her.[115]

The returnees used the camp newspapers to publicize their new emphasis. The Gila *News Courier*, for example, reported that the returnees wanted to speak to students and "all parents."[116] The returnee Clifford Nakadegawa publicized a similar message in Tule Lake. The Newell *Star* reported that he believed "resettlement to be the most important problem now facing center residents. . . . 'If people only will look at the problem squarely, they will realize that the best thing for them is to get out of here while the WRA still has machinery operating to help them in their resettlement.'"[117]

Takasugi highlighted the family resettlement work of the returnees in his report on the 1945 project. The returnees had been most effective, he argued, when engaged in informal family discussions, which often coordinated student and family resettlement plans. The council, he continued, had consciously sought "more mature returnees . . . who could get along with both Issei and Nisei, and who could serve as a liaison between the appointed WRA staff members and the residents." Although students faced many of the same obstacles in 1945 as in 1944, they remained interested in higher education. Takasugi connected this desire to a key concern: would the council remain in operation until mid-1946?[118]

While the council expressed pleasure with the results of its 1945 program, a history of the Minidoka Center noted its limited achievements. The 1945 returnees had arrived while Helen Amerman was on vacation and subsequently had been treated by administrators as "political footballs." Local conditions once again limited the effectiveness of the returnees.[119]

The Council and the Students

The council continued to help place students through the end of the war. Kiyoaki Murata, who had been in the United States for a total of only five months prior to Pearl Harbor, presented a unique case. Incarcerated at Poston, Murata resettled to Chicago, where he enrolled in Central YMCA College. Rebuffed in two attempts to gain admission to the University of Chicago, Murata contacted the council and, on its advice, decided to attend Carleton College in Northfield, Minnesota. Arriving in September 1944, Murata "found Carleton truly like a big family. . . . Although the students expressed interest in my situation and background, not one of them made reference to the fact that my country was at war with theirs." Although Murata could laugh when somebody warned a white friend of his to "be careful because he might stab you in the back," he clearly met racism while in Minnesota. Still, he was warmly received as a guest lectureer to an Army Specialized Training Program (ASTP) group at the University of Minnesota. Murata eventually earned a master's degree at the University of Chicago.[120]

The council's correspondence with students after summer 1944 increasingly centered on financial issues. Although Bodine believed that this made the letters less exciting, scholarships opened important opportunities for Nikkei. While the added thrill of battling the government might have faded, the excitement felt by the approximately one thousand students who escaped the camps for colleges via the council after summer 1944 did not abate in the council's final years (see table 3).

Contributions to the council's scholarship fund totaled $270,170.23 by June 30, 1946 (see table 4). Distributed in 1,419 grants to 966 individuals, awards averaged a little under $200, although earlier grants tended to be larger. Most of the grants were made at the council's recommendation, although some allocations were made independently. Larger churches with more Nikkei members contributed more. The Presbyterian Church, for example, awarded 195 grants worth $45,847.25. Smaller denominations donated proportionally smaller amounts. The WSSF contributed $40,743.32 in 271 grants, often to Buddhists and non–church members.[121]

Harold Ogi, a resettled student at Ohio's Muskingum College, approached the council for financial aid in late 1943. Harry Evans of the local United Presbyterian Church wrote in support, noting that Ogi had attended his church since arriving and fit "into this college community very commendably." Evans reported that the student and his fellow fraternity pledges had recently taken "over our house and served a fine spaghetti dinner for [their entire fraternity]. He made a good impression on my wife, which, under the circumstances, means a great deal."[122]

Ogi received a scholarship from Muskingum in spring 1944 that was later supplemented by a Presbyterian grant. "May I say thanks," he wrote E. Fay Campbell, "from the bottom of my heart for your scholarship grant? . . . No Christmas present was ever more appreciated." The grant, in addition to others as well as his work as a laboratory assistant in the biology depart-

Table 3. Acceptances and Enrollments, April 30, 1944–April 1946

Dates	Acceptances	Enrollments
As of April 30, 1944	3,112	2,575
May 1, 1944–December 31, 1944		
College students	502	303
Nursing students	35	21
January 1, 1945–July 31, 1945		
College students	376	220
Nursing students	14	6
August 1945		
College students	64	39
Nursing students	5	4
September 1945		
College students	59	40
Nursing students	16	16
October 1945		
College students	277	118
Nursing students	71	111
November 1945		
College students	11	10
December 1945		
College students	22	21
January 1946		
College students	35	35
February 1946		
College students	103	80
Nursing students	8	8
March 1946		
College students	36	95
Nursing students	1	1
April 1946		
College students	13	10
	4,760	3,713

Source: Acceptances and Enrollments, n.d., Box 48, NJASRC, HI. Thomas Bodine, in explaining one reason for the large discrepancy between acceptances and enrollments, noted that "[i]n the early days an educational leave was the easiest way of getting out of camp and thus a number of people applied to the Student Relocation Council for whom a chance to study was secondary to their primary desire to get out." See "From Camp to Campus," *Heart Mountain Sentinel,* 16 December, 1944, 5.

Table 4. Scholarship Allocations through June 30, 1946

Source	Students Aided	Second Year	Third Year	Total
AFSC	8	—	—	$ 1,122.00
J. M. Atherton Trust and Friend Peace Scholarships	5	2	—	800.00
Baptist	142	2	—	39,275.86
Brethren	3	—	—	400.00
Catholic	22	6	1	10,716.00
Church of the Crossroads Loan Fund	14	—	—	1,433.44
Columbia Foundation	7	1	—	2,000.00
Congregational	70	13	3	15,911.65
Disciples of Christ	13	1	—	2,384.00
Episcopal	106	22	5	26,890.12
Evangelical	9	—	—	900.00
Evangelical and Reformed	78	25	12	19,187.49
Free Methodist	12	—	—	2,297.00
Methodist	152	25	2	20,042.71
Presbyterian	195	56	13	45,847.25
Private Donations Fund	298	31	4	37,484.39
United Brethren in Christ	4	—	—	325.00
United Lutheran	10	3	1	2,410.00
WSSF	271	31	4	40,743.32
	1,419	218	45	$270,170.23

Source: Report on Scholarship Allocations, June 30, 1946, Reports, Box 49, NJASRC, HI.
Note: The council lacked complete data on the United Brethren in Christ Church and the Free Methodist Church.

ment and as head dishwasher, allowed him to pursue his "ultimate goal": helping others as a medical missionary.

The Presbyterian grant, Ogi explained, had also enabled him to serve as an ambassador of goodwill. He enthusiastically described being tapped publicly by the college's honorary fraternity for upperclass students and faculty. Although he took pride in being the only junior selected, Ogi was more pleased "in knowing that we [Nisei] at Muskingum have . . . showed to Muskingum and others that we are not so different from other Americans." He also hoped that students in the camps would be inspired by the acceptance of Nikkei on the outside.

Ogi clearly felt a close relationship with Campbell and the council, apologizing for writing at such "great length about myself. . . . I feel just like a little kid writing home to his parents trying to tell them that their investment is being used to [its] greatest capacity." He believed that the financial aid provided by the Presbyterian Church and the council had opened up opportunities for both himself and the Nikkei as a whole.[123]

John Kamiya wrote Graybill from Ohio Wesleyan in June 1946 after hearing "the very good news" of a $60.00 award from the Methodist Church Board. He planned to work in California during the summer to help meet rising college costs and then return to Ohio Wesleyan. "Although I had my ups and downs this year," he wrote, "I really enjoyed my first year of college life. Everyone here has been friendly and helpful in every respect." Kamiya was the second highest scorer on the basketball team, which compiled a record of nine wins and ten losses against "some of the most powerful teams in Ohio." He had forged, he reported, friendships with "some of the finest group of men." Kamiya described the council's closing as "a big blow to all the Nisei students" but believed "we can struggle some way through college. The helpfulness and kindness of . . . the council will always be remembered by me and surely by all the Nisei students of America."[124]

Elizabeth Emlen realized the importance of financial aid and made it a council priority during her tenure as national director. Slow WSSF disbursements exacerbated her financial concerns, especially for Buddhist and nonchurch students. Uncertainty about the continuing support of church boards added to Emlen's worry.

Emlen approached financial shortcomings by relying on local donations in raising money for Nikkei students when possible, a tested council strategy. For example, she arranged for the Massachusetts Association of Universalist Women to help finance Michi Nishiura's studies at Mount Holyoke in 1944.[125] Although the group's initial aid amounted to only $29, even a few dollars could make a significant difference. Emlen thanked the group for its support and included Nishiura's biography. Nishiura, who later published *Years of Infamy,* an important early historical study of exile and incarceration, also wrote a letter of thanks, an action encouraged by the council. The association responded by giving her an additional $36, the entirety of one meeting's collection.

Graybill appealed to the association for $90 in September 1945. Although it had not responded to Emlen's attempt to raise $20,000 in scholarship funds, Graybill hoped that it would continue to help Nishiura meet her annual college expenses, which totaled more than $1,100. Graybill wrote again in October after receiving no reply. The association, although wishing Nishiura success, did not provide additional aid, explaining that it had too many other pressing projects in fall 1945.

The scarcity of funds after fall 1944 made the council appreciative of students who returned unneeded aid. For example, Jack Furkawa returned $90 to the council in late 1944, the balance remaining from a grant that would go unused because he had entered the army. The Presbyterian Church thanked him for this gesture and assured him that the money would be given to another Nikkei student. The Presbyterians wrote, "We of course are very sorry that your schooling has been cut short at this time, but sincerely hope that you will be able to resume your studies when this horrible conflict is over."[126]

The council's finances were strained further by the government's decision to end restrictions on Nikkei enrollment. Students who resettled on their own sometimes then wrote the council for financial aid, adding to its already heavy load. For example, Jane Kono resettled at the University of Rochester's Eastman School of Music independently and then filed for financial aid in summer 1945.[127] She received $80 in July and $100 in September from the Protestant Episcopal Church. These grants did not end her financial problems, however; Father Joe Kitigawa wrote Graybill in September to explain that she still lacked the necessary funds to continue. He wrote again in October, explaining that Kono was reluctant to ask for more help.[128] Although Kono's file shows no additional aid, she did enroll for 1945–46.

The council also fielded financial requests from students who had resettled earlier. Mary Osaka left Minidoka for Iowa's University of Dubuque in fall 1945 with the help of a $150 Presbyterian grant and an additional $60 from the council.[129] She promised, since she could not adequately express her thanks, to "really . . . try to be worthy of the scholarship." Osaka described the people at the university as "very, very friendly and we have so much fun."[130]

The council granted Osaka an additional $100 from the Hattie M. Strong Foundation before the end of her first year. Graybill informed her, "Mrs. Strong has indicated that if at any time in the future, you are able to return it to the Hattie M. Strong Foundation, it would be used to help some other needy student."[131] Graybill wrote again in April 1946 and urged Osaka to work to raise money for her expenses, explaining that the $310 granted to her greatly exceeded the average for 1945–46 and that the council could not provide that much again. The council wanted to help, she assured Osaka, but would appreciate it if she could reduce her application for 1946–47 to the minimum necessary.

Shigeki Ono at Earlham also applied for additional aid in spring 1943. George D. Van Dyke, dean of the college, wrote in support of Ono. Although Ono was a B-minus student, Van Dyke praised his "attitude and citizenship" as well as his participation in athletics. "I believe," Van Dyke concluded, "in every way he is living up to the fine record that all of our Japanese American students have established at Earlham."[132]

The council could not continue to help students in spring 1946 as it had previously, in part because church boards began to turn their attention to new projects. For example, Monica Itoi wrote Presbyterian E. Fay Campbell in April 1946 after hearing him speak at the Hanover College chapel.[133] She inquired about the possibilities for financial aid in pursuing master's degree in clinical psychology. Anne Horner responded for Campbell, explaining that Presbyterian appropriations for Nikkei students were decreasing with the end of the war. "The plan," she continued, "is to absorb the entire program into the Service Loan program. Under that it will not be possible to assist graduate students unless they are preparing for church vocations. Restrictions have also been placed on the funds available specifically for Japanese American students, and I fear we will be unable to help you finance your graduate work." Horner hoped that a fellowship might be possible and suggested working before entering graduate school. "It is always a disappointment to give up a cherished plan," she counseled, "but I believe that graduate work is sometimes of more value if there have been one or two years of practical experience after college."[134]

Financial difficulties played a role in some Nikkei abandoning college after resettling. Masao Takano had applied for admission to Grinnell through Sarah Young, his journalism teacher at Tule Lake and a Grinnell graduate.[135] He arrived in August 1944 and thanked the council "for helping me get a start in 'Life.' The 'outside,' I think is just grand." Takano found a job for room and board but worried about his financial situation and asked the council to write a letter of recommendation to help him win "an academic refund."[136] The high costs of Grinnell so concerned Takano that he planned to eventually transfer to the University of Missouri. He did not, however, he assured Emlen, need a scholarship for his first year.

The registrar at Grinnell believed that Takano was too optimistic. His funds were limited, and the $100 academic refund was uncertain because, the registrar felt, he would have difficulty maintaining a B average. Takano was in a financial pinch by January and wrote the council asking for a $50 loan. Emlen promised to try, but noted that money was tight. Takano's financial crisis seemed averted by February, when a Nisei friend loaned him the money. He reported in April that his "most crucial period" was over. He restated his intent to finish four years of college, and he thanked the council for giving him "courage and confidence to continue when my feelings leaned toward defeat. Knowing that I am not alone, that your organization was ready to help me has been a great aid."[137]

Emlen searched for aid for Takano, writing Methodist ministers in Pasadena and Los Angeles, and Young offered to aid her former student with an anonymous gift of $50. The council, however, did not hear from Takano again. When Graybill wrote Grinnell for an update, the registrar reported that Takano had not enrolled for 1945–46. She attributed Takano's withdrawal to his academic record the previous year, "the poorest of any Nisei student who has attended Grinnell." The registrar faulted his uneven preparatory work and an inability to adjust to college work for his poor performance. Financial concerns were not noted, but certainly contributed to Takano's struggles. The registrar believed he had returned to Tule Lake.[138]

The council struggled with some students. Yamashita described one to Reverend Sunji Forrest Nishi, a field counselor for the Cleveland Church Federation. Katsuro Matsui had acted "undiplomatically" at Columbus's Capital University and soured the council's relations with the school. Yamashita considered Matsui "a fairly immature student [who] does not seem to know what he wants and has his mind easily changed by suggestions from others." Although the council forwarded his records to Kent State—because its policy dictated compliance with any student request—Yamashita doubted the wisdom of this. She explained,

> The more I think through the problem of higher education for Japanese American students, I am not so convinced that all of those who have applied to this Council or seem eager to attend college should really struggle in order to do so. I . . . believe that because parents have such strong ideas about higher education, some . . . have really forced themselves through four years in courses they were not fitted. With dispersion, I am hopeful that there will be broader opportunities for Nisei in general and I wonder if students, such as Katsuro, would not benefit by specialized training other than in a four year Liberal Arts College.[139]

Financial concerns delayed the resettlement of other Nikkei students. John Morita received an educational leave in fall 1942, but chose to remain in camp because of strained finances.[140] He wrote Bill Stevenson of the council's records department in May 1943 after attending an informal student resettlement meeting. Morita asked Stevenson to tell King that he remained in camp. "I wish," he pleaded, "I could attend a college on some scholarship. . . . Please don't forget about me."[141]

Woodruff Emlen attempted to place Morita at the University of New Hampshire, but the university refused to consider male Nikkei because of the presence of army units on campus. The council encouraged Morita to take advantage of the new PMGO clearance process. Yamashita also wrote in November, apologizing for leaving him "in a lurch since trying the University of New Hampshire."[142]

Correspondence with Morita did not resume until he wrote the council in July 1945. He had gained acceptance at the University of Illinois, he reported, but he might need financial aid. Elizabeth Emlen wrote that it was "grand to have first hand news of you once again," but repeated the common reply to students seeking aid: money was tight and students needed to earn as much as possible on their own.[143] The council arranged local contacts and a $75 grant per semester from the Religious Workers' Association at the University of Illinois.

Morita wrote again in July 1946. He planned to register at the University of Illinois medical school in the fall. He regretted leaving the Champaign campus: "I was only just learning what college offered me. I was just learning what help other students can be and I to them. . . . It was so different from the three idle years that I spent practically stagnating." Aware of the council's closing, he also asked for help in finding financial aid.[144] Lee W. Smyth responded to this last-minute appeal on July 10, explaining that the council had closed and referring Morita to the Hattie M. Strong Foundation.

Saying *Sayonara*

On June 7, 1946, Graybill wrote resettled students to announce the closing of the council and to say *sayonara* (good-bye). She believed that the closing of the council provided "a significant indication of the steadily progressing readjustment of the Japanese Americans throughout the country." Graybill also wrapped up council business with the students, asking for updates and explaining that transcripts from project high schools could be requested from the U.S. Office of Education. She also outlined how to deal with urgent financial problems, suggesting first looking to church boards that had previously provided aid and only then contacting the council immediately to indicate "the minimum amount of aid which you will need for the coming year. If we cannot help you from council funds, we may be able to refer you to a Foundation which has granted aid to Japanese American students." Graybill concluded her letter with an emotional message from "those staff members who have meant the most to you[:] I want to tell you how much all of us have enjoyed working with you and the other Nisei students. Good luck in whatever you undertake!"[145]

Graybill's letter inspired students to write notes of gratitude. A Nikkei graduate of Huron College in South Dakota thanked the council for its work that "can never be specifically written down nor perhaps fully appreciated." Most important, the student noted, the council deserved much of the credit for the Nisei assuming their place as American citizens.[146]

The letters that arrived after the council's closing mirrored messages that had been presented before. Many suggested that students felt an obligation to the council. Martha Fujita recalled how she had felt "like an animal being herded about [on evacuation day]—a nonentity whom no one would trust." She had approached student resettlement interviews in Santa Anita as "just another farce" and explained, "frankly I only went to be able to explain later how shallow the plan of relocating students was going to be. I was very surprised to find out then how thoroughly your system went in the matter of scholastic records and [your] understanding, sympathy and encouragement." Recalling Bodine's "many trips" and "the scores of letters" written for her, Fujita thanked the council and added that "[i]f at any time there is something I can do for you—I shall certainly expect you to call upon me."[147]

Edward and Ayako Goto wrote from Cincinnati in May 1946 to express their gratitude. "We know," they explained, "all this couldn't possibly have happened without your help. You picked us up and lifted us, and set us on our feet. . . . We hope someday soon we can help someone as you've helped us."[148] Jane Izumi wrote in January 1946 from Earlham to explain her desire to "make some individual as happy as you have made me" and to relate how Nikkei students had already begun to pay the council back. Some, she noted, had visited local churches to talk about exile and incarceration. "The people were very understanding and sympathetic," she reported. "It is a pleasure to speak to such an understanding group of individuals."[149]

Edwin Noda wrote from Kenyon College and captured a widely shared sentiment among the resettled students, explaining that the council's closing left him with "a feeling of ambiguity; a feeling of sadness in that the Council will function no more; and yet a stronger feeling of gladness that the Council need not function any more. However, this leaves one-half the work done: the other half is up to us, the students, to prove that your work . . . has not been vainly spent. You may rest assured that we shall try our best to do that job. My only hope is that I may be of some help to others someday, as the Council and other agencies have been to me."[150] Frank Yamada echoed this sentiment: "Words cannot express my sincerest appreciation, but as long as memory lives, I shall always be thankful to you."[151]

CONCLUSION:
MEMORY AND THE MEANING OF
STUDENT RESETTLEMENT

While positive memories of the council justifiably remain today, especially among the students it helped, a critical appraisal of the council and its program is necessary. The council negotiated a complex and racist wartime environment to help a group that many Americans considered disloyal only because of their ethnic origin. Success in this endeavor required compromise and resulted in part from a shared vision with the WRA.

The historical legacies of student resettlement during World War II defy simple explanation. While casting the council's story as one of heroes and villains—the council, its supporters, and the Nikkei students defeating the federal government, the WCCA, the PMGO, the WRA, reluctant college administrators, recalcitrant communities, and American racism—is tempting, such a simplistic dichotomy ignores a more nuanced story. Understanding the council's success remains incomplete so long as it is viewed as simply the result of good defeating evil.

The council's success as a voluntary agency in resettling the vast majority of students wishing to pursue higher education, in fact, clearly did not result from the inevitable triumph of right over wrong. The wartime context, especially in the early months as the war in the Pacific went badly for the United States, placed Nikkei in a tenuous position, and presented the council with serious obstacles, both private and public. The council managed to overcome these problems, but only because a number of factors worked in combination for the council and the students it hoped to help.

Thomas Bodine, on his tours of the camps, sometimes sang "Manzanar Love Song" at the beginning of his talks to groups of students. This song told the story of a boy and a girl at Manzanar who were in love, but felt that their relationship was stifled by a lack of privacy created by the many onlookers in camp. In "Manzanar Love Song," the boy complains,

Our love affair of necessity must be
A thing of public interest, not private property
    For there!: ma and pa and sis and bud
To peer and jeer when I love you and you love me.

No place to park and watch the moon go down
We can't take in a picture show or window shop the town
    We must do our romancing
    With lots of people glancing
But we don't care; just let them stare and let them frown.

The mess hall can be dinner at the Ritz
    Guayule your corsage
Since gas is rationed we must walk a bit
But we can pretend our Packard is stored at camouflage.

So we'll go on and do the best we can
You're still my favorite glamour girl and I'm your ardent fan
    It's just as good to pretend
    It's not so important when
You know it's true that I love you
    And I think you know it
    And I'll show it
When I can."[1]

While the comedic quality of Bodine performing "Manzanar Love Song" for incarcerated students is easily imagined, the song speaks on a symbolic level to the relationship between the council and the students. Any and all interactions between the two were deeply scrutinized both inside and outside the camps. These awkward conditions limited the ways the council could express and act on its desire to help the students.

Inside the assembly centers in 1942, the council and the students faced intense scrutiny from the WCCA and the hypervigilant Karl Bendetsen. The transfer of custody from the WCCA to the WRA did not erase all barriers to student resettlement, either. Although, in general, the WRA supported student resettlement, individual administrators and high school teachers in its camps sometimes discouraged Nikkei from pursuing college education. Military regulations for student resettlement often hindered efforts to resettle students. The Nikkei community also closely monitored the relationship between the council and the students. Although cynics existed and some individuals, often fearful parents, had to be convinced of the council's good intentions and the safety of their children, most inmates either actively supported or passively accepted student resettlement.

Outside the concentration camps, college administrators and communities observed the relationship between the council and the students. Administrators wanted to make sure that the council provided sufficient financial support to the students. Local communities wanted to be sure that the council could vouch for the trustworthiness of Nikkei students. The resettled students thus were always expected to be ambassadors of goodwill in their new surroundings.

Council members hoped that, even when mistakes were made and delays occurred because of the complications of wartime racism and bureaucratic processes, the students would continue to feel the deep concern of the council for them as individuals. Both the council and the students, the song implied, would have to make the best of a bad situation; the students, it seemed, would have to be satisfied with the council proving its love when it could.

The council succeeded in negotiating this at-times hostile wartime environment, in part, because of internal divisions between pragmatic easterners and crusading westerners. The cooperative approach of the more conservative council members accepted slow but steady progress in student resettlement and helped create and maintain a positive relationship with the WRA and the military. Even when the occasional excesses of more outspoken members such as Thomas Bodine upset government officials, the pragmatic orientation of the eastern group smoothed ruffled feathers. The professional focus of the easterners, with their emphasis on organization and results, fit neatly with the WRA's approach to both student and general resettlement.

Achieving a working relationship with the WRA did not, however, guarantee the council's success. In fact, the council's cooperative relationship with the Nikkei's custodians and jailers presented a potential problem: inmates distrusted the WRA and organizations too closely associated with it. Nikkei, however, always perceived an important distance between the council and the WRA. While the council promoted itself as a private agency in the concentration camps, this claim would have sounded hollow had inmates observed only the easterners' stress on cooperating with the WRA. Instead, Nikkei in the camps understood the council through individual visitors, most prominently Bodine, a crusader who criticized camp conditions and encouraged students to resettle in the way most advantageous to them, even if this meant skirting or breaking WRA regulations. Bodine also strove to create personal relationships with individual Nikkei, a West Coast emphasis from the start.

Had either faction dominated, such success as the council achieved would have been problematic. The easterners might have produced excellent relations with government agencies, but only at the cost of Nikkei distrust. The westerners might have motivated even larger numbers of incarcerated students to resettle, but only at the cost of government intransigence. Either way, an important component would have been lost. Although internal council divisions occasionally created an uncomfortable working relationship, the long-term benefits of internal divisions outweighed the short-term inconveniences.

In contrast, internal bickering at times distracted the council from helping the students. Carlisle V. Hibbard acknowledged the internal frictions in a letter to Trudy King, after both had left the council. Although Hibbard dismissed the possibility that such problems had limited the council's work, numerous clashes, often based in the division between east and west within the council, occurred throughout the council's brief history.[2] Had council members been able to put aside personal and strategic disagreements to focus on the goal that all sought—ameliorating the wrongs of exile and incarceration by helping college students resettle—energy wasted on internal bickering could have been more productively directed to helping students leave the concentration camps.

The intense dedication of council members, both eastern and western, to help Nikkei students also explains the council's success. The two groups within the council occasionally disagreed as to the best means for helping the students; both agreed, however, that student resettlement represented the best possible outcome for incarcerated young people. Council members worked hard to achieve this, often extending themselves—even according to the students—well beyond the call of duty in offering assistance. High levels of dedication and motivation enabled a small organization to accomplish a large task.

Even the dedication of the council's workers could not, however, overcome bureaucratic and racist barriers unaided. The willingness of a wide variety of individuals and organizations to cooperate provided another factor in the success of student resettlement. While the AFSC made a significant contribution to the initial creation and eventual success of the council, it alone could not have hoped to accomplish what was achieved collectively. Clarence Pickett deserves credit for recognizing this and for designing student resettlement as a project that involved all interested parties. The council's most important work, as a result, often consisted of coordinating the efforts of groups and individuals wishing to help the Japanese American students.

Financial support from foundations, especially the Carnegie Corporation and the Columbia Foundation, provided desperately needed administrative funding early on. Church boards provided monetary support for both administrative and scholarship needs while also working to open denominational schools and to build welcoming attitudes in communities receiving resettled students. The WSSF played a key role in helping Buddhist and non-Christian students attend college. Both national and local YMCAs and YWCAs also contributed much-needed funds as well as moral support. West Coast college presidents and professors urged the government to help students while their eastern college counterparts provided openings and financial aid. Without the financial and moral support of these groups, as well as innumerable individuals who provided room and board, jobs, or even small donations to the scholarship fund, the council's success would have been considerably limited.

The WRA also contributed to the council's success. The council could work in the camps, as Bodine learned after writing his critical letter about Tule Lake, because the WRA allowed it. Beyond simply permitting the council to operate, national WRA administrators, local WRA officials, and camp directors and personnel all contributed, in varying ways and degrees, to the council's program. The WRA and the council also, perhaps not surprisingly, learned from each other. Each employed, for example, similar methods in preparing local communities for the arrival of Nikkei. The WRA, for example, described how changes in local attitudes were "carefully nurtured and fostered by thousands of decent-minded citizens in hundreds of communities."[3]

Other government officials contributed to the council's success as well. President Franklin D. Roosevelt, after authorizing exile and incarceration with Executive Order 9066, promised educational opportunities for Nikkei students. John J. McCloy, the assistant secretary of war, and Adlai Stevenson, the assistant to the secretary of the navy, listened to council complaints and helped fix bottlenecks. These and other officials helped clear the way for student resettlement.

Finally, the Nikkei themselves contributed to the success of student resettlement. Camp scholarship funds provided both financial and moral support for pursuing higher education. The Issei, holding a widespread belief in the value of education, also aided the council's efforts. While some Nikkei, often parents, resisted student resettlement, the community generally proved supportive. Nikkei also assumed an increasing presence on the council during the course of the war. The students themselves, of course, also contributed to the council's success, despite their facing various problems.[4]

Many consciously and even enthusiastically became ambassadors of goodwill, and, in the process, promoted additional student resettlement.

Student resettlement, facilitated by these various factors, produced important results by allowing Nikkei to pursue higher education. Once out of the camps, Mildred Joan Smith has observed, "[t]he rectifying of wrongs inflicted upon the Japanese Americans was never a dramatic, sudden gesture, but [was a] positive accumulation of little acts of consideration and kindness."[5] The council's efforts are also of long-term importance. The historical legacies of the council and its program continue to influence the Nikkei students, their descendents, and the wider society.

Students who resettled, especially those who left prior to spring 1943, provided visible evidence to the larger community that incarceration might be ameliorated. They also played an important role as pioneers in the larger WRA plan for resettlement. As the historian Roger Daniels has argued, the success of student resettlement "was the first significant exception to a policy of mass exclusion and therefore far more important than the relatively small number of evacuees affected might indicate."[6] The students also made up a significant proportion of early resettled Nikkei. In April 1943, when only 7,600 inmates had been cleared to leave the camps, there were 1,493 resettled students. As late as May 1943, Nikkei college students outnumbered other resettlers in Nebraska and Missouri.[7]

Another important legacy of the council's work was the conscious promotion by some council members of what is now called multiculturalism. Student resettlement, from the council's perspective, promised to help not only the Nikkei students; the presence of resettled students would also foster multiculturalism in their new communities. As Bodine explained it, the council was "selling a minority group on the idea that America has a place for them and . . . helping America create the place."[8] Nao Takasugi also envisioned student resettlement reforming the larger society. Personal contacts between Nikkei and whites, he believed, could lead to "prejudice and discrimination [giving] way to understanding and friendship."[9] Bodine, Takasugi, and others like them were social reformers who must have looked on happily as Nikkei students at Nebraska Wesleyan not only joined their classmates in the classroom and on the athletic field, but also talked about their experiences on Hawaiian sugar plantations, organized an "Aloha Hop," and prepared a sukiyaki dinner to accompany a program.[10]

Multiculturalism, of course, did not blossom everywhere students arrived. For every success story like the one at Nebraska Wesleyan, other resettled students struggled with local perceptions and attitudes. For example, a resettled Nisei recalled, "[a]t Wheaton I was always one of the foreign students. No one could get it through their heads that I wasn't foreign. Like the English teacher would stop me and say, 'Oh, where are you going for Christmas? I always like to hear where the foreign students spend their vacations.'" Another Nisei at the University of Wisconsin remembered, "[t]here wasn't much interest in [exile and incarceration. The students] probably didn't know anything about camp and that I had come from a concentration camp. . . . I think the only people that were aware were the church people who were trying to help us."[11]

The history of student resettlement also helps explain at least one causal factor in the movement toward multiculturalism that thrives on college campuses today. While Asian Americans are taken as a given at universities throughout the United States today, this was not always the case. These Nikkei students are thus important not only in and of themselves. They turned out to be precursors of the "overrepresentation" of Asian American college students throughout the United States in recent decades and harbingers of the increasing multiculturalism that characterized American college campuses by the last quarter of the twentieth century. The role played by Nikkei students who chose not to return to the West Coast after World War II in spreading multicultural ideals to the broader American society deserves further attention.

The council's history also provides insight into attitudes about race, ethnic identity, and assimilation during the 1940s, disabusing the idea that student resettlement drew support only from civil libertarians with purely praiseworthy goals. While all the council's members wanted to help Nikkei students, some envisioned "helping" in a disturbing way. Paradoxically, these unenlightened ideas often coexisted side-by-side within the council with more progressive ideas.

Robert W. O'Brien's in-house history of the council presents the best evidence of the limits of liberal thought on matters of race and ethnic identity in the 1940s. O'Brien, clearly both a friend of and an advocate for Nikkei students as well as one of the earliest and most energetic workers on their behalf after Pearl Harbor, supported dispersal in his 1949 book. The Nisei students, he explained, were ideal candidates to pioneer resettlement because of their "willingness . . . to break with the Japanese community institutions, their desire to be further assimilated, their relatively loose ties to any particular area, and their status as American citizens."

O'Brien examined, in a manner common to the paternalistic, social science studies of Nikkei that typify the historiography of the day, the connection between dispersal and assimilation. He noted that the absence of Nikkei institutions in the communities students arrived in "forced [the newcomers] to mix with other American students in their social life." Dispersal helped Nikkei become, the title of O'Brien's last chapter suggested, "Americans without question." This was seen, he pointed out, in the decision of some resettled students to Americanize their Japanese names or to adopt new American names. O'Brien apparently envisioned a total assimilation that erased all "Japanese-ness" as the best outcome for Japanese Americans. Although he allowed that white Americans learned about Nikkei as a result of student resettlement, apparently this meant that whites learned that Nikkei were just like Americans once their "Japanese-ness" disappeared through assimilation.[12]

O'Brien was not the only council member to urge dispersal, which, in fact, became a common goal of both council workers and the U.S. government. The admonitions of others, such as Bodine, Trudy King, and Elizabeth Emlen, that Nikkei disperse are harder to analyze than O'Brien's forthright sociological conclusions. This advice often seems to have been motivated by a sense of self-preservation; members feared that large groups of too-conspicuous Nikkei would arouse local hostility and defeat the larger program.

Regardless of whether council calls for dispersal were aimed at assimilation or self-preservation, they fit neatly with the WRA's agenda for resettlement and presented a threat to Japanese American identity. The WRA noted in 1946 that students had played an important role in imbuing exile and incarceration, despite "all its drastic character and its high cost in the impairment of human values, [with] benefits and compensations." Resettled Nikkei and "the spectacular and highly publicized record of the Japanese American soldier" helped Nikkei reach "a higher level of acceptance than they have previously known since the first regular Japanese immigrants arrived at San Francisco in the early 1880[s]." Some of this improved reputation, seemingly, resulted from dispersal promoting assimilation. A picture of three Nikkei students walking with white students on a campus in the WRA history suggested that resettlement had enabled "[t]he Nisei [to learn] about America." Both the WRA and at least O'Brien envisioned a similar relationship between dispersal and assimilation.[13]

Faced with at best an implicit, and at times an explicit, threat of forced and total assimilation, Nikkei students worked both during and after the war to construct their own meaning for their wartime experiences. They did not simply assimilate as the WRA and at least some council members wanted; instead, students took advantage of resettlement and created their own meaning for it. The resettled students were able to do this, in part, because dispersal meant free space in which the WRA could not directly oversee them. Disagreements between the military, the WRA, and the council also provided students the opportunity to construct their own meaning from their experiences. While acculturation certainly occurred to various degrees for resettled Nikkei, the students served a more important and influential role as ambassadors of multiculturalism than as ambassadors by assimilation.

Many Nikkei students adopted the role of ambassador of goodwill, either independently or at the urging of the council and the WRA. Adopting this persona might on one level have been a self-defense mechanism—students may have feared the consequences of compiling a poor academic record or refusing to fit into their new community. Most, however, seemed to adopt the role of ambassador for less defensive reasons. Of course, performing well in college and fitting into the community benefited the student, providing a sense of belonging and a chance to establish oneself. However, some students were not just looking out for themselves; many wanted to teach America about the Nikkei and dispel stereotypes intensified by wartime rumors. They hoped that resettlement might create new opportunities after the war. The results of such efforts were not uniformly positive; the ambassador persona that resettled students adopted and the council promoted unwittingly helped lay the foundation for the stereotype of the "model minority."

The students who resettled during the war paradoxically did not have to abandon their ethnic identity completely to prove that they were "100 percent American." Instead, the students, like many ethnic groups in the United States, continued to acculturate; however, as John W. Jeffries has argued, "ethnic Americans did not plunge headlong into the melting pot [during World War II]: metaphors of 'orchestras' and 'salads' were common, . . . reflecting a sense that differing parts made a stronger whole, that unity involved respect for diversity."[14] Jeffries's argument fits neatly with Philip Gleason's broader study of changing notions of American identity, in which he suggests that World War II shaped an understanding of what it meant to be an American that stressed ideology (in other words subscribing to basic American values) over ethnicity. The war, Gleason contends, made national unity so compelling that efforts were made to reduce prejudice, improve group relations, and promote tolerance for diversity.[15]

Gleason suggests that the government successfully pursued these goals with one large exception: the exile and incarceration of Japanese Americans. However, Gleason's article only delivers the Nikkei to the concentration camps; it does not discuss the movement of many Nikkei back into mainstream society. Although the government's program certainly had many lamentable flaws and even the relatively progressive council could be remarkably rigid in thinking about issues of race at times, the Nikkei students who resettled had the freedom to maintain ties with other Japanese Americans and with their cultural heritage. Thus, the Nikkei students' experiences during World War II led to seemingly contradictory results. Indeed, Jeffries's generalizations about Native Americans and other ethnic groups seem to fit quite well for Nikkei resettled as college students, too: "the war at once underwrote assimilation and ethnic assertiveness, a paradox consistent with the wartime blend of national unity and cultural pluralism."[16]

Resettled students used this opportunity to discuss exile and incarceration in uncompromising terms with an often ill-informed or unknowing public. For example, two Nikkei students spoke on exile and incarceration at Oberlin's Finney Chapel on March 2, 1943. Dave Okada argued that anti-Japanese agitation had started prior to the twentieth century when "[e]conomic pressure groups, political opportunists, [and] jingoistic press . . . all united to make the public aware of the Yellow Peril." He told his listeners that "old prejudices and fears"—and not military necessity—had resulted in exile and incarceration. Kenji Okuda suggested that Nisei were increasingly "uncertain of themselves and their future [and were being] slowly overcome by an enervating sense of indifference within the secluded confines of their cities."[17] Another resettled student spoke in Kansas City because "[t]hese people didn't look on us as Americans. They looked on us as Japanese, as the enemy. No matter how much you said 'We're Americans,' they just didn't accept that. You had to be blue-eyed, blonde, white to be an American."[18]

Nikkei women who resettled as students took different paths after the war. Some moved toward further acculturation, while others moved back more fully into the Japanese American community. In both cases, of course, Nikkei women continued to face both racial and gender discrimination. Leslie A. Ito argues, however, that women continued to play an important role as preservers of Japanese culture, regardless of whether they returned to the Nikkei community or stayed in the East and continued to acculturate.[19]

Sumiko Kobayashi chose to live in Philadelphia with her family after graduating from Drew University in 1946.[20] She was not "forced," however, by either her time at Drew or her life after the war on the East Coast, to assimilate to the point of losing her identification with the Japanese American community or her connections to her Japanese heritage.

Instead, while making a living as a computer programmer, Kobayashi maintained a strong ethnic identity. Kobayashi became an active leader of the local chapter of the JACL. She also spent two years in Japan, starting in 1952, as a civilian employee of the U.S. Army. After returning to the United States, Kobayashi continued to promote a Japanese American identity and to preserve the Nikkei connection to their Japanese heritage. She supported the Japanese House and Garden in Fairmont Park. She also participated in Philadelphia's annual Folk Fairs, which celebrated the diverse ethnic heritage of the area. Kobayashi joined the Pan Asian Association of Philadelphia and supported its efforts to unite the local Asian community in an effort to "[p]romote cross-cultural understanding among Asians and between the Asian community and others."[21] In 1987, Kobayashi organized a photography exhibit for the Pan Asian Association. Her prepared text for the display suggests a refusal to assimilate, even after almost forty years in the East. "These photo exhibits illustrate," Kobayashi explained, "how Americans from various Asian backgrounds are adopting to new ways in the United States, yet are retaining proudly their unique customs which reflect the long history, richness and diversity of the cultures from which they come."[22]

As a member of the JACL, Kobayashi was active in the movement for redress in the 1980s.[23] She also spearheaded the local chapter's cooperation with the Balch Institute for Ethnic Studies in cosponsoring two Japanese American exhibits in 1984. One of these, "The Japanese American Experience," ran through summer 1985 and attracted more than 8,500 visitors, the most successful turnout since the Balch opened in 1971.

Kobayashi also worked to honor the council's efforts by donating to the fledgling Nisei Student Relocation Commemorative Fund in 1981. The fund had been created by a group of New England Nisei in 1980. As Nobu Hibino later remembered, a group who had resettled during the war were talking at a picnic and wondered, "Gee, we wouldn't have even been here if it wasn't for the American Friends and the [council]. Why can't we do something about some other group that's now in the same predicament we were back in the forties?" The group eventually decided to help Southeast Asian refugee students pursue higher education. Hibino located as many resettled students as possible, and, within one year, the group raised $2,000.[24] Kobayashi attended that organization's first ceremony on June 5, 1982, which honored the AFSC for its role in student resettlement during World War II. Elizabeth and Woodruff Emlen, former council workers, hosted a brunch the next day for the participants. Kobayashi also later helped organize the second awards ceremony held in Philadelphia in 1990.

The Nisei Student Relocation Commemorative Fund has since awarded scholarships to Southeast Asian refugee students each year, working through local committees organized to raise money to supplement the fund's contribution and to award scholarships. A San Francisco committee awarded eight scholarships of $500 each in 1983. The 2001 ceremony demonstrated the dramatic growth of the fund over its first twenty years. In that year, thirty-eight students received scholarships totaling $37,500.[25]

Kesaya E. Noda's 1982 account of the fund's origin explains its continued operation in 2001. Noda, a third-generation Japanese American whose father had been helped by the council, rhetorically asked, "In remembering our past, do we focus on our rage and sense of hopelessness or do we seek freedom—the means to increase our strength? Do we focus upon ourselves as an isolated and wronged minority or, acknowledging the injustice, do we seek to move forward, linking ourselves with others who are struggling now?"[26]

The Nikkei college students of World War II, in choosing to resettle, sought freedom and strength; in the process, they transformed the WRA's and O'Brien's focus on assimilation to their own purposes, reintegrating themselves into the wider society without sacrificing their connections to the Japanese American community and their Japanese cultural heritage. This transformation is embodied in the fund's work, which ignores the assimilative component of student resettlement in drawing its own meaning from the council and its program.

The fund also emulates the council in trying to establish lasting personal relationships with the students it helps. Its 1996 newsletter noted that the fund's philosophy of *ongaeshi*—recognizing and returning thanks for acts of kindness—led it to keep in touch with those it aided. The 1995 newsletter printed excerpts from student letters that echo, in expressing thanks, describing the college experience, and apologizing for not writing more often, Nikkei letters to the council fifty years earlier.[27]

The council's work to resettle Japanese American students during what John Dower has described as a racialized "war without mercy" provides an important perspective on the American home front.[28] The council's history is a reminder that racism comes in a variety of guises and sometimes can even be present in those who genuinely desire to help. Perhaps one of the most important legacies of the council is the profoundly optimistic statement each Japanese American student made about his or her future in the United States by resettling. These students did not act alone; even in the midst of racism and war, interested individuals and organizations stepped forward to aid the students as best they could. The history of Japanese American student resettlement thus illuminates the worst and the best of America, highlighting not only the prevailing racism, but also the efforts of a few to mitigate it.

APPENDIX I:
ATTENDEES AT MAY 29, 1942,
MEETING IN CHICAGO

John W. Abbott, Chief Investigator, House Committee Investigating National Defense Migration
Frank Aydelotte, Institution for Advanced Studies
Robbins W. Barstow, President, Hartford Theological Seminary
Mrs. H. S. Bechtolt, United Lutheran Women's Mission Board
Naomi Binford, AFSC
J. J. Braun, Board of National Missions of the Evangelical and Reformed Church
Barbara Cary, International House, Chicago
Alfred E. Cohn, International Student Service
Harold W. Colvin, YMCA
Joseph Conard, Friends Center, San Francisco
James A. Crain, Disciples of Christ
Mildred Cummings, West Coast Baptist Home Mission
Mark A. Dawber, ABHMS
John Everton, Dean of the Chapel, Grinnell College
Robert W. Gammon, Congregation Education Society
Bess Goodykoontz, Assistant Commissioner of Education
E. R. Hedrick, Vice President, University of California
Rufus Jones, Haverford College
Mrs. Sylvester Jones, Friends Women's Missionary Union
Alden D. Kelley, University Commission of the Church Boards of Education, Episcopal Church
Mrs. Edwin Kinney, Women's American Baptist Home Mission
Arthur M. Knudsen, Board of American Missions, United Lutheran Church
C. S. Marsh, Vice President, American Council on Education
Mrs. G. M. Martin, Baptist Home Mission
Mike Masaoka, JACL
W. O. Mendenhall, President, Whittier College
Mrs. I. E. Metcalf, Disciples of Christ Department of Home Missions

173

Edwin Morgenroth, AFSC
John W. Nason, President, Swarthmore College
John Oliver Nelson, Board of Christian Education, Presbyterian Church
Robert W. O'Brien, University of Washington
Clarence Pickett, AFSC
John Provinse, WRA
Marian B. Reith, YWCA
Francis X. Riley, staff member, House Committee Investigating National Defense Migration
Mrs. J. N. Rodeheaver, Women's Division of Christian Service, Methodist Church
Wilmina Rowland, WSSF
Marjorie Schauffler, AFSC
Frederick A. Schiotz, American Lutheran Conference University Commission
Frank Harron Smith, affiliation unknown
Guy E. Snavely, Association of American Colleges
Roy Sorenson, National Council YMCA
Henry H. Sweets, Secretary of Committee on Christian Education, Presbyterian Church
J. W. Thomas, ABHMS
George A. Weiland, Protestant Episcopal National Council, Department of Domestic Missions
M. R. Zigler, General Ministerial Board, Church of the Brethren

APPENDIX 2:

ATTENDEES AT SEPTEMBER 29, 1943, MEETING IN NEW YORK CITY

Members of the Council

Paul Braisted, Program Secretary, Hazen Foundation

E. Fay Campbell, Director, Department of Colleges and Theological Seminaries, Presbyterian Church

C. Reed Cary, Assistant Executive Secretary, AFSC

William F. DeLong, Board of National Missions, Evangelical and Reformed Church

Walter C. Eells, Executive Secretary, American Association of Junior Colleges

Eleanor French, Executive Secretary, National Student Council, YWCA

Carolus P. Harry, Secretary, Board of Education, United Lutheran Church in America

John W. Nason, President, Swarthmore College

Clarence Pickett, Executive Secretary, AFSC

Mrs. Lenore E. Porter, Secretary of Student Work, Board of Mission and Church Extension of the Methodist Church

John H. Provinse, Chief, Community Management Division, WRA

Alfred Schmalz, Clergyman, Congregational Christian Church, Darien, Connecticut

Guy E. Snavely, President, Association of American Colleges

Roscoe L. West, President, Association of State Teachers Colleges

Alternates

DeWitt C. Baldwin, Board of Missions and Church Extension of the Methodist Church, New York

M. Eleanor Doney for E. Fay Campbell, Director, Department of Colleges and Theological Seminaries, Presbyterian Church

Allan P. Farrell, S.J., for Edward B. Rooney, Executive Director, Jesuit Educational Association

Edmonia Grant for Eleanor French, Executive Secretary, National Student Council, YWCA
Mary W. S. Hayes for Mr. Robert Cullum, WRA, New York City
Teiko Ishida for Mike Masaoka, National Secretary, JACL
Edith E. Loury for Mark A. Dawber, Executive Secretary, Home Missions Council
Toru Matsumoto for George Rundquist, Committee for Resettlement of Japanese Americans

Guests

Marjorie Elkus, Executive Director, Columbia Foundation
Robertson M. Fort, AFSC, Chicago
Willis G. Hoekje, Committee for Resettlement of Japanese Americans
Wilmer J. Kitchen, YMCA, New England Branch
Edwin C. Morgenroth, Executive Secretary, AFSC, Chicago
Marian B. Reith, National West Coast Secretary, YWCA, Los Angeles, California
Sumi Yamaguchi, Committee for Resettlement of Japanese Americans

Staff Members

Thomas R. Bodine
Elizabeth B. Emlen
Woodruff J. Emlen
Robert King Hall
C. V. Hibbard
Trudy King
William G. Stevenson
Kay Yamashita

NOTES

Abbreviations

AFSC	American Friends Service Committee
BI	Balch Institute for Ethnic Studies
FBI	Federal Bureau of Investigation
FDRL	Franklin D. Roosevelt Library
HI	Hoover Institution
NA	National Archives
NACP	National Archives, College Park
NICC	National Intercollegiate Christian Council
NJSRC	National Japanese Student Relocation Council
NJASRC	National Japanese American Student Relocation Council
NRF	No-Records Folder
NSRC-WC	National Student Relocation Council-West Coast
OSU	Ohio State University
PHS	Presbyterian Historical Society
PSU	Pennsylvania State University
RG	Record Group
SHSW	State Historical Society of Wisconsin
SIS	Social-Industrial Section, AFSC
UBC	United Brethren in Christ
UNC	University of North Carolina
WCCA	Wartime Civil Control Administration
WDC	Western Defense Command
WRA	War Relocation Authority
WRU	Western Reserve University
WSSF	World Student Service Fund

Introduction

1. Quoted in Yoo, *Growing Up Nisei,* 102.

2. The term *Nikkei,* meaning "Japanese people," refers to Japanese Americans. *Issei* refers to Japanese immigrants to the United States. *Nisei* refers to second-generation Japanese Americans.

3. Eisenhower briefly served as the first director of the WRA, the civilian agency created to run the concentration camps. He left the WRA for the Office of War Information in mid-June 1942. Dillon S. Myer replaced Eisenhower as the WRA director on June 17.

4. *Internment,* the most frequently used term to describe Nikkei incarceration during the war, refers to a legal process in which enemy aliens can be detained during times of war. Thus, use of the term *internment* (as well as *evacuation, relocation,* and *projects,* among others) employs euphemistic language. Although some historians point to the close association of the term *concentration camp* with Nazi death camps to argue against the use of that term, *concentration camp* is, in fact, the most appropriate term. See Daniels, "Words Do Matter."

5. Although the newly formed organization typically used the title National Student Relocation Council early on, the title National Japanese American Student Relocation Council was used as early as June 1942. I use *council* in referring to the organization. See Executive Committee Minutes, July 9, 1942, 64.508, #1, 4–9/42, Subject-Classified General Records, Headquarters, Records of the WRA, RG 210, National Archives (hereafter cited NA).

6. The idea of Nikkei serving as "ambassadors" was not entirely new. Kazuo Kawa, for example, attempted to explain the East to the West in the 1920s. See Yu, *Thinking Orientals,* 108; Takahashi, *Nisei/Sansei,* 37, 49–53, 80.

7. Matsunaga Letter, August 5, 1943, Letters, July–September 1943, Box 7, Bodine, Hoover Institution (hereafter cited HI); "Candidates Tell Goals in Student Relocation Plan," *Santa Anita Pacemaker,* 11 July 1942, 2.

8. Notes for Bodine Talks, Box 8, Bodine, HI.

9. "Masuda and Kamitsuka Honored at Farewell Social," *Poston Press Bulletin,* 11 August 1942, 2.

10. "Students Bear a Great Burden," *Santa Anita Pacemaker,* 11 July 1942, 4.

11. For more on the model minority stereotype, see Daniels, *Asian America,* 317–21; Okihiro, *Storied Lives,* xiv.

12. Matsumoto, *Farming the Home Place,* 133.

13. Barstow, "Help for Nisei Students," 836–37.

14. Daniels, *Concentration Camps,* 2–6; Moriyama, *Imingaisha,* 2–10.

15. In 1940, 93,717 Japanese Americans lived in California, 14,565 lived in Washington, and 4,071 lived in Oregon. In contrast, 2,734 Japanese Americans lived in Colorado, 2,538 lived in New York, 2,210 lived in Utah, and 1,191 lived in Idaho, the four states with the next largest Japanese American populations in

1940. No other state had more than 650 Japanese American residents. Daniels, *Asian America*, 156, 289.

16. Daniels, *Concentration Camps*, 6–8; Daniels, *Asian America*, 134–35; Daniels, *Politics of Prejudice*, 9.

17. Daniels, *Asian America*, 137; Daniels, *Concentration Camps*, 9.

18. Conte, "Overseas Study in the Meiji Period," vi–viii; Daniels, *Asian America*, 104; Daniels, *Politics of Prejudice*, 11.

19. Daniels, *Concentration Camps*, 9–21.

20. Daniels, *Asian America*, 156.

21. See Yoo, *Growing Up Nisei*.

22. Takahashi, *Nisei/Sansei*, 41, 28–44, 74; Daniels, *Concentration Camps*, 22–24; Daniels, *Asian America*, 130, 133, 156, 165, 172–78.

23. Uchida, *Desert Exile*, 46–48.

24. University of Washington, "Interrupted Lives."

25. See University of Washington, "Interrupted Lives."

26. Daniels, *Asian America*, 338; Daniels, *Concentration Camps*, 83, 104; Daniels, Taylor, and Kitano, *Japanese Americans*, xiv–xix, 74; Drinnon, *Keeper of Concentration Camps*, 33; Girdner and Loftis, *Great Betrayal*, 122. On Roosevelt's role, see Robinson, *By Order of the President*.

Chapter 1: Creating the National Japanese American Student Relocation Council

1. Form Letter, April 10, 1942, Historical Council Material (I), Box 9, NJASRC, HI.

2. AFSC Oral History Interview #409.

3. Roger Daniels, *Concentration Camps*, 74–84; Daniels, Taylor, and Kitano, *Japanese Americans*, xvi.

4. The National YMCA issued resolutions that called for the protection of the Nikkei's Constitutional rights, asked local associations to help resettlers, appointed Masao Satow to work with Japanese Americans, and published articles that emphasized the racist motivations behind exile and incarceration. See Fisher, *Public Affairs and the Y.M.C.A.*, 5, 140; Fisher, "Our Two Japanese-American Policies," 961–963; Fisher, "Our Two Japanese Refugees," 424–426.

5. Information for NICC (File II) (note that this notation is used throughout for file numbers), April 2, 1942 (c), Historical Council Material (II), Box 10, NJASRC, HI.

6. Information Concerning American Born Japanese Students Facing Evacuation, University of California and San Francisco Bay District, Spring, 1942 (c), Historical Council Material (I), Box 9, NJASRC, HI; Hall, "Japanese American College Students," 51–52.

7. In addition to teaching in the sociology department, O'Brien was the assistant dean of arts and sciences and the adviser of the Japanese Student Club at the Uni-

versity of Washington. Immediately active in student resettlement efforts, O'Brien served briefly as national director of the council and later wrote a history of it, *The College Nisei.* See University of Washington, "Interrupted Lives."

8. O'Brien, *College Nisei,* 135-37; Total Number and Percentage Distribution, n.d., Historical Council Material (I), Box 9, NJASRC, HI; Preliminary Report on the Number of American Students of Japanese Ancestry, n.d., Historical Council Material (I), Box 9, NJASRC, HI; Conard (Executive Secretary, Student Relocation Committee) to Deutsch, May 2, 1942, Monroe E. Deutsch (Provost, University of California, Berkeley), Box 6, NJASRC, HI. Student resettlement advocates seriously underestimated the total number of Nikkei students in California, Oregon, and western Washington in 1941. Although their initial estimate of 2,313 later proved too low, student relocation workers generally believed it to be fairly accurate throughout the war.

9. Information for NICC (II), April 2, 1942 (c); Conard to West Coast Colleges Wishing to Help, April, 1942 (c), 64.508, #1, 4–7/42, Subject-Classified General Records, Headquarters, Records of the WRA, RG 210, NA.

10. Deutsch (1879–1955) received his bachelor's, master's, and doctoral degrees from the University of California. After working as a professor of Latin, Deutsch was named vice president and dean of the university in 1930. He served in this position until his retirement in 1947.

11. Information for NICC (II), April 2, 1942 (c); Okihiro, *Storied Lives,* 30; Daniels, *Asian America,* 242–243.

12. University of Washington, "Interrupted Lives."

13. Quoted in Japanese Evacuation Report #7, March 26, 1942, Folder 20, Box 32, M99–097, Howard K. Beale Papers, State Historical Society of Wisconsin (hereafter cited SHSW).

14. Okihiro, *Storied Lives,* 132–33; AFSC Oral Interview #405.

15. Hall, "Japanese American College Students," 48.

16. O'Brien, *College Nisei,* 111–14.

17. For quotes from Obata in this paragraph and the subsequent one, see Hill, *Chiura Obata's Topaz Moon,* 1, 5, 16–17, 109; Okihiro, *Storied Lives,* 90; Hall, "Japanese American College Students," 57–58; Japanese American National Museum, press release.

18. Betty Ikeda is a pseudonym. For Ikeda, see Betty Ikeda File, Box 115, NJASRC, HI; "Nisei Student Relocation Report," *Rohwer Outpost,* 1 November 1944, 1, 4. The council, after initially deciding to offer information and advice, but not scholarships, to students outside the camps, eventually provided all Nikkei students the same help.

19. See Wertheimer, "Admitting Nebraska's *Nisei.*"

20. Quoted in Okihiro, *Storied Lives,* 77–78. See also Wertheimer, "Admitting Nebraska's *Nisei*"; Ito, "Loyalty and Learning," 50–51.

21. Franz Woodworth, Mayor of Athens, Ohio, to B. T. Grover, Director of Pub-

lic Relations of Ohio University, September 15, 1942. See Ohio University File, Box 75, NJASRC, HI.

22. Jack Takiguchi and Masao Umino are pseudonyms. Takiguchi left the West Coast voluntarily after an FBI investigation because of defense research being conducted at his old school, the California Institute of Technology. Umino, a student at the University of California, left the West Coast on May 5 before evacuation to an assembly center. Takiguchi received his bachelor's degree in September 1943, and Umino received his bachelor's degree in May 1943. For Takiguchi and Umino, see Ohio University File, Box 75, NJASRC, HI; College Questionnaire, Ohio University File; Takiguchi and Umino to O'Brien, November 5, 1942, Ohio University File; Nao Takasugi, Student Relocation Council, to Carl Spicer, Relocation Officer, June 18, 1945, WRA-Cleveland, Box 22, NJASRC, HI; *1993 Ohio University Alumni Directory*, 604, 688; George W. Bain, Head of Archives and Special Collections, Ohio University, e-mail to author, 3 August 2000.

23. Umino letter, February 19, 1943, Notes for Bodine Talks, Box 8, Bodine, HI. The WRA received a report in January 1943 that a group planned to give Nikkei arriving at Greenville College in Illinois the "treatment." Despite the school's assurances that local opposition had decreased, the council sent students there only in 1944–45. See Hall, "Japanese American College Students," 253–54.

24. For Nakata, see Okihiro, *Storied Lives*, 4–7.

25. Report on the Japanese Evacuation Situation, March 8, 1942, Mills Reports, Box 105, NJASRC, HI.

26. Second Report on the Japanese Evacuation Situation, March 24, 1942, Mills Reports, Box 105, NJASRC, HI.

27. Taylor knew Nikkei students at Berkeley and was a member of the Committee on American Principles and Fair Play. Alexander, a leading Southern liberal involved with the Commission on Interracial Cooperation in Atlanta, worked with the labor division and the minorities branch of the Office of Production Management. See Dykeman and Stokely, *Seeds of Southern Change; American National Biography*.

28. Taylor to Alexander, March 17, 1942, US Government-War Production Board, Box 20, NJASRC, HI; O'Brien, *College Nisei*, 61. Alexander to Wickard, March 25, 1942, and Carl Hamilton, Assistant to the Secretary of Agriculture, to Alexander, April 1, 1942, are cited in Hall, "Japanese American College Students," 47, 53, 58. Eisenhower to Wickard, April 1, 1942, is quoted in Daniels, *Concentration Camps*, 91.

29. Welles to Eleanor Roosevelt, May 9, 1942, Box 378, Series 70, Correspondence with Government Departments, Eleanor Roosevelt Papers, Franklin D. Roosevelt Library (hereafter cited FDRL); Eleanor Roosevelt to Welles, April 6, 1942, Box 378, Series 70, Correspondence with Government Departments, Eleanor Roosevelt Papers, FDRL.

30. Okihiro, *Storied Lives*, 30–34; Hall, "Japanese American College Students," 152.

31. After receiving his bachelor's degree from Grinnell College in 1935, Conard worked for the AFSC between 1935 and 1948. Conard resigned as the council's West Coast director in October 1942 to finish his master's degree work before going to work for the AFSC in San Francisco in February 1943. See "Joseph Conard," *The Phoenix.*

32. Conard to Cary (Assistant Executive Secretary, AFSC), April 14, 1942, Committees and Organizations: National Student Relocation Council-West Coast (hereafter cited NSRC-WC), Japanese-American Relocation, Social-Industrial Section (hereafter cited *SIS*), 1942, AFSC; Conard to West Coast Colleges Wishing to Help, April, 1942 (c); Okihiro, *Storied Lives,* 30-31.

33. Conard to Cary, April 14, 1942; Conard to West Coast Colleges Wishing to Help, April, 1942 (c); Robert W. O'Brien, *College Nisei,* 61. The West Coast committee included Robert W. O'Brien of the University of Washington; M. D. Woodbury of the University YMCA in Seattle; Karl Onthank of the University of Oregon; Dr. Dorothy Swaine Thomas, a professor of rural sociology at the University of California; Leila Anderson of the University YWCA at Berkeley; Dr. Monroe E. Deutsch, the vice president and provost at the University of California, Mills; and Marian Reith of the YWCA. Educators from Southern California were to be added later. The Central committee was staffed by people located in Northern California and included Thomas; Anderson; Harry Kingman of the YMCA; Alice Hoyt of the University of California; Alfred Fisk of San Francisco State College; Elton Trueblood of Stanford; Annie Cloe Watson of the International Institute in San Francisco; Alice James of the University YWCA at the University of California; Al Stone, a University of California student; Harold Jacoby of the College of the Pacific; Tom Shibutani, a student studying the problems of relocation; and Chitoshi Yanaga of University of California's political science department.

34. The idea of dispersing Nikkei existed prior to World War II. William Jennings Bryan had suggested dispersal while serving as secretary of state in the Wilson administration. President Roosevelt also hoped in a June 12, 1944, memorandum that the WRA program would result in the dispersal of Japanese Americans away from the West Coast. See Daniels, "William Jennings Bryan and the Japanese," 236; Daniels, *Asian America,* 286-88; Daniels, *Concentration Camps,* 153.

35. Bulletin No. 2, May 18, 1942, Committees and Organizations: NSRC-WC, Japanese-American Relocation, SIS, 1942, AFSC.

36. Conard to West Coast Colleges Wishing to Help, April 1942 (c).

37. Conard to Cary, April 14, 1942.

38. Ibid.

39. Daniels, *Concentration Camps,* 85.

40. Ibid, 85-97.

41. Conard to West Coast Colleges Wishing to Help, April, 1942 (c); Conard to Deutsch, April 5, 1942, Monroe E. Deutsch, Box 6, NJASRC, HI.

42. Conard to Deutsch, April 5, 1942.

43. Bulletin No. 1, May 6, 1942, Committees and Organizations: NSRC-WC, Japanese-American Relocation, SIS, 1942, AFSC.

44. Conard to Cary, April 14, 1942; Conard to West Coast Colleges Wishing to Help, April, 1942 (c).

45. Conard to West Coast Colleges Wishing to Help, April, 1942 (c); Conard to Deutsch, April 5, 1942; Conard to Cary, April 14, 1942.

46. Okihiro, *Storied Lives*, 32–33, 78; Hall, "Japanese American College Students," 66–67.

47. Report of Progress, up to July 25, 1942, 64.508, #1, April–September 1942, Subject-Classified General Records, Headquarters, Records of the WRA, RG 210, NA.

48. Conard to West Coast Colleges Wishing to Help, April, 1942 (c); Conard to Deutsch, April 5, 1942.

49. Conard to Cary, April 14, 1942; Conard to West Coast Colleges Wishing to Help, April, 1942 (c); O'Brien, *College Nisei*, 62.

50. Statement of the Rapporteurs of the Group Meeting, April 29, 1942, Steering Committee-Pre-Student Relocation, Box 38, NJASRC, HI; O'Brien, *College Nisei*, 62; Edgar J. Fisher, Assistant Director, Institute of International Education, to Charles Thomson, Chief, Division of Cultural Relations, Department of State, June 1, 1942, 811.42794/116–121, Records of the Department of State, RG 59, National Archives, College Park (hereafter cited NACP).

51. Third Report on the Japanese Evacuation Situation, April 15, 1942, Mills Reports, Box 105, NJA SRC, HI.

52. Conard to Deutsch, April 5, 1942; Conard to West Coast Colleges Wishing to Help, April, 1942 (c); Conard to Cary, April 14, 1942; Conard to Ade, April 24, 1942, 64.508, #1, 4–9/42, Subject-Classified General Records, Headquarters, Records of the WRA, RG 210, NA; Cary to Booth, Schmoe, Conard, April 9, 1942, Committees and Organizations: NJASRC, Japanese-American Relocation, SIS, 1942, AFSC.

53. Conard to West Coast Colleges Wishing to Help, April, 1942 (c); Conard to Cary, April 14, 1942; Conard to Ade, April 24, 1942.

54. Hall, "Japanese American College Students," 59–60.

55. Hall, "Japanese American College Students," 60–61. Sproul's letters to Tolan on April 7, Roosevelt on April 24, and Wallace on May 1 are located in Robert G. Sproul, Box 36, NJASRC, HI.

56. Sproul to Wallace, May 1, 1942, Robert G. Sproul, Box 17, NJASRC, HI. Sproul had encouraged Nikkei students to act as "cultural ambassadors" prior to the war and likely believed that resettlement was beneficial to both the receiving communities and the students themselves. See Takahashi, *Nisei/Sansei*, 52.

57. Proposal for the Continued Collegiate Training of Citizens of Japanese Ancestry Forced by Evacuation Orders to Interrupt Studies, n.d., Robert G. Sproul, Box 17, NJASRC, HI; Tolan Committee, For Release April 14, 1942, 64.501, #1, 4–12/42, Subject-Classified General Files, Headquarters, Records of the WRA, RG 210, NA.

58. E. H. Wiecking to Eisenhower, April 14, 1942, 64.501, #1, 4–12/42, Subject-Classified General Files, Headquarters, Records of the WRA, RG 210, NA. Defense Health and Welfare Services was part of the Federal Security Agency.

59. Boekel to Ade, April 30, 1942, 000.8–Schools (Civilian), Volume I, Central Correspondence, WCCA and Civil Affairs Division, Western Defense Command (hereafter cited WDC) and Fourth Army, RG 338, NACP; Daniels, *Concentration Camps*, 99–100.

60. Eisenhower to Sproul, May 6, 1942, 64.501, #1, 4–12/42, Subject-Classified General Files, Headquarters, Records of the WRA, RG 210, NA.

61. Rowalt to Eisenhower, April 24, 1942, 64.501, #1, 4–12/42, Subject-Classified General Files, Headquarters, Records of the WRA, RG 210, NA; Zook to Eisenhower, April 3, 1942, 64.500, Subject-Classified General Files, Headquarters, Records of the WRA, RG 210, NA; Rowalt to Eisenhower, April 23, 1942, A17, NA; Rowalt to Eisenhower, April 24, 1942; Telephone Call, Eisenhower to Rowalt, April 24, 1942, 64.501, #1, 4–12/42, Subject-Classified General Files, Headquarters, Records of the WRA, RG 210, NA; Barstow to Cary, August 7, 1942, Committees and Organizations: NJASRC, Japanese-American Relocation, SIS, 1942, AFSC; Eisenhower to Warne, April 28, 1942, 64.501, #1, 4–12/42, Subject-Classified General Files, Headquarters, Records of the WRA, RG 210, NA; Eisenhower to Studebaker, April 28, 1942, 64.501, #1, 4–12/42, Subject-Classified General Files, Headquarters, Records of the WRA, RG 210, NA.

62. See Pickett, *For More Than Bread; American National Biography*. For additional details on Pickett's relationship with Eleanor Roosevelt, see American Friends Service Committee, "Eleanor Roosevelt Connection."

63. Memo, Eisenhower to Provinse, May 5, 1942, 64.501, #1, 4–12/42, Subject-Classified General Files, Headquarters, Records of the WRA, RG 210, NA. Eisenhower's autobiography is vague: "I must confess that I am still distressed by the excuses I received from the educators I approached. All declined. Then someone suggested that I telephone Clarence Pickett, the prominent Quaker leader" (Eisenhower, *The President Is Calling*, 120); Hall, "Japanese American College Students," 82.

64. Cary to Booth, Schmoe, Conard, April 9, 1942. Frank Aydelotte (1880–1956) had been president of Swarthmore College from 1921 to 1939, before he moved on to the Institute for Advanced Studies in Princeton, New Jersey. His successor, John W. Nason, had worked closely with Aydelotte at Swarthmore. Nason would later chair the Student Relocation Council. For Aydelotte, see Blanshard, *Aydelotte*; Clark, *Distinctive College*.

65. Cary to Aydelotte, Felix Morely, Nason, April 23, 1942, Frank Aydelotte, Box 2, NJASRC, HI; Pickett to Alexander, March 31, 1942, US Government-War Production Board, Box 20, NJASRC, HI; Aydelotte to Pickett, April 18, 1942, Frank Aydelotte, Box 2, NJASRC, HI.

66. Eisenhower to Pickett, May 5, 1942, Historical Council Material (II), Box 10, NJASRC, HI.

67. Eisenhower to Sproul, May 6, 1942. Similarly, Roosevelt approved relatively liberal treatment for conscientious objectors in work camps, but insisted on private-sector funding.

68. Most churches adopted a "cautious patriotism" that attempted to balance political realism and religious idealism. See Sittser, *Cautious Patriotism*, 12.

69. Pickett to Eisenhower, May 15, 1942, WRA-DC, 5/5/42–9/15/42, Box 26, NJASRC, HI.

70. Barstow (1890–1962) received a bachelor's of divinity degree from the Hartford Theological Seminary in 1916 and, after serving as a chaplain in World War I and at various churches, became president of the Hartford Theological Seminary in 1930. He resigned in 1944 to become director of the Commission for World Council Service of the American Committee for the World Council of Churches. See Robbins Barstow Archive, Hartford Seminary Library.

71. Pickett to Barstow, May 9, 1942, Robbins Barstow, Box 2, NJASRC, HI.

72. Ibid.

73. O'Brien, *College Nisei*, 87; Smith, "Backgrounds," 60–62. Letter is quoted in Girdner and Loftis, *Great Betrayal*, 337. A number of Nikkei attended University of Idaho later during the war.

74. Fisher, "What Race Baiting Costs America," 1009–11.

75. Pickett to Barstow, May 9, 1942.

76. Conard to Cary, May 7, 1942, AFSC (Volume II), Box 2, NJASRC, HI; Cary to Conard, May 7, 1942, National Student Relocation Committee-Early Development, Box 103, NJASRC, HI; Cary to Conard, May 14, 1942, National Student Relocation Committee-Early Development, Box 103, NJASRC, HI; Cary to Mendenhall, May 13, 1942, W. O. Mendenhall, Box 13, NJASRC, HI; Mendenhall to Cary, May 8, 1942, W. O. Mendenhall, Box 13, NJASRC, HI.

77. Conard to Cary, May 7, 1942; Cary to Conard, May 14, 1942.

78. Mendenhall to Cary, May 8, 1942; Mendenhall to Cary, May 16, 1942, W. O. Mendenhall, Box 13, NJASRC, HI.

79. Cary to Conard, May 14, 1942; Cary to Conard, May 7, 1942; Conard to Cary, May 7, 1942.

80. Mendenhall to Cary, May 8, 1942; Mendenhall to Cary, May 16, 1942; Cary to Mendenhall, May 13, 1942.

81. Cary to Conard, May 14, 1942; Conard to Cary, May 7, 1942.

82. Barstow to Pickett, May 16, 1942, Robbins Barstow, Box 2, NJASRC, HI; Cary to Conard, May 7, 1942; Hall, "Japanese American College Students," 90–91.

83. Cary to Mendenhall, May 13, 1942.

84. Adams to Fryer, May 19, 1942, WRA-DC, 5/5/42–9/15/42, Box 26, NJASRC, HI; Adams to Eisenhower, May 22, 1942, 64.501, #1, 4–12/42, Subject-Classified General Files, Headquarters, Records of the WRA, RG 210, NA. For Adams, see James, *Exile Within*, 37.

85. Adams to Eisenhower, May 22, 1942; Provinse to Pickett, May 25, 1942, WRA-DC, 5/5/42–9/15/42, Box 26, NJASRC, HI.

86. Eisenhower, *The President Is Calling,* 120–21; Daniels, *Concentration Camps,* 99–100.

87. Daniels, *Concentration Camps,* 99–100.

88. McCloy based his support for exile and incarceration on national security concerns, responding to Attorney General Francis Biddle's opposition reportedly by remarking that Biddle was "putting a Wall Street lawyer in a helluva box, but if it is a question of the safety of the country [and] the Constitution. . . . Why the Constitution is just a scrap of paper to me." McCloy later testified that, given the context of the times, exile and incarceration had been reasonable, thoughtful, and humane. The policy was, he argued forty years later, "in accordance with the best interests of the country." See Daniels, *Concentration Camps,* 55, 145; Daniels, *Asian America,* 337–38.

89. Eisenhower to McCloy, May 18, 1942, 64.501, #1, 4–12/42, Subject-Classified General Files, Headquarters, Records of the WRA, RG 210, NA.

90. McCloy to Pickett, May 21, 1942, 000.8–Schools (Civilian), Volume #I, Central Correspondence, WCCA and Civil Affairs Division, WDC and Fourth Army, RG 338, NACP.

91. International Student Service Executive Committee Meeting, May 20, 1942, Box 2068, Series 130, News Items, Eleanor Roosevelt Papers, FDRL.

92. Bodine to Pickett, May 23, 1942, Committees and Organizations: NSRC-WC, Japanese-American Relocation, SIS, 1942, AFSC.

93. Barstow to Binford, June 1, 1942, Robbins Barstow, Box 2, NJASRC, HI.

94. Bodine to Conard, Pickett, Cary, and Booth, May 26, 1942, Committees and Organizations: NSRC-WC, Japanese-American Relocation, SIS, 1942, AFSC.

95. See Pickett, *For More Than Bread,* 157–58.

96. Memo, Provinse to Eisenhower, June 5, 1942, 64.501, #1, 4–12/42, Subject-Classified General Files, Headquarters, Records of the WRA, RG 210, NA; List of Persons Invited to Japanese Student Relocation Meeting Held on May 29, 1942, Chicago, Illinois, n.d., 64. 501, 4–12/42, Subject-Classified General Files, Headquarters, Records of the WRA, RG 210, NA; List of Persons Who Attended the Japanese Student Relocation Meeting, Chicago, May 29, 1942, n.d., 64.501, 4–12/42, Subject-Classified General Files, Headquarters, Records of the WRA, RG 210, NA; O'Brien, *College Nisei,* 62; Hall, "Japanese American College Students," 167.

97. Digest of Points Presented at Chicago conference, Box 5, NJASRC, HI.

98. Memo, Provinse to Eisenhower, June 5, 1942; Hall, "Japanese American College Students," 133.

99. Digest of Points Presented at Chicago Conference; Hall, "Japanese American College Students," 108–10.

100. Hall, "Japanese American College Students," 100, 122.

101. Digest of Points Presented at Chicago Conference; Okihiro, *Storied Lives,* 38; O'Brien, *College Nisei,* 62–63; Hall, "Japanese American College Students," 111; Memo, Provinse to Eisenhower, June 5, 1942.

102. Memo, Provinse to Eisenhower, June 5, 1942; Digest of Points Presented at Chicago Conference; Hall, "Japanese American College Students," 110–11.

103. Digest of Points Presented at Chicago Conference.

104. Schauffler to Pickett and Barston [sic], May 31 and June 1, 1942, Committees and Organizations: NSRC-Chicago Conference, Japanese-American Relocation, SIS, 1942, AFSC.

Chapter 2: Living in Hope and Working on Faith, Summer 1942

1. "Diplomas Go to 250 Friday," Santa Anita Pacemaker, 24 June 1942; "Students from 34 Schools Graduate," Santa Anita Pacemaker, 27 June 1942, 1–2.

2. For Ota, see Girdner and Loftis, Great Betrayal, 337; Graybill, "Nisei," 110; Lillian Ota File, Box 113, NJASRC, HI.

3. Ota to Conard, August 30, 1942, Lillian Ota File.

4. Quoted in Girdner and Loftis, Great Betrayal, 337. Ota graduated from Wellesley in 1943 and enrolled at Yale. Ota received her master's degree in Far Eastern history from Yale on June 22, 1944. She remained at Yale for her doctoral degree and completed her dissertation, "The Sino-Japanese War of 1894–1895: A Study in Asian Power Politics," in 1951. Ota cowrote two books: John Embree and Lillian Ota, Bibliography of the Peoples and Cultures of Mainland Southeast Asia (1950) and Floyd Dotson and Lillian Ota Dotson, The Indian Minority of Zambia, Rhodesia, and Malawi (1968).

5. See, for example, "From Camp to College," July 1944, WRA-DC, 8/44–, Box 24, NJASRC, HI; Howard K. Beale to Edward R. Bartlett, Dean of DePauw University, DePauw University File, Box 61, NJASRC, HI; Inouye, "Higher Education," 19 August 1944, Heart Mountain Sentinel, 5.

6. Inouye, "Higher Education." See also Advance Release, October 22, 1944, WRA-DC, Release on Student Relocation, Box 28, NJASRC, HI; Beale to Bartlett, May 28, 1943, DePauw, Box 61, NJASRC, HI.

7. George Tamaki is a pseudonym. For Tamaki, see George Tamaki File, Box 112, NJASRC, HI.

8. Quotations from Letters of Reference, George Tamaki File.

9. O'Brien to Reed, January 25, 1943, National Information Bureau, Box 14, NJASRC, HI.

10. Barstow's Interim Report, June 29, 1942, Minutes, 1942–46, Box 87, NJASRC, HI.

11. Pickett to Conard, June 12, 1942, AFSC, Box 103, NJASRC, HI; Barstow to Conard, August 14, 1942, Robbins W. Barstow, Box 110, NJASRC, HI; Conard to Barstow, June 6, 1942, Pacific Coast Branch, –6/42, Box 36, NJASRC, HI; Confidential Report on Activities, May 30 to June 6, 1942, June 6, 1942, 64.508, #1, 4–9/42, Subject-Classified General Records, Headquarters, Records of the WRA, RG 210, NA.

12. See Cary to Nason, December 8, 1942, Committees and Organizations: NSRC-WC, Japanese-American Relocation, SIS, 1942, AFSC. Barstow resigned as national director in August after only three months. The historian Howard K. Beale served as interim director briefly before Robert W. O'Brien assumed the directorship in fall 1942. Carlisle V. Hibbard replaced O'Brien and served from March 4, 1943, to March 31, 1944. Helga Swan then served until November 15, 1944. Elizabeth Emlen replaced Swan and directed the council until August 1, 1945. Ann Graybill followed Emlen and oversaw the council until its close in summer 1946.

13. Trudy King (1916-69) had worked during summer 1941 at a Quaker camp in Georgia. She then joined Thomas Bodine and others to train for overseas AFSC work. Although King was not a Quaker, she wanted to act constructively while the war raged. She joined the council in late June and left in April 1944. See Hayashi, *Face of the Enemy,* 49-51.

14. King Report, September 5, 1942, Committees and Organizations: NSRC-WC, Japanese-American Relocation, SIS, 1942, AFSC.

15. Beale to Frank P. Graham, President, University of North Carolina at Chapel Hill, November 14, 1942, Department of History Files, University Archives, Wilson Library, University of North Carolina at Chapel Hill (hereafter cited UNC).

16. King to Jones, July 1, 1942, Committees and Organizations: NSRC-WC, Japanese-American Relocation, SIS, 1942, AFSC.

17. Barstow's Interim Report, June 29, 1942.

18. Report to the Executive Committee, August 4, 1942, Philadelphia Office (8-9/42), Box 38, NJASRC, HI.

19. Conard to Barstow, July 31, 1942, Committees and Organizations: NSRC-WC, Japanese-American Relocation, SIS, 1942, AFSC.

20. Barstow to Conard, August 14, 1942.

21. All quotes from King are from the letter from King to Schauffler, August 18, 1942, Committees and Organizations: NSRC-WC, Japanese-American Relocation, SIS, 1942, AFSC.

22. NSRC: Preliminary Tabulation of 939 Questionnaires, July 18, 1942, 000.8-Schools and Colleges, Volume #I, Central Correspondence, WCCA and Civil Affairs Division, WDC and Fourth Army, RG 338, NACP; Barstow to Marks, August 10, 1942, WRA-DC, 5/5/42-9/15/42, Box 26, NJASRC, HI; Report of Progress, up to July 25, 1942, 64.508, #1, 4-9/42, Subject-Classified General Records, Headquarters, Records of the WRA, RG 210, NA; Tentative Minutes Steering Committee Meeting, October 23, 1942, Pacific Coast Branch-Steering Committee Minutes, Box 36, NJASRC, HI; 1308 Students, November 5, 1942, Box 48, NJASRC, HI.

23. Joe Conard's Suggestions to Raters, July 26, 1942, Pacific Coast Branch-Japanese Situation (SF), 7-8/42, Box 35, NJASRC, HI.

24. Okihiro, *Storied Lives,* 39; Joe Conard's Suggestions to Raters.

25. Minutes of the Steering Committee Meeting, August 12, 1942, Steering Committee-Pre-Student Relocation, Box 38, NJASRC, HI.

26. N.S.R.C.: Its Purpose and Functions, May 27, 1943, Historical Council Material (II), Box 10, NJASRC, HI.

27. Nason to Pickett, October 20, 1942, AFSC-General Correspondence, Box 2, NJASRC, HI; N.S.R.C.: Its Purpose and Functions.Nason (1905–2001) attended Yale and Harvard for a master's degree in philosophy and studied as a Rhodes Scholar at Oxford. He accepted a teaching job at Swarthmore in 1931. Between 1931 and 1940, Nason first taught philosophy and then served as an assistant to President Frank Aydelotte. Nason considered himself a "Quaker by conviction" (Clark, *Distinctive College,* 216); see Lewis, "John W. Nason"; Okihiro, *Storied Lives,* 128–29; Executive Committee Minutes, February 27, 1945, Minutes, 1942–46, Box 87, NJASRC, HI.

28. N.S.R.C.: Its Purpose and Functions; Nason to Bodine, January 13, 1943, Committees and Organizations: NJSRC-Philadelphia, Japanese-American Relocation, SIS, 1943, AFSC; Pickett to Ackerman, May 19, 1942, A-General Correspondence, Box 1, NJASRC, HI.

29. Johnson to Members of the Executive Committee, December 1, 1942, Internal Correspondence-12/42, Box 19, Nason, HI; Barstow to Binford, June 1, 1942, Barstow, Box 2, NJASRC, HI; Conard to Reith, September 1, 1942, Reith, Box 16, NJASRC, HI; Minutes of Executive Committee, October 30, 1942, Minutes, 1942–46, Box 87, NJASRC, HI.

30. Sittser, *Cautious Patriotism,* 172–75.

31. Thomas to Barstow, July 15, 1942, Baptist (I), Box 92, NJASRC, HI; Thomas to Cope, June 2, 1942, Baptist (I), Box 92, NJASRC, HI. John W. Thomas of the ABHMS replaced Nason as council chair in 1945. See Okihiro, *Storied Lives,* 128–29; Executive Committee Minutes, February 27, 1945.

32. Many Jewish organizations, like African American groups, were slow to protest exile and incarceration because of their deep investment in Allied war aims, their need to prove their loyalty, their focus on their own agendas, and their fear of both anti-Semitism at home and for the safety of Jews abroad. See Greenberg, "Black and Jewish Responses," 3–37.

33. Memo of Office Conversation with Rabbi Arthur J. Lelyveld, August 8, 1942, Jewish Peace Fellowship, Box 96, NJASRC, HI; Lelyveld to Hibbard, April 8, 1943, Jewish Peace Fellowship, Box 96, NJASRC, HI; Ziegler to Pickett, July 13, 1942, United Brethren in Christ (hereafter cited UBC), Box 100, NJASRC, HI.

34. For an example of the form letter, see Barstow to Thomas, July 28, 1942, Baptist (I), Box 92, NJASRC, HI.

35. Matsumoto, *Beyond Prejudice,* 50; Brubaker to O'Brien, February 15, 1943, Brethren Service Committee (hereafter cited as Brethren *SC*), Box 93, NJASRC, HI; Brubaker to Hibbard, April 12, 1943, Brethren SC, Box 93, NJASRC, HI; Porter to Binford, July 24, 1942, Methodist (I), Box 96, NJASRC, HI; Bodine to McMillan, January 1, 1943, WRA-Central Utah Relocation Project (I), Box 29, NJASRC, HI; Summary, May 20, 1943, Evangelical, Box 95, NJASRC, HI; Procedure in Allocat-

ing Presbyterian Board Funds to Japanese American Students Now in Projects, May 10, 1943, Presbyterian (II), Box 98, NJASRC, HI.

36. Barstow to Ziegler, July 17, 1942 UBC, Box 100, NJASRC, HI.

37. Methodist Japanese-American Student Relocation Committee, December 9, 1942, Methodist (I), Box 96, NJASRC, HI; Summary, May 20, 1943; Methodist Japanese-American Student Relocation Committee, December 5, 1942, Methodist (I), Box 96, NJASRC, HI; Methodist Japanese-American Student Relocation Committee, December 7, 1942, Methodist (I), Box 96, NJASRC, HI; Methodist Japanese-American Student Relocation Committee, December 8, 1942, Methodist (I), Box 96, NJASRC, HI.

38. Statistical Summary, January 23, 1943, Presbyterian Forms and Reports, Box 99, NJASRC, HI.

39. Barstow to Ziegler, July 17, 1942; Barstow to Thomas, August 28, 1942, Baptist (I), Box 92, NJASRC, HI; Cordier to Whom It May Concern, August 7, 1942, Brethren SC, Box 93, NJASRC, HI; Brubaker to Barstow, August 11, 1942, Brethren SC, Box 93, NJASRC, HI; Brubaker to Misc., August 19, 1942, Brethren SC, Box 93, NJASRC, HI; Nelson to Binford, September 4, 1942, Presbyterian (I), Box 98, NJASRC, HI; Colvin to O'Brien, November 13, 1942, YMCA (I), Box 34, NJASRC, HI.

40. Executive Committee Minutes, August 31, 1942, Minutes of Council Meetings, Box 87, NJASRC, HI.

41. Bodine to Nason, January 23, 1943, Committees and Organizations: NSRC-WC, Japanese-American Relocation, SIS, 1943, AFSC; Status of Scholarship Funds, "about 2/43," Reports, Box 49, NJASRC, HI.

42. United for the Future, n.d., WSSF-Publicity Material, Box 102, NJASRC, HI.

43. Uprooted Students, n.d., WSSF-Publicity Material, Box 102, NJASRC, HI.

44. Bendetsen, one of the "prime architects" of exile and incarceration, based his concerns for national security in racism, arguing that Nikkei "must be regarded as potential enemies, if put to the test of being present during an invasion by an army of their own race." He defended exile and incarceration as an example of America's "justice and humanity" in handling the process in an "American way." Bendetsen, who boasted of creating and directing exile and incarceration after the war, later explained that he had only been following orders (qtd. in Daniels, *Concentration Camps,* 92–93). See Girdner and Loftis, *Great Betrayal,* 17; Daniels, *Concentration Camps,* 45, 92–93, 102; Daniels, *Asian America,* 337.

45. Conard to Barstow, August 4, 1942, Robbins W. Barstow, Box 110, NJASRC, HI; Conard to Bendetsen, June 16, 1942, 000.8–Schools and Colleges, Volume #I, Central Correspondence, WCCA and Civil Affairs Division, WDC and Fourth Army, RG 338, NACP; Dedrick to Boekel, June 11, 1942, 000.8–Schools (Civilian), Volume #I, Central Correspondence, WCCA and Civil Affairs Division, WDC and Fourth Army, RG 338, NACP; Goebel to Conard, June 25, 1942, 000.8–National Student Relocation Council, Volume #I, Central Correspondence, WCCA and Civil Affairs Division, WDC and Fourth Army, RG 338, NACP; Evans to Operations

Branch, TSO Division, June 14, 1942, 000.8–Schools (Civilian), Volume #I, Central Correspondence, WCCA and Civil Affairs Division, WDC and Fourth Army, RG 338, NACP; Ashworth to Nichols, July 2, 1942, 000.8–Schools (Civilian), Volume #I, Central Correspondence, WCCA and Civil Affairs Division, WDC and Fourth Army, RG 338, NACP.

46. Nineteen-Point Agreement, June 19, 1942, 64.501, #1, 4–12/42, Subject-Classified General Files, Headquarters, Records of the WRA, RG 210, NA.

47. Conard to Bendetsen, June 21, 1942, 64.501, 4–12/42, Subject-Classified General Files, Headquarters, Records of the WRA, RG 210, NA; Memo, Ashworth to All Chiefs of Interior Police at Assembly Centers, June 19, 1942, 000.8–Schools (Civilian), Volume #I, Central Correspondence, WCCA and Civil Affairs Division, WDC and Fourth Army, RG 338, NACP; Ashworth to Nichols, July 2, 1942; Hall, "Japanese American College Students," 126, 139.

48. Japanese Student Relocation, n.d., Publicity, Box 37, NJASRC, HI.

49. Bendetsen to Conard, July 3, 1942, 64.501, 4–12/42, Subject-Classified General Files, Headquarters, Records of the WRA, RG 210, NA; Evans to Chief, Property, Security and Regulations Division, July 2, 1942, 000.8–Schools (Civilian), Volume #I, Central Correspondence, WCCA and Civil Affairs Division, WDC and Fourth Army, RG 338, NACP.

50. Baker to M. M. Tozier, Acting Chief, Office of Reports, WRA, July 4, 1942, 64.501, #1, 4–12/42, Subject-Classified General Files, Headquarters, Records of the WRA, RG 210, NA.

51. Bodine to Pickett and Barstow, July 4, 1942, Pacific Coast Branch, 7–8/42, Box 35, NJASRC, HI.

52. Japanese Student Relocation (Version 2), n.d., Box 47, NJASRC, HI.

53. Bodine to Conard, July 30, 1942, Publicity, Box 37, NJASRC, HI.

54. Conard to Barstow, July 15, 1942, Barstow (–7/31/42), Box 38, NJASRC, HI; Harris to unknown, August 7, 1942, West Coast Office (8–12/42), Box 38, NJASRC, HI.

55. Bendetsen to Sproul, November 6, 1942, 000.8–Schools and Colleges, Volume #I, Central Correspondence, WCCA and Civil Affairs Division, WDC and Fourth Army, RG 338, NACP; Report to the Executive Committee, August 4, 1942; Barstow to Chittum, September 3, 1942, Wooster, Box 59, NJASRC, HI; Sproul to Bendetsen, October 22, 1942, 000.8–Schools and Colleges, Volume #I, Central Correspondence, WCCA and Civil Affairs Division, WDC and Fourth Army, RG 338, NACP.

56. Executive Committee Minutes, July 9, 1942, 64.508, #1, 4–9/42, Subject-Classified General Records, Headquarters, Records of the WRA, RG 210, NA; Minutes Steering Committee Meeting, September 30, 1942, Pacific Coast Branch–Steering Committee Minutes, Box 56, NJASRC, HI.

57. Bendetsen to Tate, August 3, 1942, 000.8–Schools (Civilian), Volume #I, Central Correspondence, WCCA and Civil Affairs Division, WDC and Fourth Army, RG 338, NACP.

58. Boekel to Bendetsen, September 8, 1942, 323.3–WCCA, Central Correspondence, WCCA and Civil Affairs Division, WDC and Fourth Army, RG 338, NACP; Early Leaves, n.d., Leave Clearances, Box 12, NJASRC, HI; Ediphone Record, Bendetsen and Hall, October 6, 1942, 000.8–Schools (Civilian), Volume #I, Central Correspondence, WCCA and Civil Affairs Division, WDC and Fourth Army, RG 338, NACP.

59. DeWitt to McCloy, October 5, 1942, J. L. DeWitt, Central Correspondence, WCCA and Civil Affairs Division, WDC and Fourth Army, RG 338, NACP.

60. Report of Progress, up to July 25, 1942, 64.508, #1, 4–9/42, Subject-Classified General Records, Headquarters, Records of the WRA, RG 210, NA.

61. Provinse to Myer, July 27, 1942, 64.501, #1, 4–12/42, Subject-Classified General Files, Headquarters, Records of the WRA, RG 210, NA.

62. Early Leaves, n.d.; Memorandum of Agreement between the War Relocation Authority and the War Department concerning the relocation of evacuee Japanese American students in inland schools and colleges, n.d., 64.501, #1, 4–12/42, Subject-Classified General Files, Headquarters, Records of the WRA, RG 210, NA.

63. Nason to Provinse, October 8, 1942, 64.507, #1, Subject-Classified General Records, Headquarters, Records of the WRA, RG 210, NA; Memo, Provinse to Myer, July 29, 1942, 64.501, #1, 4–12/42, Subject-Classified General Files, Headquarters, Records of the WRA, RG 210, NA; Executive Committee Minutes, July 9, 1942; Morris to Barstow, July 11, 1942, Barstow (-7/31/42), Box 38, NJASRC, HI; Sigler to Myer, August 20, 1942, 64.501, 4–12/42, Subject-Classified General Files, Headquarters, Records of the WRA, RG 210, NA; Barstow to Marks, July 30, WRA-DC, 5/5/42–9/15/42, Box 26, NJASRC, HI; Conard to Deutsch, September 2, 1942, WRA-DC, 5/5/42–9/15/42, Box 26, NJASRC, HI.

64. E. Emlen to Provinse, January 11, 1945, WRA-Washington (II), Box 23, NJASRC, HI; Memo, E. Emlen to Bodine, January 4, 1945, Bodine-Field Reports, Box 3, NJASRC, HI; Provinse to All Project Directors and Relocation Area Supervisors, January 3, 1945, WRA-Washington (II), Box 23, NJASRC, HI; Nason to Paul, January 2, 1945, 64.501, Subject-Classified General Files, Headquarters, Records of the WRA, RG 210, NA.

65. Barstow's Interim Report, June 29, 1942; N.S.R.C.: Its Purpose and Functions; Hall, "Japanese American College Students," 143; Beale to Lafabregue, October 26, 1942, 521.2, Colleges and Universities, Central Utah Files, Subject-Classified General Files, Records of the Relocation Centers, Records of the WRA, RG 210, NA; Provinse to Barstow, June 24, 1942, US Government-WCCA, Box 20, NJASRC, HI; Provinse to Myer, June 26, 1942, 64.501, #1, 4–12/42, Subject-Classified General Files, Headquarters, Records of the WRA, RG 210, NA.

66. Conard to Provinse, July 15, 1942, WRA-DC, 5/5/42–9/15/42, Box 26, NJASRC, HI; Barstow to Conard, July 2, 1942, Barstow (–7/31/42), Box 38, NJASRC, HI; Conard to Bearn, July 21, 1942, B-General, Box 2, NJASRC, HI; Barstow to Aydelotte, July 31, 1942, Frank Aydelotte, Box 2, NJASRC, HI.

67. Barstow to Conard, July 16, 1942, Barstow (-7/31/42), Box 38, NJASRC, HI;

Cary to Aydelotte, June 26, 1942, Committees and Organizations: NJASRC, Japanese-American Relocation, SIS, 1942, AFSC; Barstow to Conard, July 13, 1942, Barstow (–7/31/42), Box 38, NJASRC, HI.

68. Schauffler to Morris, Conard, Berkeley Staff, David Henley, Reith, Esther Rhoades and Clare Brown Harris, Bob O'Brien, July 15, 1942, Committees and Organizations: NJASRC, Japanese-American Relocation, SIS, 1942, AFSC.

69. Schauffler to Morris, Conard, Henley, Rhoades, and O'Brien, July 17, 1942, Committees and Organizations: NJASRC, Japanese-American Relocation, SIS, 1942, AFSC.

70. Japanese Problem, July 22, 1942, Committees and Organizations: NJASRC, Japanese-American Relocation, SIS, 1942, AFSC.

71. Barstow to Aydelotte, July 31, 1942; Barstow to Conard, July 29, 1942, Pacific Coast Branch, 7–8/42, Box 35, NJASRC, HI.

72. Schauffler to Conard, July 27, 1942, Majorie Schauffler, Box 17, NJASRC, HI.

73. Barstow to Conard, August 17, 1942, Robbins W. Barstow, Box 110, NJASRC, HI; Nason to Aydelotte, August 8, 1942, Frank Aydelotte, Box 2, NJASRC, HI; Barstow to Marks, August 3, 1942, WRA-DC, 5/5/42–9/15/42, Box 26, NJASRC, HI.

74. Barstow to Conard, August 17, 1942; A Report to the Executive Committee from the Director, August 25, 1942, Philadelphia Office (8–9/42), Box 38, NJASRC, HI.

75. Dunbar to Hibbard, April 23, 1943, WRA-DC, 4/1/43–5/31/43, Box 25, NJASRC, HI.

76. Provinse to Beale, November 10, 1942, 64.508, #2, 10–12/42, Subject-Classified General Records, Headquarters, Records of the WRA, RG 210, NA; Barstow to Conard, August 14, 1942; Marks to Bodine, August 2, 1942, WRA-DC, 5/5/42–9/15/42, Box 26, NJASRC, HI; Barstow to Cary, August 7, 1942, Committees and Organizations: NJASRC, Japanese-American Relocation, SIS, 1942, AFSC; Executive Committee Minutes, August 31, 1942; Beasley to Bendetsen, September 5, 1942, 000.8–Schools and Colleges, Volume #I, Central Correspondence, WCCA and Civil Affairs Division, WDC and Fourth Army, RG 338, NACP.

77. Mary Tanaka is a pseudonym. Pillard to Conard, October 8, 1942, Antioch File, Box 53, NJASRC, HI.

78. Fressa Baker Inman (director of admissions, Antioch) to W. Emlen, March 23, 1943, Antioch File.

79. Minutes of the Steering Committee Meeting, August 12, 1942; McCloy to Myer, August 5, 1942, 64.504, #1, Subject-Classified General Records, Headquarters, Records of the WRA, RG 210, NA.

80. Provinse to McCloy, November 5, 1942, 64.501, 4–12/42, Subject-Classified General Files, Headquarters, Records of the WRA, RG 210, NA; Baker to Johnston and Taylor, November 13, 1942, 64.500, College Educational Problems, Jerome Center, Denson, Arkansas, Subject-Classified General Files, Records of the Relocation Centers, Records of the WRA, RG 210, NA.

81. Beale to Marks, December 2, 1942, WRA-DC, 11/1/42–12/30/42, Box 26, NJASRC, HI; Beale to Provinse, November 30, 1942, WRA-DC, 11/1/42–12/30/42, Box 26, NJASRC, HI; Hall, "Japanese American College Students," 218.

82. Beale to Provinse, November 30, 1942; Hall, "Japanese American College Students," 218.

83. Beale to Marks, December 9, 1942, WRA-DC, 11/1/42–12/30/42, Box 26, NJASRC, HI; Marks to Beale, December 4, 1942, WRA-DC, 11/1/42–12/30/42, Box 26, NJASRC, HI.

84. Marks to Beale, December 15, 1942, WRA-DC, 11/1/42–12/30/42, Box 26, NJASRC, HI.

85. Quoted in "Tops Class," *Manzanar Free Press,* 16 May 1942, 1.

86. Early Leaves, n.d.; Bodine Memo, July 1, 1942, WRA-DC, May 5, 1942–September 15, 1942, Box 26, NJASRC, HI; E. Emlen to Campbell, July 17, 1943, Presbyterian Forms and Reports, Box 99, NJASRC, HI.

87. Graybill, "Nisei," 109.

88. Executive Committee Minutes, August 31, 1942, Minutes of Council Meetings, Box 87, NJASRC, HI; King to Edward B. Marks Jr., Administrative Assistant, Community Management Division, WRA, September 29, 1942, WRA-DC, 6/6/42–10/31/42, Box 25, NJASRC, HI.

89. Provinse to Nason, September 29, 1942, 64.501, 4–12/42, Subject-Classified General Files, Headquarters, Records of the WRA, RG 210, NA.

90. Myer to Nason, September 25, 1943, WRA-DC, 9/1/43–11/30/43, Box 24, NJASRC, HI.

91. See Barstow to Clarence E. Josephson (president, Heidelberg College), July 10, 1942, Heidelberg File, Box 65, NJASRC, HI.

92. See Barstow to Lincoln B. Hale (president, Evansville College), August 27, 1942, Evansville File, Box 62, NJASRC, HI.

93. See Evansville File; Ashland File, Box 54, NJASRC, HI; Defiance File, Box 60, NJASRC, HI.

94. Daniels, *Concentration Camps,* 99.

95. Kostka to Barstow, July 22, 1942, College of Chestnut Hill File, Box 57, NJASRC, HI; Naomi Binford (AFSC) to Kostka, July 23, 1942, College of Chestnut Hill File; Notre Dame College File, Box 74, NJASRC, HI.

96. Fall to Barstow, June 23, 1942, Hiram, Box 66, NJASRC, HI; Evansville File; Daniels, *Concentration Camps,* 99; Hall, "Japanese American College Students," 150–51, 155–56.

97. Hibbard to Browning, April 1, 1944, Pittsburgh File, Box 76, NJASRC, HI.

98. Page to Barstow, June 29, 1942, Pikeville File, Box 76, NJASRC, HI; Excerpts from letter received in Philadelphia Office, June 4, 1942, Pikeville File.

99. Barstow to Page, July 3, 1942, Pikeville File.

100. Wilkins to Sieg, March 19, 1942, Oberlin College Subject Files: Japanese Americans, Oberlin College Archives; University of Washington, "Interrupted Lives."

101. Barstow to Ruth T. Forsyth (Secretary to the President, Oberlin), August 20, 1942, Oberlin File, Box 75, NJASRC, HI.

102. James C. McCullough to King, August 27, 1942, Oberlin File.

103. Barstow to Forsythe, September 16, 1942, Oberlin File.

104. Editorial from *Oberlin News-Tribune,* 1 October 1942, Oberlin File.

105. Hall, "Japanese American College Students," 223–24.

106. Bodine to Shirrell, June 17, 1942, 521.2, Colleges and Universities, Tule Lake Relocation Center Central Files, Subject-Classified General Files, Records of the Relocation Centers, Records of the WRA, RG 210, NA; "School Site Selected, Nisei Eligible to Teach," *Manzanar Free Press,* 2 June 1942, 1.

107. Yamato Ichihashi to Ray Lyman Wilbur, Stanford President, July 3, 1942, quoted in Chang, *Morning Glory,* 130.

108. "Relocation of Students," *Santa Anita Pacemaker,* 4 July 1942, 1–2.

109. "All Students Must Answer Quiz," *Tulean Dispatch,* 7 July 1942, 3.

110. "Student Relocation Council Formed to Help Scholars Here," *Tulean Dispatch,* 4 July 1942, 5; "Friends Service Committee Confer to Speed Work for Student Relocation," *Manzanar Free Press,* 9 July 1942, 1; Morris to Cary, et al., July 28, 1942, Homer Morris, Box 36, NJASRC, HI.

111. Bodine to Shirrell, June 17, 1942.

112. "Largest Group of Students Leaves Project," *Tulean Dispatch,* 23 September 1942, 1; "Students Urged to File Questionnaire," *Poston Press Bulletin,* 16 August 1942.

113. "Your Opinion Please!," *Tanforan Totalizer,* 8 August 1942, 7; "Education Column," *Tanforan Totalizer,* 12 September 1942.

114. "Eduction Column," *Tanforan Totalizer,* 12 September 1942.

115. See "Scholarships," *Tanforan Totalizer,* 22 August 1942, 5, and Ohio State University, Box 75, NJASRC, HI. For a sketch of Kikuchi and his work for the Japanese Evacuation and Resettlement Study in Chicago, see Yoo, *Growing Up Nisei,* 156–58.

116. "Your Opinion Please!" *Tanforan Totalizer,* August 8, 1942.

117. Letter, October 6, 1942, Letters, October 1942, Box 7, Bodine, HI.

118. Jack Ozaki and Masao Sugiyama are pseudonyms. Ozaki Letter, September 29, 1942, Letters, April–September 1942, Box 7, Bodine, HI; "Candidates Tell Goals in Student Relocation Plan," *Santa Anita Pacemaker,* 11 July 1942, 2; Sugiyama Letter, July 7, 1942, Selected Letters, April–September 1942, Box 7, Thomas R. Bodine, HI.

119. "Education Column," *Tanforan Totalizer,* 12 September 1942.

Chapter 3: In "Free America," Fall 1942–Summer 1943

1. Chiya Veronica Asado is a pseudonym. For Asado, see Excerpts from Student Letters, Box 105, NJASRC, HI; Asado Letter, February 14, 1943, Letters, February

1943, Box 7, Bodine, HI; Excerpt from Asado's letter of January 28, 1946, Letters, Box 7, Bodine, HI.

2. "Free America," *Topaz Times,* 10 June 1943, 2.

3. Nason to Pickett, October 20, 1942, AFSC-General Correspondence, Box 2, NJASRC, HI; Beale to Arai, March 3, 1943, A General Correspondence, Box 1, NJASRC, HI; Marks to Bodine, January 13, 1943, WRA-DC, 1/43, Box 25, NJASRC, HI; Hall, "Japanese American College Students," 168.

4. Bodine to Nason, January 23, 1943, Committees and Organizations: NSRC-WC, Japanese-American Relocation, SIS, 1943, AFSC.

5. For the WSSF, see WSSF-1942, Box 101, NJASRC, HI; WRA-DC, 11/1/42–12/30/42 File, Box 26, NJASRC, HI; Japanese Student Fund: Financial Statement, December 30, 1942, Administration: Finance-Budgets, Japanese-American Relocation, SIS, 1942, AFSC; Bodine to Nason, January 23, 1943.

6. Barstow to Thomas, July 28, 1942, Baptist (I), Box 92, NJASRC, HI; Bodine to Nason, January 23, 1943; Japanese Student Fund: Financial Statement, December 30, 1942; Hibbard to Beale, Bodine, B. Emlen, W. Emlen, King, and Morris, March 26, 1943, Job Opportunities, Box 11, NJASRC, HI; Bodine to E. Emlen, May 22, 1943, WRA-Central Utah Student Aid Committee (I), Box 29, NJASRC, HI.

7. Bob Ishida is a pseudonym. See College of Wooster File, Box 59, NJASRC, HI.

8. W. Emlen to Jess J. Petty, Director of Admissions, Baldwin-Wallace, June 15, 1945, Baldwin-Wallace File, Box 54, NJASRC, HI; A. L. Roberts, War Service Unit, Board of National Missions, Presbyterian Church, to George Inouye, September 30, 1943, Correspondence re: Japanese American students (I-L), Box 1, RG 37, Presbyterian Historical Society (hereafter cited PHS).

9. Quoted in Taylor, *Jewel of the Desert,* 125.

10. "Topaz Scholarship Fund Organized," *Topaz Times,* 11 May 1943, 4; "$168.79 Received in Scholarship Fund," *Topaz Times,* 19 May 1943, 4; "Scholarship Committee Concentrates on Fund Raising," *Topaz Times,* 10 June 1943, 4; "Students to Sell Tags to Aid SSAF," *Topaz Times,* 19 June 1943, 3; "Scholarship Fund Hits Half-Way Mark of Goal, *Topaz Times,* 26 June 1943, 3; "SSAF Boosted to $3,080.93," *Topaz Times,* 20 July 1943, 2.

11. "Scholarship Fund Tops $1,000 with Aid of PTA," *Tulean Dispatch,* 25 August 1943, 1.

12. Nason to Bodine, January 30, 1943, Committees and Organizations: NJSRC-Philadelphia, Japanese-American Relocation, SIS, 1943, AFSC. The Columbia Foundation had been established in 1940 to support world peace, human and civil rights, the environment, urban life, and the arts. The Columbia Foundation provided a second grant of $10,000 to the council in January 1944. See Columbia Foundation, "About"; Russell, "Furthering the Public Welfare, 1929–1991"; Columbia Foundation Grants: Actual Payment by Program Area, Report GF4, Columbia Foundation Papers; Hibbard to Elkus, January 22, 1944, Columbia Foundation Papers.

13. Bodine to O'Brien, January 6, 1943, Committees and Organizations: NSRC-WC, Japanese-American Relocation, SIS, 1943, AFSC; O'Brien to Beale, November

2, 1942, Pacific Coast Branch-Japanese Situation (San Francisco), 11–12/42, Box 35, NJASRC, HI; O'Brien to Bodine, January 14, 1943, Philadelphia Office (1/43–), Box 38, NJASRC, HI.

14. Bodine to Nason, January 23, 1943.

15. Nason to Bodine, January 13, 1943, Committees and Organizations: NJSRC-Philadelphia, Japanese-American Relocation, SIS, 1943, AFSC.

16. O'Brien to Bollman, January 30, 1943, Evangelical, Box 95, NJASRC, HI; Bodine to West Coast Committee, January 27, 1943, John Nason-1943, Box 13, NJASRC, HI; Executive Committee Minutes, January 28, 1943, Philadelphia Office (1/43–), Box 38, NJASRC, HI.

17. Executive Committee Minutes, February 3, 1943, Minutes of Council Meetings, Box 87, NJASRC, HI; Distribution by Denomination of Students, n.d., Churches: General Material, Box 100, NJASRC, HI.

18. A Report to the Executive Committee from the Director, August 25, 1942; Report to the Executive Committee, August 4, 1942.

19. Pickett to Barstow, May 9, 1942, Robbins Barstow, Box 2, NJASRC, HI.

20. Elliot to Biddle, November 28, 1942, 64.501, #1, 4–12/42, Subject-Classified General Files, Headquarters, Records of the WRA, RG 210, NA.

21. Andrews to Kilgore, January 5, 1943, US Government-Congress, Box 19, NJASRC, HI; Andrews to Kilgore, December 3, 1942, US Government-Congress, Box 19, NJASRC, HI; Freeman to Kilgore, December 29, 1942, US Government-Congress, Box 19, NJASRC, HI. State legislatures in Iowa and Pennsylvania also protested student resettlement. See Myer to W. J. Scarborough, Secretary of the Senate, Iowa, n.d., 64.501, 4–12/42, Subject-Classified General Files, Headquarters, Records of the WRA, RG 210, NA; Esther Rhoades to Beale, April 22, 1943, Temple File, Box 82, NJASRC, HI.

22. Myer to Gearhart, December 15, 1942, 64.501, 4–12/42, Subject-Classified General Files, Headquarters, Records of the WRA, RG 210, NA; Myer to Scarborough, n.d., 64.501, 4–12/42, Subject-Classified General Files, Headquarters, Records of the WRA, RG 210, NA; Myer to Mundt, February 12, 1943, 64.502, #1, Subject-Classified General Files, Headquarters, Records of the WRA, RG 210, NA; Myer to McKellar, March 4, 1943, 64.502, #1, Subject-Classified General Files, Headquarters, Records of the WRA, RG 210, NA.

23. O'Brien to Kilgore, January 28, 1943, US Senate-Kilgore Correspondence, Box 20, NJASRC, HI; Johnson to Kilgore, February 19, 1943, US Senate-Kilgore Correspondence, Box 20, NJASRC, HI.

24. The *American Historical Review* noted that "Professor Beale combined his concern for academic freedom with a crusading interest in religious freedom, racial democracy, civil liberties, and international peace. He sustained these values in all circles and all circumstances." See Beale to Newsome, August 13, 1942, Department of History Files, University Archives, Wilson Library, UNC; Beale to Newsome, September 1, 1942, Department of History Files, University Archives, Wilson Library, UNC; Beale to Frank P. Graham, President, UNC, September 8, 1942, De-

partment of History Files, University Archives, Wilson Library, UNC; "Historical News and Comments: Howard K. Beale Obituary"; "Recent Deaths: Howard K. Beale."

25. Schauffler to O'Brien, September 25, 1942, Committees and Organizations: NJASRC, Japanese-American Relocation, SIS, 1942, AFSC; Beale to Graham, November 14, 1942, Department of History Files, University Archives, Wilson Library, UNC.

26. Beale to Bodine, October 6, 1942, Folder 13, Box 32, MSS 99–097, Howard K. Beale Additions, SHSW.

27. Beale to Nason, December 4, 1942, Internal Correspondence -12/42, Box 19, Nason, HI.

28. Beale to Nason, October 24, 1942, NJASRC-Organization and Goals, Box 21, Nason, HI.

29. Beale to Nason, October 24, 1942; Beale to Nason, December 4, 1942.

30. Beale to Nason, December 4, 1942.

31. Beale to Nason, December 5, 1942, Internal Correspondence -12/42, Box 19, Nason, HI.

32. Beale to Nason, December 20, 1942, Internal Correspondence -12/42, Box 19, Nason, HI.

33. Beale to Nason, December 4, 1942; Cary to Nason, December 8, 1942, Committees and Organizations: NSRC-WC, Japanese-American Relocation, SIS, 1942, AFSC.

34. Bodine to Nason, December 31, 1942, Internal Correspondence -12/42, Box 19, Nason, HI.

35. Nason to Deutsch, January 13, 1943, Nason-1943, Box 13, NJASRC, HI.

36. Beale to Nason, December 4, 1942.

37. Beale to Nason, December 4, 1942.

38. Beale to Nason, December 4, 1942; Cary to Nason, December 8, 1942.

39. King Report, September 5, 1942, Committees and Organizations: NSRC-WC, Japanese-American Relocation, SIS, 1942, AFSC. King is quoted in Cary to Nason, December 8, 1942.

40. Beale to Nason, December 4, 1942.

41. Beale to Nason, December 4, 1942; Rhoades to Shirrell, October 28, 1942, 521.2, Colleges and Universities, Tule Lake Central Files, Subject-Classified General Files, Records of the Relocation Centers, Records of the WRA, RG 210, NA.

42. Beale to Graham, November 14, 1942; Beale to Newsome, November 14, 1942, Department of History Files, University Archives, Wilson Library, UNC; Executive Committee Minutes, June 9, 1943, Minutes, Box 89, NJASRC, HI. Beale worked in the council's placement department in Philadelphia through the spring, when he left the council. See Beale to Newsome, June 22, 1943, Department of History Files, University Archives, Wilson Library, UNC.

43. Bodine to O'Brien, January 6, 1943.

44. Jones to Nason, December 27, 1942, Committees and Organizations: NSRC-WC, Japanese-American Relocation, SIS, 1942, AFSC.

45. Bodine to Nason, December 24, 1942, Committees and Organizations: NSRC-WC, Japanese-American Relocation, SIS, 1942, AFSC.

46. Personnel Analysis, December 24, 1942, Committees and Organizations: NSRC-WC, Japanese-American Relocation, SIS, 1942, AFSC.

47. Beale to Nason, December 4, 1942.

48. Beale to Nason, December 20, 1942.

49. History of Student Relocation in Minidoka WRA, October 4, 1945, WRA-Minidoka (V), Box 32, NJASRC, HI.

50. Woodruff, a Quaker pacifist, had worked in banking for five years after graduating from Haverford and also attended Harvard Business School. He left for San Francisco one month after his marriage, because student resettlement qualified as work "of national significance" with his draft board. Emlen left the council in mid-summer 1944. See Okihiro, *Storied Lives,* 130; Swan to All SR Counselors, July 25, 1944, Counselors-Letters and Memos (I), Box 33, NJASRC, HI.

51. Hibbard came to the council after sixteen years as general secretary of the University of Wisconsin YMCA. He served as the council director for almost thirteen months, leaving on March 31, 1944. See Hibbard to Connor, July 1, 1943, Richard Connor, Box 6, NJASRC, HI; Hibbard to Irvine, October 23, 1943, Marietta File, Box 70, NJASRC, HI; Hibbard to Harbert, March 31, 1944, US Government-PMGO, Box 20, NJASRC, HI.

52. W. Emlen to Nason, March 18, 1943, Committees and Organizations: NJSRC-Philadelphia, Japanese-American Relocation, SIS, 1943, AFSC.

53. Nason to Cary, March 22, 1943, Committees and Organizations: NJSRC-Philadelphia, Japanese-American Relocation, SIS, 1943, AFSC.

54. Elizabeth Emlen had developed a sense of social responsibility while she was a student at Vassar. She moved west with Woodruff Emlen, her husband of one month, and became active in student resettlement work. She left the council on August 1, 1945. See Okihiro, *Storied Lives,* 129–30; Hiraoka to Nason, July 30, 1945, John Nason-1945, Box 14, NJASRC, HI; E. Emlen to the Council Members, July 3, 1945, Council Members, Box 6, NJASRC, HI.

55. Nason to Bodine, January 4, 1943, Nason-1943, Box 13, NJASRC, HI; Nason to Deutsch, January 13, 1943.

56. Bodine to O'Brien, January 6, 1943; Bodine to Nason, December 24, 1942; Bodine and Deutsch to West Coast Committee, January 27, 1943, Nason-1943, Box 13, NJASRC, HI; Bodine to O'Brien, January 6, 1943.

57. Bodine to Pickett, June 7, 1943, Committees and Organizations: NJSRC-Philadelphia, Japanese-American Relocation, SIS, 1943, AFSC.

58. Hoover to Myer, December 16, 1942, 64.507, #1, Subject-Classified General Records, Headquarters, Records of the WRA, RG 210, NA.

59. Myer to Hoover, December 22, 1942, 64.507, #1, Subject-Classified General Records, Headquarters, Records of the WRA, RG 210, NA.

60. Memo, Hibbard to Emlen, August 11, 1943, US Government-FBI, Box 19, NJASRC, HI.

61. Hall, "Japanese American College Students," 185–95; University of Cincinnati File, Box 22, NJASRC, HI.

62. Hibbard to Myer, June 23, 1943, WRA-DC, 6/1/43–8/31/43, Box 25, NJASRC, HI.

63. King to Dunbar, June 20, 1943, 64.501, 4–12/42, Subject-Classified General Files, Headquarters, Records of the WRA, RG 210, NA; W. Emlen to Myer, June 23, 1943, 64.505, #1, Subject-Classified General Records, Headquarters, Records of the WRA, RG 210, NA; Dunbar to W. Emlen, July 10, 1943, WRA-DC, 6/1/43–8/31/43, Box 25, NJASRC, HI.

64. Myer to Hibbard, June 18, 1943, Leave Clearances, Box 12, NJASRC, HI.

65. Myer to Zacharias, June 25, 1943, 64.505, #1, Subject-Classified General Records, Headquarters, Records of the WRA, RG 210, NA.

66. Zacharias to Myer, July 1, 1943, 64.503, #2, Subject-Classified General Files, Headquarters, Records of the WRA, RG 210, NA; King to Dunbar. Zacharias had supported a proposal by Elmer Davis and Milton Eisenhower to allow Nikkei, "after individual test," to enlist in the military. See Daniels, *Concentration Camps,* 146–47.

67. Dunbar to Hibbard, July 1, 1943, WRA-DC, 6/1/43–8/31/43, Box 25, NJASRC, HI.

68. Memo, n.d., US Government-Navy, Box 19, NJASRC, HI; Memo, NJASRC to Nason, July 26, 1943, Nason-1943, Box 13, NJASRC, HI.

69. Nason to Provinse, July 31, 1943, WRA-DC, 6/1/43–8/31/43, Box 25, NJASRC, HI.

70. E. Emlen to Nason, August 1, 1945, Financial Memorandums, 1943–45, Box 19, Nason, HI; Holland to Provinse, August 9, 1943, 64.505, #1, Subject-Classified General Records, Headquarters, Records of the WRA, RG 210, NA.

71. Dunbar Memo for File, August 12, 1943, 64.410, #1, Subject-Classified General Files, Headquarters, Records of the WRA, RG 210, NA.

72. Hibbard Phone Conversation with Myer, August 27, 1943, WRA-DC, 6/1/43–8/31/43, Box 25, NJASRC, HI; Hibbard to Myer, August 20, 1943, WRA-DC, 6/1/43–8/31/43, Box 25, NJASRC, HI; Hibbard to Frase, August 27, 1943, 64.503, #2, Subject-Classified General Files, Headquarters, Records of the WRA, RG 210, NA.

73. Hibbard to Frase, August 27, 1943.

74. University of Southern California Dental Students Case Letters, Box 80, NJASRC, HI; Hall, "Japanese American College Students," 201–5.

75. Melvin D. Brown, Dean of Freshmen, to NSRC, July 6, 1943, Washington and Jefferson File, Box 83, NJASRC, HI. See also Ball State File, Box 54, NJASRC, HI; Centre College File, Box 57, NJASRC, HI; Bowling Green State University File, Box 55, NJASRC, HI.

76. Ralph E. Hill, Registrar, to Hibbard, April 6, 1943, University of Louisville File, Box 69, NJASRC, HI.

77. Tirey to Conard, October 6, 1942, Indiana State Teachers College File, Box 67, NJASRC, HI.

78. Sara King Harvey to Beale, November 7, 1942, Indiana State Teachers College File.

79. Herbert T. Gebert, Dean and Registrar, to Hall, September 1, 1943, Thiel File, Box 82, NJASRC, HI; Goshen File, Box 64, NJASRC, HI.

80. Hibbard to Dabney, October 22, 1943, Ashland Junior College File, Box 54, NJASRC, HI.

81. Defiance File, Box 60.

82. See Bodine to Mary Koppius, Secretary, YWCA, University of Cincinnati, December 4, 1942, University of Cincinnati File (I); W. Emlen to Jess J. Petty, Director of Admissions, Baldwin-Wallace, June 15, 1945, Baldwin-Wallace File, Box 54, NJASRC, HI; W. Emlen to C. L. Murray, Registrar, June 26, 1943, Ball State File; Denison File, Box 60, NJASRC, HI; Fenn College File, Box 63, NJASRC, HI; Goshen File.

83. Herrick to Mary C. Megilligan, NJASRC, October 23, 1942, Fenn College File, Box 63, NJASRC, HI.

84. Herrick to O'Brien, July 16, 1943, Fenn College File.

85. Miami University File, Box 70, NJASRC, HI.

86. For Wilmington, see Wilmington College File, Box 85, NJASRC, HI; Watson and Watson, *Our Life Together,* 110–11.

87. Watson and Watson, *Our Life Together,* 110.

88. For Cincinnati, see University of Cincinnati File.

89. College Questionnaire, University of Cincinnati File.

90. Beale to O'Brien, November 13, 1942, Pacific Coast Branch-Japanese Situation (San Francisco), 11–12/42, Box 35, NJASRC, HI; Holliday to King, February 13, 1943, Cincinnati (I), Box 58, NJASRC, HI; Holliday to NJASRC, October 12, 1943, Cincinnati (I), Box 58, NJASRC, HI.

91. Inouye, *Odyssey,* Book II, Section T, 1–2, 6.

92. Ibid., Book II, Section T, 3.

93. Okihiro, *Storied Lives,* 94.

94. For Allegheny College, see Allegheny File, Box 53, NJASRC, HI; College Questionnaire, Allegheny File.

95. Hibbard to Betty Bugbee, Allegheny College Christian Council, May 1, 1943, Allegheny File.

96. Otterbein File, Box 75, NJASRC, HI.

97. For Bowling Green, see Bowling Green State University File.

98. Nao Takasugi, NJASRC, to Robert Cullum, Relocation Supervisor, June 28, 1945, WRA-Cleveland, Box 22, NJASRC, HI.

99. For Heidelberg, see Heidelberg File, Box 65, NJASRC, HI; Josephson Letter, June 2, 1943, Letters, June 1943, Box 7, Bodine, HI.

100. Quoted in Hall, "Japanese American College Students," 251.

101. College Questionnaire, Heidelberg File.

102. Frances Lemke, Dean of College, to Hall, September 22, 1943, Heidelberg File.

103. Bodine to Clarence E. Josephson, President, Heidelberg, January 11, 1943, Heidelberg File.

104. University of Toledo File, Box 82, NJASRC, HI; Okihiro, *Storied Lives*, 83. See also George Sakata's essay in "Nisei Students Speak," 246–47.

105. For Earlham, see Earlham College File, Box 62, NJASRC, HI; Hall, "Japanese American College Students," 226–41.

106. College Questionnaire, Earlham College File.

107. Dennis to Barstow, June 24, 1942, Earlham College File.

108. Dennis to Barstow, August 21, 1942, Earlham College File.

109. The Junior Order of United American Mechanics was organized in the 1840s by laborers upset by immigrant competition and became a leading nativist organization by the 1890s that promoted the exclusion of Asian immigrants in the early twentieth century. See Higham, *Strangers in the Land,* 57, 80, 173–74.

110. Excerpt from *Richmond Palladium,* 29 September 1942, Earlham College File.

111. Faye Whitenack to Dennis, September 30, 1942. Quoted in Hall, "Japanese American College Students," 235.

112. Editorial from the *Earlham Post,* 6 October 1942, Earlham College File.

113. Tanaka, "Earlham College," 4–5.

114. Dennis to E. Emlen, September 22, 1943, Earlham College File.

115. Hall, "Japanese American College Students," 205–13; Minutes of the Executive Committee, October 30, 1942.

116. Memo Provinse to Eisenhower, June 5, 1942.

117. "Students Advised on Relocation," *Topaz Times,* 16 December 1942.

118. "Philip Glick Addresses Council, Unit One," *Poston Press Bulletin,* 1 September 1942, 1.

119. "Permanent Resettlement Sought," *Denson Communiqué,* 4 December 1942, 1.

120. Okihiro, *Storied Lives, 67.*

121. Yeiz Kato is a pseudonym. Kato Letter, October 10, 1942, Letters, October 1942, Box 7, Bodine, HI.

122. Dohi Letter, November 25, 1942, Letters, 4–12/42, Box 7, Bodine, HI. See also Okihiro, *Storied Lives,* 68, 71.

123. American-Japanese Students Enrolled at Asbury College, Fall '43, Asbury College File, Box 54, NJASRC, HI. For Asbury College, see also Okihiro, *Storied Lives, 92.*

124. See Noble, "Masaye Nakamura's Personal Story," 37–40.

125. George Oda and Helen Harada are pseudonyms. Dohi Letter, November 25, 1942; Kato Letter, October 10, 1942; Letter, July 27, 1943, Letters, July–September 1943, Box 7, Bodine, HI; Ishimaru Letter, February 28, 1943, Letters, Box 7, Bodine, HI; Graybill, "Nisei," 111; Okihiro, *Storied Lives,* 121; Paul Swain Havens,

President, Wilson College, to W. Emlen, February 19, 1943, Reports and Publicity, Box 48, NJASRC, HI.

126. From Camp to College, July 1944, WRA-DC, August 1944–, NJASRC, HI.

127. Yoshi Higa and Bob Nakata are pseudonyms. Higa Letter, January 27, 1943, Letters, January 1943, Box 7, Bodine, NJASRC, HI; Nakata Letter, June 22, 1943, Letters, June 1943, Box 7, Bodine, NJASRC, HI.

128. Sumiko Kanno is a pseudonym. Kanno to Emlen, May 30, 1943, Letters, 5/43, Box 7, Bodine, HI.

129. Form Letter, April 29, 1943, 64.500, Subject-Classified General Files, Headquarters, Records of the WRA, RG 210, NA.

130. Ito, "Loyalty and Learning," 41–42.

131. Student Letter, October 20, 1942, Letters, October 1942, Box 7, Bodine, NJASRC, HI.

132. Ishimaru Letter, February 28, 1943.

133. Student Letter, April 16, 1943, Letters, April 1943, Box 7, Bodine, HI. Thomas Bodine, in annotating his papers at the Hoover Institution, thought that "Life Begins with Freedom" made an excellent title, perhaps for a book on student resettlement that he planned to write. Bodine never wrote his book, but Thomas James did use the proposed title for an article.

134. Quoted in Brokaw, *Greatest Generation*, 216–23.

135. Quoted in "Still the Greatest Country."

136. Okuda Letter, November 28, 1942, Letters, 11–12/42, Box 7, Bodine, HI; Conard to Marks, September 12, 1942, 64.508, #1, Subject-Classified General Records, Headquarters, Records of the WRA, RG 210, NA.

137. Okuda Letter, March 12, 1943, Letters, March 1943, Box 7, Bodine, HI.

138. Student Letter, March 22, 1943, Letters, March 1943, Box 7, Bodine, HI; Okuda Letter, March 12, 1943.

139. Bodine to Hibbard, May 5, 1943, Bodine-Field Reports, Box 3, NJASRC, HI; Hibbard to Vivian Hauser, Chair, Student University Religious Council, Ohio State, October 20, 1943, Ohio State File, Box 75, NJASRC, HI; E. Emlen to Evelyn Hunter, Dean of Women, Mount Union, October 22, 1943, Mount Union File, Box 73, NJASRC, HI.

140. "Kenji Okuda Reflects on Local Nisei's Apathy," *Rohwer Outpost*, 7 October 1944, 3; "Kenji Okuda to Speak at YBA," *Outpost*, 30 September 1944, 3; Background of Minidoka Center, October 4, 1945, WRA-Minidoka (V), Box 32, NJSRC, HI; "Oberlin Nisei Is Student Prexy," *Tulean Dispatch*, 8 April 1943, 3; "Kenji Okuda," *Minidoka Irrigator*, 10 April 1943, 3.

141. Form Letter, July 14, 1943, NRF-A, Box 40, NJASRC, HI; King to Student, January 25, 1943, Letters, January 1943, Box 7, Bodine, HI.

142. Beale to Student, May 6, 1943, Student File, Box 115, NJASRC, HI.

143. George Hara is a pseudonym. Sugiyama to Denny Wilcher, NJASRC, February 13, 1943, Letters, February 1943, Box 7, Bodine, HI; Okihiro, *Storied Lives*, 60; Hara Letter, January 27, 1943, Letters, January 1943, Box 7, Bodine, HI.

144. Okihiro, *Storied Lives,* 58.

145. Ito, "Japanese American Women," 4–5; Ito, "Loyalty and Learning," 14–20, 30; Matsumoto, "Japanese American Women," in Ruiz and DuBois, *Unequal Sisters,* 439–47.

146. Mary Tanaka is a pseudonym. See Ito, "Loyalty and Learning," 20–21, 24–29.

147. Jack Emoto is a pseudonym. Emoto to King, July 9, 1943, William Emoto File, Box 114, NJASRC, HI.

148. George Ogawa is a pseudonym. Ogawa Letter, April 26, 1943, Letters, 4/43, Box 7, Bodine, HI.

149. See Student File, Box 115, NJASRC, HI.

150. Sumiko Mary Okita is a pseudonym. King to Okita, August 16, 1943, Okita, Box 113, NJASRC, HI.

151. "O'Brien Meets Students," *Heart Mountain Sentinel,* 19 December 1942, 1; "NSRC Aids Over 300," *Granada Pioneer,* 29 November 1942, 1; "College Plans Encouraging," *Rohwer Outpost,* 18 November 1942, 2.

152. "NSRC Permit Supervisor Makes Whirlwind Visit," *Gila News Courier,* 23 February 1943, 3; "Student Aid Speeded Up for Fall," *Heart Mountain Sentinel,* 27 February 1943, 8.

153. "Bodine Here On Visit," *Minidoka Irrigator,* 27 February 1943, 3.

154. Bodine Speeches, February 1943, Speeches, Box 1, Bodine, HI.

155. "Bodine Here to Interview," *Gila News Courier,* 25 May 1943, 1; "Thomas R. Bodine to Visit Center," *Topaz Times,* 11 May 1943, 1; "NSRC Delegate Coming," *Topaz Times,* 13 May 1943, 4; "NSRC Director to Speak Tonight," *Poston Chronicle,* 1 June 1943, 1; "High School Hears Talk," *Granada Pioneer,* 12 May 1943, 4; Thomas P. [*sic*] Bodine Speaks to SCA," *Heart Mountain Sentinel,* 31 July 1943, 3; "Nisei Students Are Attending Colleges in the Middlewest," *Heart Mountain Sentinel,* 31 July 1943; "Bodine Encourages Student Relocation," *Manzanar Free Press,* 12 June 1943, 1.

156. "Outlook for Student Relocation Bright," *Heart Mountain Sentinel,* 13 February 1943, 5.

157. O'Brien to Jones, January 6, 1943, Pacific Coast Branch-Japanese Situation (San Francisco), 1/43, Box 35, NJASRC, HI.

158. From Camp to College, Box 47, NJASRC, HI.

159. "The S.R.C., Its Purpose and Functions," *Minidoka Irrigator,* 19 June 1943, 6.

160. "Student Relocation Places 500 in Schools," 20 December 1942, 3.

161. "1136 Attending Colleges from Relocation Centers," *Tulean Dispatch,* 10 August 1943, 1–2; "Sixty More Colleges Cleared for Student Relocation," *Tulean Dispatch,* 26 January 1943, 2; "N.S.R.C.: Record Is Reviewed," *Tulean Dispatch,* 9 March 1943, 3.

162. "Student Secretary Visits Project," *Heart Mountain Sentinel,* 19 September 1942, 4; "284 Colleges on Approved List for Evacuees," *Minidoka Irrigator,* 19 December 1942, 3; "Nisei Girl Offered Tuition to College," *Minidoka Irrigator,* 7 Au-

gust 1943, 5; "Opportunity for Girls to Attend College Made," *Tulean Dispatch,* 5 August 1943, 1; "Des Moines," *Granada Pioneer,* 17 July 1943, 1; "Nursing Schools Now Open for Enrollment," *Rohwer Outpost,* 3 February 1943, 2.

163. "Preparing for the Future," *Minidoka Irrigator,* 25 December 1942, 1.

164. "Editorial: Student Relocation," *Rohwer Outpost,* 11 November 1942, 4; "Editorial: For Student Aid," *Rohwer Outpost,* 25 August 1943, 6.

165. "School Swell Says Tanaka," *Tulean Dispatch,* 1 February 1943, 2; "Letter to Editor," *Denton Tribune,* 27 April 1943, 3; "Former Resident Gives Advice," *Heart Mountain Sentinel,* 7 August 1943, 5; "Students," *Topaz Times,* 27 October 1942, 3.

166. "Attempt to Oust Former Postonians from Park College," *Poston Press Bulletin,* 10 September 1942, 1–2; Girdner and Loftis, *Betrayal,* 337; Daniels, *Concentration Camps,* 101; Okihiro, *Storied Lives,* 69–71; Smith, "Backgrounds," 57–60; Hall, "Japanese American College Students," 241–48. See also Park College, "Nisei."

167. Noble, "Masaye Nakamura's Personal Story," 39–40.

168. "Students," *Times,* 27 October 1942, 3.

169. "Former Resident Gives Advice," *Heart Mountain Sentinel,* 7 August 1943, 8.

170. "Fourteen Residents Leave on Student Relocation," *Tribune,* 26 February 1943, 5; "San Francisco Office of Ntl. Student Relocation Council Moves to Philadelphia," *Poston Chronicle,* 18 February 1943; "Relocated Students Goodwill Ambassadors," *Rohwer Outpost,* 6 February 1943, 3.

171. "Scholarship," *Granada Pioneer,* 21 January 1943, 2; "Collegiate Dance Hailed Successful," *Manzanar Free Press,* 30 November 1942, 1.

172. "*Time* Tells of Nisei Activities in College," *Granada Pioneer,* 26 June 1943, 3.

173. Beale to Lafabregue, December 8, 1942, WRA-Central Utah Relocation Project (I), Box 29, NJASRC, HI.

174. "College Group," *Manzanar Free Press,* 28 October 1942, 3; "Inter-Collegiate," *Manzanar Free Press,* 7 November 1942; "Collegiate Dance Hailed Successful," *Manzanar Free Press,* 30 November 1942, 1.

175. "Student Association," *Topaz Times,* 16 January 1943, 4; "'Music Revue' Student Benefit," *Topaz Times,* 4 May 1943, 7.

176. Lafabregue to NSRC Director, March 12, 1943, WRA-Central Utah (I), Box 29, NJASRC, HI; Beale to Lafabregue, April 4, 1943, WRA-Central Utah (I), Box 29, NJASRC, HI.

177. "Relocated Students Goodwill Ambassadors," *Rohwer Outpost,* 6 February 1943; King Report, September 5, 1942, Committees and Organizations: NSRC-WC, Japanese-American Relocation, SIS, 1942, AFSC.

178. Brief Report of Progress, December 24, 1942, Pacific Coast Branch-Japanese Situation (San Francisco), 11–12/42, Box 35, NJASRC, HI; Megilligan to Brown, November 4, 1942, B-General (III), Box 3, NJASRC, HI; Bodine to West Coast Committee, January 27, 1943.

179. N.S.R.C.: Its Purpose and Functions, May 27, 1943, Historical Council Material (II), Box 10, NJASRC, HI.

Chapter 4: Change and New Challenges in a World at War, Fall 1943–Summer 1944

1. Mary Murata is a pseudonym. Murata to King, September 12, 1943, Murata File, Box 113, NJASRC, HI.

2. Iijima graduated with an A.B. with honors and was admitted to Harvard Law School. Mineta looked forward to a career in medicine. Mineta's brother Norman later served in the House of Representatives. Brothers College, Drew University Yearbook, 1944, Box 3, Sumiko Kobayashi Collection, Balch Institute (hereafter cited BI); "Topazans Attain College Records," *Topaz Times*, 4 November 1944, 3; AFSC Oral History Interview #402, AFSC Archives, Philadelphia. For Iijima's recollections of his incarceration experience, see Inada, *Only What We Could Carry*, 3–7. Iijima's diary is in the Bancroft Library. For Drew University and Mineta, see also Okihiro, *Storied Lives*, 71, 91, 100–102.

3. Brothers College, Drew University Yearbook, 1945, Box 3, Kobayashi, BI.

4. See Kobayashi Collection, BI; AFSC Oral History Interview #402.

5. See Nisei Student Relocation Commemorative Fund *Newsletter*, Fall 2001, 11; Okihiro, *Storied Lives*, 132–33; Executive Committee Minutes, February 27, 1945.

6. Minutes of the Second Plenary Meeting, September 29, 1943, Minutes, Box 88, NJASRC, HI.

7. Nason to Myer, October 5, 1943, 64.502, #1, Subject-Classified General Files, Headquarters, Records of the WRA, RG 210, NA.

8. Hibbard to Myer, October 18, 1943, 64.410, #1, Subject-Classified General Files, Headquarters, Records of the WRA, NA.

9. To Council Members, October 8, 1943, Nason Letter, Box 89, NJASRC, HI.

10. Conversation [with] W.R.A., November 19, 1943, WRA-DC, 9/1/43–11/30/43, Box 24, NJASRC, HI.

11. Minutes of the Executive Committee, November 24, 1943, Minutes, 1942–46, Box 87, NJASRC, HI.

12. Bodine to Kingman, October 28, 1943, Committee on American Principles and Fair Play, Box 5, NJASRC, HI; Bodine to Nason, November 18, 1943, John Nason-1943, Box 13, NJASRC, HI.

13. Martha Fujita to E. Emlen, November 20, 1943, Student Letters, Box 105, NJASRC, HI.

14. Kodama to Bodine, October 26, 1943, WRA-Heart Mountain (II), Box 31, NJASRC, HI.

15. "Kodama Raps Discontinuing Student Council," *Heart Mountain Sentinel*, 30 October 1943, 1.

16. WRA-Semi-Annual Reports, Box 28, NJASRC, HI; From Camp to College,

July, 1944, WRA-DC, 8/44–, Box 24, NJASRC, HI; Hall, "Japanese American College Students," 193.

17. Myer to Nason, November 22, 1943, Leave Clearances, Box 12, NJASRC, HI.

18. Conversation [with] W.R.A., November 19, 1943; Minutes of the Executive Committee, November 24, 1943.

19. The PMGO adopted a different point of view toward Nikkei and the issue of loyalty in a memo about Nikkei enlisted men who made disloyal statements to avoid overseas combat. The PMGO stated, "[i]n determining whether the subject is dangerously disloyal statements [to that effect] . . . will not alone be deemed sufficient to justify transfer to a special organization but all the facts will be considered." See Ulio, Adjutant General, Memo, August 20, 1944, 014.3114–General, Mail and Records Branch, Classified Decimal File, Administrative Division, Provost Marshal General, RG 389, NACP.

20. Ulio Memo, October 14, 1943, 014.3114–General, Mail and Records Branch, Classified Decimal File, Administrative Division, Provost Marshal General, RG 389, NACP; Instructions, n.d., 014.3114–General, Mail and Records Branch, Classified Decimal File, Administrative Division, Provost Marshal General, RG 389, NACP.

21. From Camp to College, July 1944.

22. Form Letter, October 28, 1943, Student, Box 113, NJASRC, HI.

23. King Memo, February 1, 1944, US Government-PMGO, Box 19, NJASRC, HI.

24. Nason to Wilkins, January 18, 1944, Oberlin, Box 75, NJASRC, HI; Newsletter-VIII, January 5, 1944, 410.123, Student Relocation, Colorado River, Subject-Classified General Files, Records of the Relocation Centers, Records of the WRA, RG 210, NA; Proscribed Colleges, March 28, 1944, Counselors-Letters and Memos, Box 34, NJASRC, HI.

25. Form Letter, February 19, 1944, Letters to Colleges with Divided Campuses, Box 90, NJASRC, HI.

26. Hibbard to Dunbar, February 5, 1944, 64.501, Subject-Classified General Files, Headquarters, Records of the WRA, RG 210, NA; Hibbard to Tovan, February 5, 1944, 64.501, Subject-Classified General Files, Headquarters, Records of the WRA, RG 210, NA; Hibbard to Harbert, February 28, 1944, 64.503, #3, Subject-Classified General Files, Headquarters, Records of the WRA, RG 210, NA; Survey of Educational Institutions, Japanese American Branch, General File, 1942–46, PMGO, RG 389, NACP.

27. Hibbard to Harbert, March 31, 1944, NJASRC, Box 1730, PMGO, RG 389, NACP; Provinse to Hibbard, March 2, 1944, NJASRC, Box 1730, PMGO, RG 389, NACP.

28. John Haynes Holmes, Arthur Garfield Hayes, and Roger N. Baldwin, Director, to Stimson, December 13, 1943, Educational Institutions, PMGO, RG 389, NACP; McCloy to American Civil Liberties Union, January 4, 1944, Educational Institutions, PMGO, RG 389, NACP.

29. King Memo, February 1, 1944.

30. Excerpt from letter of 3/7/44 from Hibbard to Bodine, March 7, 1944, WRA-DC, 3/1/44–7/31/44, Box 24, NJASRC, HI; Dunbar to Hibbard, January 22, 1944, WRA-DC, 12/1/43–2/29/44, Box 24, NJASRC, HI.

31. Swan served as the council director for a little less than eight months, leaving on November 15, 1944. See Provinse to Swan, November 11, 1944, WRA-DC, 8/44–, Box 24, NJASRC, HI; Prepared for *New York Times,* June 24, 1944, *New York Times,* Box 14, NJASRC, HI.

32. Provinse to Swan, August 5, 1944, WRA-DC, 8/44–, Box 24, NJASRC, HI; Nason to Provinse, August 10, 1944, WRA-DC, 8/44–, Box 24, NJASRC, HI; Provinse to Nason, August 12, 1944, WRA-DC, 8/44–, Box 24, NJASRC, HI.

33. Provinse to Swan, August 5, 1944.

34. Council Minutes, January 19, 1944, Minutes, Box 88, NJASRC, HI.

35. Hibbard to Stafford, February 17, 1944, WRA-Minidoka (II), Box 32, NJASRC, HI.

36. Nason to Myer, March 27, 1944, Copies, Box 89, NJASRC, HI.

37. Balderston to Cary, April 20, 1944, Copies, Box 89, NJASRC, HI; Rhoades to Cary, April 5, 1944, Copies, Box 89, NJASRC, HI.

38. Deutsch to Hibbard, April 6, 1944, 64.410, #2, Subject-Classified General Files, Headquarters, Records of the WRA, RG 210, NA.

39. Myer to Nason, April 14, 1944, WRA-DC, 3/1/44–7/31/44, Box 24, NJASRC, HI.

40. Provinse to Nason, June 5, 1944, 64.410, #2, Subject-Classified General Files, Headquarters, Records of the WRA, RG 210, NA.

41. Minutes of Executive Committee, May 10, 1944, Minutes, 1942–46, Box 87, NJASRC, HI; Letter to College Representatives on Council, May, 1944, Box 89, NJASRC, HI.

42. Council Minutes, June 15, 1944, Minutes, Box 88, NJASRC, HI.

43. See Kent State University File, Box 68, NJASRC, HI.

44. Marion Kobara is a pseudonym. Stopher to Stevenson, November 20, 1943, Kent State University File.

45. Kobara to Yamashita, October 29, 1944, Kent State University File.

46. For Muskingum College, see Muskingum College File, Box 73, NJASRC, HI.

47. For Kinji Hiramoto, see Hiramoto Diary and Kinji Hiramoto letter to author, 27 March 2002.

48. Frank Ito is a pseudonym.

49. W. Emlen to McKnight, June 12, 1943, Muskingum College File.

50. McKnight to King, August 5, 1943, Muskingum College File.

51. See Indiana Technical College File, Box 67, NJASRC, HI.

52. Keene to FBI, October 6, 1942, Indiana Technical College File.

53. Keno to Stevenson, November 10, 1943, Indiana Technical College File.

54. For examples of failed attempts, see Georgetown College File, Box 63,

NJASRC, HI; State Teachers College, Indiana, Pennsylvania, Box 76, NJASRC, HI.

55. Hibbard to Haentzschel, October 23, 1943, Valparaiso File, Box 83, NJASRC, HI; Okihiro, *Storied Lives*, 90.

56. For Case, see Case School of Applied Science File, Box 57, NJASRC, HI.

57. Theodore M. Focke to Robert L. Kelly, September 14, 1942, Case File.

58. Beale to Willard E. Nudd, Registrar, May 26, 1943, Case File.

59. For DePauw, see DePauw University File, Box 61, NJASRC, HI.

60. Wildman to Provinse, October 20, 1942, DePauw File.

61. Bartlett to Hibbard, February 3, 1944, DePauw File.

62. Hibbard to Bartlett, January 31, 1944, DePauw File.

63. For Tri-State College, see Tri-State College File, Box 87, NJASRC, HI

64. Roush to Hibbard, March 6, 1944, Tri-State College File.

65. Vaughn to Hibbard, January 11, 1944, Morehead State Teachers College File, Box 72, NJASRC, HI.

66. Hibbard to Vaughn, January 14, 1944, Morehead State File.

67. Brown to W. Emlen, May 29, 1944, Kenyon File, Box 68, NJASRC, HI.

68. For Bluffton College, see Bluffton College File, Box 55, NJASRC, HI.

69. For a general history of the U.S. Cadet Nurse Corps, see U.S. Public Health Service, *Cadet Nurse Corps;* Honan, "Lucille Petry Leone." For the council's work with pharmacy students, see Worthen, "Nisei Pharmacists"; Worthen, "Nisei Students."

70. Mabel Kuba is a pseudonym. See Mabel Kuba File, Box 43, NJASRC, HI.

71. Form Letter, November 4, 1943, Kuba File.

72. Newsletter VI, September 24, 1943, 64.500, Student Relocation, Minidoka Central Files, Subject-Classified General Files, Records of the Relocation Centers, Records of the WRA, RG 210, NA. For the form letter on nursing, see Hibbard to Lettie Christenson, Director of Nursing, Christ Hospital, Cincinnati, Ohio, Box 58, NJASRC, HI.

73. See Pennsylvania Hospital School of Nursing File, Box 76, NJASRC, HI; St. Luke's and Children's Medical Center File, Box 78, NJASRC, HI; Methodist Hospital-Philadelphia File, Box 70, NJASRC, HI.

74. See St. Mary's Hospital File, Box 79, NJASRC, HI.

75. St. Louis to Hibbard, March 6, 1944, St. Vincent Hospital File, Box 79, NJASRC, HI.

76. See Fairview Park Hospital File, Box 62, NJASRC, HI.

77. Cunningham to Hibbard, February 9, 1944, Northeastern Hospital File, Box 74, NJASRC, HI.

78. Peeler to Hibbard, February 11, 1944, Osteopathic Hospital File, Box 75, NJASRC, HI.

79. Ferris to Hibbard, November 24, 1943, White Cross Hospital File, Box 85, NJASRC, HI.

80. Leonis to Hibbard, January 29, 1944, St. Alexis Hospital File, Box 78, NJASRC, HI.

81. Wivel to Hibbard, December 22, 1943, Indianapolis City Hospital File, Box 67, NJASRC, HI.

82. See McKay, "Problem of Student Nurses."

83. Jane Nemoto is a pseudonym. See Jane Nemoto, Box 113, NJASRC, HI.

84. Paul Kasai is a pseudonym. Student Letter to King, October 13, 1943, Selected Letters, Box 7, Bodine, HI.

85. Swan to V. F. Schwalm, President, Manchester College, July 17, 1944, Manchester College File, Box 69, NJASRC, HI.

86. For Marietta College, see Marietta College File, Box 70, NJASRC, HI.

87. Schoonover to Bodine, January 8, 1943, Marietta File.

88. "Japanese-American Student Adds Cosmopolitan Atmosphere to Marietta College Campus," *The Olio,* 12 February 1943, 1.

89. Irvine to King, October 1, 1943, Marietta File.

90. Bodine note, n.d., Box 7, Bodine, HI.

91. George Hata is a pseudonym. Hibbard to Hata, December 9, 1943, Marietta File.

92. Okihiro, *Storied Lives,* 96.

93. Smith, "Backgrounds," 64, 68.

94. *'44 Ramblings,* June 1944, Yearbook, Shapp, BI. Some Nikkei carried this strategy with them into their new surroundings, using sports to gain acceptance. See Austin, "'A Finer Set of Hopes and Dreams'"; Franks, *Crossing Sidelines.*

95. *Victoria,* 1943, Denson High School, BI.

96. Yamate Form Letter, April 20, 1944, WRA-Central Utah Student Aid Committee (I), Box 29, NJASRC, HI; Minutes of the Meeting of the Topaz Student Aid Fund Committee, April 14, 1944, WRA-Central Utah Student Aid Committee (I), Box 29, NJASRC, HI. On the educational system at Topaz, see Taylor, *Jewel of the Desert,* 125–27.

97. Harris to Okamoto, April 2, 1945, 410.123, Student Relocation, Colorado River, Subject-Classified General Files, Records of the Relocation Centers, Records of the WRA, RG 210, NA; Hibbard to Masuda, June 5, 1943, 410.123, Student Relocation, Colorado River, Subject-Classified General Files, Records of the Relocation Centers, Records of the WRA, RG 210, NA; Hinson to E. Emlen, January 8, 1945, 410.123, Student Relocation, Colorado River, Subject-Classified General Files, Records of the Relocation Centers, Records of the WRA, RG 210, NA.

98. E. Emlen to Lynn, March 30, 1944, WRA-Heart Mountain (II), Box 31, NJASRC, HI; Sheldon to Bodine, August 18, 1944, WRA-Gila River (II), Box 30, NJASRC, HI; E. Emlen to Sheldon, August 31, 1944, WRA-Gila River (II), Box 30, NJASRC, HI.

99. Form Letter, n.d., Contributions-Student Drive, Box 6, NJASRC, HI.

100. Student to Bodine, August 13, 1943, Letters, 7–9/43, Box 7, Bodine, HI.

101. See AFSC Oral History Interview #402, AFSC Archives, Philadelphia; Interview Notes on Student, March 23, 1944, NRF-O, Box 41, NJASRC, HI.

102. "Relocation of Students," *Heart Mountain Sentinel*, 12 August 1944, 31.

103. AFSC Oral History Interview #409.

104. Student to Hibbard, November 9, 1943, Letters, Box 105, NJASRC, HI.

105. Excerpt, May 25, 1944, Letters, 1944, Box 7, Bodine, HI.

106. Ross to Woodruff Emlen, October 14, 1943, WRA-Cleveland, Box 22, NJASRC, HI.

107. Hibbard to Ross, October 19, 1943, WRA-Cleveland, Box 22, NJASRC, HI.

108. Student to King, November 18, 1943, Notes for Bodine Talks, Box 8, Bodine, HI.

109. "Pros, Cons of Trade Vs. College," *Minidoka Irrigator*, 16 September 1944, 5.

110. Hibbard to Henry C. Patterson, October 12, 1943, WRA-Philadelphia, Box 23, NJASRC, HI.

111. Bodine to Hibbard, March 12, 1944, Committees and Organizations: NJSRC-Correspondence, Japanese-American Relocation, SIS, 1944, AFSC; Zimmerman to Hibbard, June 29, 1943, 410.123, Student Relocation, Colorado River, Subject-Classified General Files, Records of the Relocation Centers, Records of the WRA, RG 210, NA; Hibbard to Zimmerman, July 8, 1943, 410.123, Student Relocation, Colorado River, Subject-Classified General Files, Records of the Relocation Centers, Records of the WRA, RG 210, NA; Zimmerman to Hibbard, July 26, 1943, 410.123, Student Relocation, Colorado River, Subject-Classified General Files, Records of the Relocation Centers, Records of the WRA, RG 210, NA.

112. Conversation [with] W.R.A., 19 November 1943; Balderston to Nason, February 12, 1943, Committees and Organizations: NJSRC-Philadelphia, Japanese-American Relocation, SIS, 1943, AFSC.

113. Myer to Nason, November 22, 1943, WRA-DC, 9/1/43–11/30/43, Box 24, NJASRC, HI.

114. Bodine Speech, n.d., Speeches, Box 1, Bodine, HI; N.S.R.C.: Its Purpose and Functions, May 27, 1943.

115. Shigeki Yasutake is a pseudonym. Notes for Bodine Talks, Box 8, Bodine, HI. On the Selective Service and Japanese Americans, see Daniels, *Asian America,* 248–54.

116. Advance Release, October 22, 1944, WRA-DC, Releases on Student Relocation, Box 28, NJASRC, HI.

117. Yamashita Letter, March 13, 1944, Student File, Box 114, NJASRC, HI.

118. From Camp to College, July, 1944; E. Emlen to Pusey, March 22, 1944, WRA-Manzanar (I), Box 32, NJASRC, HI; E. Emlen to Roberts, April 25, 1944, E. Emlen Correspondence, Box 1, RG 37, PHS; "NSRC Field Director Bodine Urges Draft Age Boys to Start College," *Topaz Times,* 24 May 1944, 1.

119. See Stevenson to Student, September 17, 1943, NRF-A, Box 43, NJASRC, HI; W. Emlen to Student, April 11, 1944, NRF-O, Box 41, NJASRC, HI.

120. Masao Yano is a pseudonym. King to Yano, September 25, 1943, Box 113, NJASRC, HI.

121. Mary Watanabe is a pseudonym. See Watanabe File, NRF-K, Box 43, NJASRC, HI.

122. Ayako Obano is a pseudonym. Obano to Bodine, December 2, 1942, University of Cincinnati File, Box 58, NJASRC, HI.

123. Saburo Baba is a pseudonym. Baba to W. Emlen, August 21, 1943, Letters, 7–9/43, Box 7, Bodine, HI.

124. See, for example, Student Files, Box 114, NJASRC, HI.

125. Ken Ota is a pseudonym. See Ken Ota File, Box 114, NJASRC, HI.

126. Hibbard to Fred W. Ross, September 3, 1943, WRA-Cleveland, Box 22, NJASRC, HI; W. Emlen to Amerman, April 7, 1944, WRA-Minidoka (III), Box 32, NJASRC, HI.

127. Yoshie Chida is a pseudonym. See Chida File, Box 114, NJASRC, HI.

128. Bodine Notes, May 17, 1943, Chida File.

129. Chida to King, December 21, 1943, Chida File.

130. Hibbard to James G. Lindley, Project Director at Granada, February 18, 1944, Bodine, Subject-Classified General Files: Granada, Records of the Relocation Centers, Records of the WRA, RG 210, NA; Hibbard to Stafford, February 17, 1944; Bodine to Lindley, December 1, 1943, Bodine, Subject-Classified General Files: Granada Relocation Center, Records of the Relocation Centers, Records of the WRA, RG 210, NA.

131. Newsletter-III, July 14, 1943, 64.500, Student Relocation, Minidoka Central Files, Subject-Classified General Files, Records of the Relocation Centers, Records of the WRA, RG 210, NA.

132. Newsletter-VI, September 24, 1943, 64.500, Student Relocation, Minidoka Central Files, Subject-Classified General Files, Records of the Relocation Centers, Records of the WRA, RG 210, NA.

133. Bodine to Swan, June 1, 1944, Bodine-Field Reports, Box 3, NJASRC, HI.

134. Bodine to Swan, April 30, 1944, Committees and Organizations: NJSRC-Correspondence, Japanese-American Relocation, SIS, 1944, AFSC.

135. Bodine to Hibbard, March 12, 1944.

136. Notes on Student Relocation Counselors, January 25, 1944, Counselors-Letters and Memos (I), Box 33, NJASRC, HI; Bodine to Swan, April 22, 1944, Committees and Organizations: NJSRC-Correspondence, Japanese-American Relocation, SIS, 1944, AFSC.

137. Bodine to Hibbard, March 18, 1944, Committees and Organizations: NJSRC-Correspondence, Japanese-American Relocation, SIS, 1944, AFSC.

138. Notes on Student Relocation Counselors, January 25, 1944.

139. Beginning in February 1943, Tule Lake became a segregation camp for those

who the WRA viewed as disloyal or as troublemakers. Thus, morale there was distinctly different. See Daniels, *Asian America,* 260–65.

140. Bodine is quoted in Memo, E. Emlen to Swan, April 21, 1944, Bodine-Field Reports, Box 3, NJASRC, HI.

141. AFSC Oral History Interview #405, AFSC Archives, Philadelphia; Bodine to Provinse, June 10, 1944, Homer Morris, Box 13, NJASRC, HI.

142. Bodine to Swan, April 22, 1944.

143. Bodine to Swan, April 30, 1944.

144. Bodine to Swan, May 2, 1944, Committees and Organizations: NJSRC-Correspondence, Japanese-American Relocation, SIS, 1944, AFSC.

145. Bodine to Swan, June 1, 1944.

146. *Cardinal and Gold,* Summer 1943, High School Publications, Potts, BI.

147. Bodine to Hibbard, June 14, 1943, Committees and Organizations: NJSRC-Philadelphia, Japanese-American Relocation, SIS, 1943, AFSC.

148. Takahashi to Hibbard, June 18, 1943, WRA-Manzanar (I), Box 32, NJASRC, HI.

149. Nason to Jones, April 7, 1944, Committees and Organizations: NJSRC-Correspondence, Japanese-American Relocation, SIS, 1944, AFSC; Rhoades to Cary, April 5, 1944.

150. See Bodine to Stafford, July 24, 1944, 64.500, Student Relocation, Minidoka Central Files, Subject-Classified General Files, Records of the Relocation Centers, Records of the WRA, RG 210, NA.

151. Bob Sasahara is a pseudonym. See Bodine to Sasahara, July 21, 1944, 64.500, Student Relocation, Minidoka Central Files, Subject-Classified General Files, Records of the Relocation Centers, Records of the WRA, RG 210, NA.

152. Bodine to Sasahara, July 21, 1944; Bodine to Returnee Student, August 17, 1944, Letters to and about Returnees, Box 12, NJASRC, HI; Bodine to Returnee Student, August 3, 1944, Letters to and about Returnees, Box 12, NJASRC, HI.

153. Bodine to Returnee Student, August 17, 1944.

154. Bodine to Returnee Student, August 3, 1944.

155. Sasahara to Bodine, July 28, 1944, Letters to and about Returnees, Box 12, NJASRC, HI; Sasahara to Bodine, August 24, 1944, Student Letters, Box 105, NJASRC, HI.

156. Final Composite Report of the Returnee Nisei College Leaders, Summer 1944, Box 44, NJASRC, HI.

157. Final Composite Report of the Returnee Nisei College Leaders, Summer 1944.

Chapter 5: Closing Down and Saying *Sayonara,* 1944–46

1. For Nobuko Emoto, see Correspondence re: Japanese American students (E–H), Box 1, RG 37, PHS.

2. Emoto to Chapman, June 9, 1944, Correspondence re: Japanese American students (E–H).

3. Lee to Reverend E. Fay Campbell, Presbyterian Church, June 20, 1945, Correspondence re: Japanese American students (E–H).

4. Quillian to Campbell, July 3, 1945, Correspondence re: Japanese American students (E–H).

5. Bodine Note, n.d., Selected Letters, Box 7, Bodine, HI.

6. Executive Committee Minutes, October 3, 1944, Minutes, 1942–46, Box 87, NJASRC, HI; Miller to Myer, September 4, 1944, PMG's Letter of 1944, Box 89, NJASRC, HI; Nason to Hawkins, October 27, 1944, Abington Memorial Hospital, Box 53, NJASRC, HI; Form Letter, September 13, 1944, Provost Marshal General's Letter of 1944, Box 89, NJASRC, HI.

7. Report on Meeting with WRA, September 21, 1944, WRA-DC, 8/44–, Box 24, NJASRC, HI; Myer to Nason, September 30, 1944, WRA-DC, 8/44–, Box 24, NJASRC, HI; Provinse to All Project Directors, December 26, 1944, 64.508, NSRC, Rohwer Central Files, Subject-Classified General Files, Records of the Relocation Centers, Records of the WRA, RG 210, NA. See also Untitled, n.d., Miscellaneous Items/General Correspondence, Box 2, RG 37, PHS; Amendment to WRA Handbook, No. 130.46, Release No. 168, November 30, 1944, WRA-Colorado River (II), Box 33, NJASRC, HI; WRA Handbook, November 30, 1944, "WRA Handbook," Management Files, Headquarter Records, Records of the WRA, RG 210, NA.

8. Nason to Hawkins, October 27, 1944.

9. Bodine to E. Emlen, November 29, 1944, Bodine-Field Reports, Box 3, NJASRC, HI; E. Emlen to Nason, February 19, 1945, Nason-1945, Box 14, NJASRC, HI.

10. Graybill, who befriended the Emlens while she worked for the YWCA in Philadelphia, had extensive experience with the YWCA. Although unaware of the council and the concentration camps until she met the Emlens, Graybill decided to go to work for the council because she had known a Nisei woman through her YWCA work, respected the work of the AFSC, and was honored by Elizabeth Emlen's request that she join. Graybill was elevated to council director on August 1, 1945, and oversaw the closing of the council through June 30, 1946. Okihiro, *Storied Lives*, 129; Takasugi to Paul, August 1, 1945, WRA-Washington (II), Box 23, NJASRC, HI; Nisei Student Relocation Commemorative Fund *Newsletter*, Fall 2001, 7.

11. E. Emlen to Ramsdell, December 14, 1944, 64.508, NSRC, Rohwer Relocation Center Central Files, Subject-Classified General Files, Records of the Relocation Centers, Records of the WRA, RG210, National Archives; Myer to All Project Directors, September 10, 1945, 64.508, #7, May–October 1945, Subject-Classified Center Files, Headquarters, Records of WRA, RG210, National Archives; Memo, re: Conference with Dr. N. E. Viles, Head, Education Section, and Dr. Hugo Walters, Head of the Center Liaison Office, WRA, Friday, September 7, September 12, 1945,

WRA-Washington (II); "Notes on West Coast Colleges," Schools, March 23, 1945, Los Angeles Area Office, Subject-Classified General Files, Records of Relocation Offices, Records of the WRA, RG 210, NA.

12. Stafford and Harker to E. Emlen, n.d., 64.500, Student Relocation, Minidoka Central Files, Subject-Classified General Files, Records of the Relocation Centers, Records of the WRA, RG 210, NA; Report on Student Relocation, Poston I, 1944, January 20, 1945, 410.123, Student Relocation, Colorado River, Subject-Classified General Files, Records of the Relocation Centers, Records of the WRA, RG 210, NA; Hinson to E. Emlen, June 25, 1945, 410.123, Student Relocation, Colorado River, Subject-Classified General Files, Records of the Relocation Centers, Records of the WRA, RG 210, NA.

13. Stafford and Harker to E. Emlen, n.d.; Harker to E. Emlen, March 16, 1945, WRA-Minidoka (IV), Box 32, NJASRC, HI; Harker to E. Emlen, March 21, 1945, WRA-Minidoka (III), Box 32, NJASRC, HI.

14. Ramsdell to E. Emlen, March 12, 1945, 64.508, NSRC, Rohwer Central Files, Subject-Classified General Files, Records of the Relocation Centers, Records of the WRA, RG 210, NA; Yamashita to Hinson, June 6, 1944, 410.123, Student Relocation, Colorado River, Subject-Classified General Files, Records of the Relocation Centers, Records of the WRA, RG 210, NA; Stafford and Harker to E. Emlen, n.d.

15. History of Student Relocation in Minidoka WRA, October 4, 1945, WRA-Minidoka (V), Box 32, NJASRC, HI.

16. A Brief Outlook on Japanese Relocation, n.d., 64.502, Public Comments, Manzanar Central Files, Subject-Classified General Files, Records of the Relocation Centers, Records of the WRA, RG 210, NA.

17. Daniels, *Concentration Camps,* 153–55.

18. Graybill to Hinson, August 18, 1945, 410.123, Student Relocation, Colorado River, Subject-Classified General Files, Records of the Relocation Centers, Records of the WRA, RG 210, NA.

19. Bodine to E. Emlen, November 20, 1944, Committees and Organizations: NJSRC-Correspondence, Japanese-American Relocation, SIS, 1944, AFSC.

20. Bodine to Provinse, December 5, 1944, 64.508, #5, Subject-Classified General Files, Headquarters, Records of the WRA, RG 210, NA; Bodine to Provinse, February 12, 1945, 64.508, #5, Subject-Classified General Files, Headquarters, Records of the WRA, RG 210, NA.

21. Bodine to Provinse, December 5, 1944.

22. Eleanor Gerard has written about her experiences at Topaz in Daniels, Taylor, and Kitano, *Japanese Americans.* For more on Gerard, see Taylor, *Jewel of the Desert,* 98, 193; Smith, *Democracy on Trial,* 233.

23. Quoted from Bodine to Provinse, February 12, 1945; Bodine to Provinse, December 5, 1944.

24. Bodine to Provinse, February 12, 1945.

25. Bodine to E. Emlen, November 25, 1944, Bodine-Field Reports, Box 3, NJASRC, HI.

26. Bodine to Provinse, December 5, 1944

27. Bodine to E. Emlen, November 20, 1944.

28. Nason to Hawkins, October 27, 1944; Swan to Rhoades and Schmoe, October 19, 1944, Floyd Schmoe, Box 17, NJASRC, HI.

29. Campbell to Chapman, November 11, 1944, Chapman Correspondence, Box 1, RG 37, PHS.

30. Council Minutes, December 15, 1944, Minutes, Box 88, NJASRC, HI; Bodine to Nason, December 7, 1944, Bodine-Field Reports, Box 3, NJASRC, HI.

31. Present Status of Operations, n.d., AFSC-General Correspondence, Box 2, NJASRC, HI.

32. Council Minutes, December 15, 1944.

33. Myer to Nason, April 14, 1944, WRA-DC, 3–7/44, Box 24, NJASRC, HI.

34. Provinse to All Project Directors, December 26, 1944.

35. Fisher, "Unsnaring the Nisei Tangle," 1285.

36. Reith to E. Emlen, October 11, 1944, Marian Reith, Box 16, NJASRC, HI; Girdner and Loftis, Betrayal, 379–80.

37. Extracts from Tom Bodine's reports concerning proposed West Coast Student Relocation Office, Bodine-1944, Box 4, NJASRC, HI; Bodine to Nason, December 7, 1944.

38. Council Minutes, December 15, 1944; E. Emlen to Reith, January 16, 1945, Marian Reith, Box 16, NJASRC, HI; Executive Committee Minutes, February 27, 1945, Minutes, 1942–46, Box 87, NJASRC, HI.

39. Bodine to E. Emlen, December 23, 1944, Bodine-Field Reports, Box 3, NJASRC, HI.

40. E. Emlen to Nason, December 21, 1944, Nason-1944, Box 13, NJASRC, HI; Ickes Memo, December 19, 1944, WRA-Washington (II), Box 23, NJASRC, HI.

41. Executive Committee Minutes, February 27, 1945. The council did not follow through on the planned letter when the WRA would not pay for it. See Letter to Relocated Students, Box 104, NJASRC, HI; E. Emlen to the Council Members, July 3, 1945, Council Members, Box 6, NJASRC, HI.

42. Final Summary of Guidance Counselor, n.d., Relocation (General), Heart Mountain Central Files, Subject-Classified General Files, Records of the Relocation Centers, Records of the WRA, RG 210, NA.

43. A. E. Dyar, Director, to WRA, August 7, 1945, Schools, Los Angeles Area Office, 331, Subject-Classified General Files, Records of Relocation Offices, Records of the WRA, RG 210, NA.

44. Gretchen Hoff, Owner-Director, Glendale Secretarial College, August 9, 1945, Schools, Los Angeles Area Office, 331, Subject-Classified General Files, Records of Relocation Offices, Records of the WRA, RG 210, NA.

45. Bond to WRA, August 6, 1945, Schools, Los Angeles Area Office, 331, Subject-Classified General Files, Records of Relocation Offices, Records of the WRA, RG 210, NA.

46. MacKay to Manzanar Guidance Counselor, July 30, 1945, Schools, Los An-

geles Area Office, 331, Subject-Classified General Files, Records of Relocation Offices, Records of the WRA, RG 210, NA.

47. Florence N. Brady, Occidental Registrar, to Earl L. Kelley, WRA District Relocation Officer, August 10, 1945, Schools, Los Angeles Area Office, 331, Subject-Classified General Files, Records of Relocation Offices, Records of the WRA, RG 210, NA; Memo, G. L. Ash to Raymond Booth, WRA District Relocation Officer, April 5, 1945, Schools, Los Angeles Area Office, 331, Subject-Classified General Files, Records of Relocation Offices, Records of the WRA, RG 210, NA.

48. E. Emlen to McKee, April 26, 1945, Advisory Committee for Evacuees, Box 1, NJASRC, HI; McKee to E. Emlen, April 23, 1945, Advisory Committee for Evacuees, Box 1, NJASRC, HI.

49. Memo, E. Emlen to Thomas, May 23, 1945, Thomas, Box 18, NJASRC, HI.

50. E. Emlen to the Council Members, July 3, 1945.

51. E. Emlen to Nason, August 1, 1945, Financial Memorandums, 1943–45, Box 19, Nason, HI.

52. Council Minutes, September 14, 1945, Minutes of Council Meetings, Box 87, NJASRC, HI; Executive Committee Minutes, December 19, 1945, Minutes, 1942–46, Box 87, NJASRC, HI; Council Minutes, February 26, 1946, Minutes of Council Meetings, Box 87, NJASRC, HI; Student Relocation Newssheet, March 1, 1946, 64.508A, #1, Subject-Classified General Files, Headquarters, Records of the WRA, RG 210, NA.

53. Council Minutes, May 9, 1946, Minutes, Box 88, NJASRC, HI; Graybill and Thomas Report, n.d., Committees and Organizations: NJASRC, Japanese-American Relocation, SIS, 1946, AFSC.

54. Myer to Graybill, May 6, 1946, WRA-Washington (I), Box 23, NJASRC, HI.

55. Myer to Thomas, June 24, 1946, NAT to NAZ, Chronological File-General Alphabetical, NA-NR, Washington Office Files, WRA, RG 210, NA. See also Myer to Smyth, June 24, 1946, Subject-Classified General Files, Headquarters, Records of the WRA, RG 210, NA.

56. Myer to Nason, March 16, 1945, WRA-Washington(II), Box 23, NJASRC, HI.

57. Thomas to Myer, June 18, 1946, WRA-Washington (I), Box 23, NJASRC, HI.

58. For Cincinnati, see University of Cincinnati File, Box 58, NJASRC, HI, and Chapter 3.

59. Holliday to King, April 24, 1943, University of Cincinnati File.

60. King to Holliday, May 5, 1943, University of Cincinnati File.

61. E. Emlen to Brintons, November 25, 1944, Brinton, Box 4, NJASRC, HI.

62. Fletemeyer to E. Emlen, December 19, 1944, WRA-Cincinnati, Box 22, NJASRC, HI.

63. See Franklin and Marshall File, Box 63, NJASRC, HI.

64. See Lebanon Valley College File, Box 68, NJASRC, HI.

65. Quoted in Hays to Takasugi, June 18, 1945, WRA-Colorado River (III), Box 33, NJASRC, HI.

66. Takasugi to Hays, n.d., Lebanon Valley College File.

67. For Susquehanna, see Susquehanna College File, Box 81, NJASRC, HI.

68. Smith to E. Emlen, July 27, 1945, Susquehanna File.

69. E. Emlen to Smith, July 31, 1945, Susquehanna File.

70. For Geneva College, see Geneva College File, Box 63, NJASRC, HI; Leslie J. McKinney, Office of the Registrar, Geneva, to Conard, September 15, 1942, Geneva College File.

71. For Juniata, see Juniata College File, Box 67, NJASRC, HI.

72. Shizu Katase is a pseudonym. Yamashita to Pat Reith, Peace Section, AFSC, December 1, 1944, Juniata College File.

73. For Western Reserve University (hereafter WRU), see WRU File, Box 84, NJASRC, HI.

74. Simon to Barstow, June 29, 1942, WRU File; Linehan, "Japanese American Resettlement," 54-80.

75. Beale to Leutner, November 3, 1942, WRU File; O'Brien, *College Nisei*, 88.

76. Swan to Nishi, August 11, 1944, WRU File.

77. Nishi to Swan, September 19, 1944, Cleveland Church Federation, Box 5, NJASRC, HI; O'Brien, *College Nisei*, 88.

78. For the University of Pennsylvania, see University of Pennsylvania File, Box 76, NJASRC, HI; Robinson, "Admission Denied."

79. Gates to Barstow, June 25, 1942, University of Pennsylvania File.

80. "Philadelphia Nisei Discriminated at University of Pennsylvania," *Topaz Times*, 7 June 1944, 2. Despite Nakano's statement on the lack of discrimination at the University of Pennsylvania, she had faced prejudice at least twice: a librarian attempted to deny her access to the library after Pearl Harbor, and the university did not allow women to use the student union in Houston Hall. Robinson, "Admission Denied."

81. Bodine to Peterson, February 8, 1945, Penn State University (hereafter PSU) File, Box 76, NJASRC, HI. The student noted was likely Chihiro Kikuchi, who attended Penn as a part-time graduate student in 1944-45. By 1945, the Graduate School of Medicine and Wharton had enrolled Nikkei. Robinson, e-mail to author, 20 July 2001; Takasugi to Jannet S. Walker, Relocation Officer, WRA's New York Resettlement Office, Section 200.1 of WRA's New York Resettlement Office, RG 210, Subgroup 18, NA.

82. See http://www.upenn.edu/gazette/0300/0300letters.html; http://www.upenn.edu/gazette/0500/0500letters.html.

83. For Ohio State University (hereafter OSU), see OSU File, Box 75, NJASRC, HI.

84. Dakan to Hibbard, November 26, 1943, WRA-Columbus, Box 22, NJASRC, HI.

85. Dakan to W. Emlen, May 24, 1944, OSU File.

86. Dakan to Swan, June 30, 1944, OSU File.

87. For the University of Utah, see Thompson to LeRoy E. Cowles, President,

University of Utah, June 18, 1943, Accession 23, Box 9, Folder 9, University of Utah Archives; Wiesenberg, "Japanese-American Students." For an overview of student resettlement in Utah, see Welker, "Utah Schools," 4–20.

88. Spicer to E. Emlen, March 10, 1945, WRA-Cleveland, Box 22, NJASRC, HI.

89. Spicer to E. Emlen, March 31, 1945, WRA-Columbus, Box 22, NJASRC, HI.

90. Takasugi to Spicer, April 3, 1945, WRA-Columbus, Box 22, NJASRC, HI.

91. For Pennsylvania State University (hereafter PSU), see PSU File, Box 76, NJASRC, HI.

92. Linegar to Pickett, July 14, 1942, PSU File.

93. Beale to Dutcher, September 26, 1942, PSU File.

94. Hetzel to Hibbard, April 29, 1943, PSU File.

95. White to Hibbard, November 9, 1943, PSU File.

96. Mary Gorai is a pseudonym. Bodine to Ottis Peterson, Acting Chief of the Relocation Division, February 8, 1945, PSU File.

97. E. Emlen to Yager, April 10, 1945, WRA-Philadelphia, Box 23, NJASRC, HI.

98. E. Emlen to Yager, May 29, 1945, WRA-Philadelphia.

99. E. Emlen to Yager, June 11, 1945, WRA-Philadelphia.

100. Mather to Robert M. Cullum, Relocation Supervisor, October 5, 1945, WRA-Philadelphia.

101. Hetzel to Risk, October 16, 1945, WRA-Philadelphia.

102. Snyder to Hetzel, October 18, 1945, WRA-Philadelphia.

103. Snyder to Graybill, October 19, 1945, WRA-Philadelphia.

104. See Indiana University File, Box 67, NJASRC, HI.

105. Hall, "Japanese American College Students," 156–58.

106. Beale to Conard, September 25, 1942, Pacific Coast Branch, 9–10/42, Box 36, NJASRC, HI.

107. Kohlmeier to Nason, December 16, 1942, Indiana University File.

108. For Berea College, see Berea College File, Box 55, NJASRC, HI; Okihiro, *Storied Lives,* 81–82.

109. Bodine to Provinse, December 5, 1944; E. Emlen to Tsurokai, November 16, 1944, WRA-Heart Mountain (II), Box 31, NJASRC, HI; E. Emlen to Hinson, February 2, 1945, WRA-Colorado River (II), Box 33, NJASRC, HI.

110. Bodine to Provinse, February 12, 1945; Amache Hi Newsletter, February 26, 1945, WRA-Granada (II), Box 30, NJASRC, HI.

111. Report on Student Relocation, Poston I, 1944, January 20, 1945; Hinson to E. Emlen, January 8, 1945, 410.123, Student Relocation, Colorado River, Subject-Classified General Files, Records of the Relocation Centers, Records of the WRA, RG 210, NA.

112. Manning to Camp I Community Council, n.d., 410.123, Student Relocation, Colorado River, Subject-Classified General Files, Records of the Relocation Centers, Records of the WRA, RG 210, NA; Memo, Powell to Community Council, February 13, 1945, 410.123, Student Relocation, Colorado River, Subject-Classified General Files, Records of the Relocation Centers, Records of the WRA, RG 210, NA;

Harris to Suzuki, February 26, 1945, 410.123, Student Relocation, Colorado River, Subject-Classified General Files, Records of the Relocation Centers, Records of the WRA, RG 210, NA.

113. Poston I Scholarship Committee: Policies, May 1945, 410.123, Student Relocation, Colorado River, Subject-Classified General Files, Records of the Relocation Centers, Records of the WRA, RG 210, NA.

114. Training Program, n.d., WRA-Washington (II), Box 23, NJASRC, HI.

115. Takasugi to Gerard, May 10, 1945, WRA-Central Utah (IV), Box 29, NJASRC, HI; Hinson to Takasugi, May 15, 1945, 410.123, Student Relocation, Colorado River, Subject-Classified General Files, Records of the Relocation Centers, Records of the WRA, RG 210, NA.

116. "Student Aiders to Open Office," *Gila News Courier,* 16 July 1945, 1; "Student Aiders Begin Interview," *Gila News Courier,* 21 July 1945, 3.

117. "Clifford Nakadegawa," *Newell Star,* 19 October 1945, 3.

118. Final Composite Report-Student Returnee Project, Summer 1945, Box 44, NJASRC, HI.

119. History of Student Relocation in Minidoka WRA, October 4, 1945.

120. Murata, *An Enemy,* 11, 152–54, 181, 189.

121. Report on Scholarship Allocations, June 30, 1946, Reports, Box 49, NJASRC, HI.

122. Harold Ogi is a pseudonym. Evans to E. Emlen, December 20, 1943, Selected Letters, 10–12/43, Box 7, Bodine, HI.

123. Ogi to Campbell, December 10, 1944, Letters, Box 105, NJASRC, HI; E. Emlen Memo, April 20, 1944, College Letters, Box 106, NJASRC, HI.

124. John Kamiya is a pseudonym. Kamiya to Graybill, June 10, 1946, Student Letters, Box 105, NJASRC, HI.

125. See Massachusetts Association of Universalist Women File, Box 13, NJASRC, HI; Ito, "Japanese American Women," 1; Weglyn, *Years of Infamy.*

126. Assistant to the Secretary to Furkawa, December 27, 1944, Correspondence re: Japanese American students (E–H).

127. Jane Kono is a pseudonym. See Jane N. Kono File, Box 115, NJASRC, HI.

128. Kitigawa later wrote and edited several books, including *The History of Religions* (1959), *Modern Trends in World Religions* (1959), *Religion in Japanese History* (1966), *The History of Religions* (1967), *Religions of the East* (1968), *Myths and Symbols* (1969), *Understanding Modern China* (1969), and *American Refugee Policy* (1984).

129. Mary Osaka is a pseudonym. See Mary Osaka File, Box 115, NJASRC, HI.

130. Osaka to Graybill, September 6, 1945, Osaka File.

131. Graybill to Osaka, April 16, 1946, Osaka File.

132. Shigeki Ono is a pseudonym. Van Dyke to E. Emlen, April 13, 1945, Letters, 1945–46, Box 7, Bodine, HI.

133. For Itoi, see Correspondence re: Japanese American students (I–L), Box 1, RG 37, PHS.

134. Horner to Itoi, May 3, 1946, Correspondence re: Japanese American students (I–L).

135. Masao Takano is a pseudonym. See Masao Takano File, Box 114, NJASRC, HI.

136. Takano to Yamamoto, August 30, 1944, Takano File.

137. Takano to E. Emlen, April 17, 1945, Takano File.

138. Bethana McCandless, Registrar, Grinnell, to Graybill, April 8, 1946, Takano File.

139. Katsuro Matsui is a pseudonym. Yamashita to Nishi, January 17, 1945, Cleveland Church Federation, Box 5, NJASRC, HI.

140. John Morita is a pseudonym. For Morita, see John Morita File, Box 113, NJASRC, HI.

141. Morita to Stevenson, May 14, 1943, Morita File.

142. Yamashita to Morita, November 12, 1943, Morita File.

143. E. Emlen to Morita, August 2, 1945, Morita File.

144. Morita to Graybill, July 8, 1946, Morita File.

145. Form Letter, June 7, 1946, NRF-W, Box 42, NJASRC, HI.

146. Student to Graybill, June 19, 1946, Letters, Box 105, NJASRC, HI.

147. Fujita to E. Emlen, October 10, 1945, Student Letters, Box 105, NJASRC, HI. For Fujita, see Graybill, "Nisei," 109.

148. Edward and Ayako Goto are pseudonyms. Edward and Ayako Goto to NJASRC, May 14, 1946, Letters, Box 105, NJASRC, HI.

149. Jane Izumi is a pseudonym. Izumi to Graybill, January 14, 1946, Letters, 1945–46, Box 7, Bodine, HI.

150. Edwin Noda is a pseudonym. Noda to Graybill, June 8, 1946, Selected Letters, 1945–46, Box 7, Bodine, HI.

151. Frank Yamada is a pseudonym. Yamada to NJASRC, February 16, 1946, Letters, 1945–46, Box 7, Bodine, HI.

Conclusion

1. Manzanar Love Song, n.d., Speeches, Box 1, Bodine, HI. Guayule is a plant that the Manzanar authorities cultivated, with little success, to alleviate the wartime rubber shortage.

2. Hibbard to King, July 2, 1945, King Papers, Box XIV.

3. U.S. WRA, *W.R.A.,* 193.

4. Smith argues that racism and financial concerns presented the most frequent troubles for students. See Smith, "Backgrounds," 89–108.

5. Smith, "Backgrounds," 146.

6. Daniels, *Concentration Camps,* 97.

7. O'Brien, *College Nisei,* 111–14.

8. Bodine to Hibbard, March 12, 1944, Committees and Organizations: NJSRC-Correspondence, Japanese-American Relocation, SIS, 1944, AFSC.

9. Takasugi to Alice M. Drake, Director, Department of Christian Education, March 29, 1945, Eastern Pennsylvania Young People's Conference, Box 7, NJASRC, HI.

10. Okihiro, *Storied Lives*, 96.

11. Ito, "Loyalty and Learning," 58–59.

12. See O'Brien, *College Nisei*, 114–24.

13. U.S. WRA, *W.R.A.*, 30–31, 189–93.

14. Jeffries, *Wartime America*, 134.

15. Gleason, "Americans All," 484–85, 500–501, 511–16.

16. Jeffries, *Wartime America*, 136.

17. Japanese-American Relocation: Three Short Talks Given in Finney Chapel on March 2, 1943, by Students of Oberlin College, Oberlin College Subjects File: Japanese Americans, Oberlin College Archives.

18. Ito, "Japanese American Women," 10.

19. Ito, "Loyalty and Learning," 48, 90–91.

20. See the Sumiko Kobayashi Papers, BI.

21. Asian/Pacific-American Heritage Week Pan Asian Festival program, 1986, Kobayashi, Box 12, File 3, BI.

22. No Title, 1987, Kobayashi, Box 13, File 1, BI.

23. See Maki, Kitano, and Berthold, *Achieving the Impossible*.

24. AFSC Oral History Interview #409, AFSC Archives, Philadelphia. See also Ito's essay in Okihiro, *Storied Lives*, 140–51.

25. "2001 Awards Ceremony," NSRC Fund Newsletter, Fall 2001.

26. Noda is quoted in "To Extend Helping Hands Once Offered Us: Nisei Student Relocation Commemorative Fund." A copy of this pamphlet can be found in the Sumiko Kobayashi Papers, Box 22, BI.

27. NSRC Fund Newsletter, Fall 1996; NSRC Fund Newsletter, Fall 1995; Ito in Okihiro, *Storied Lives*, 149.

28. See Dower, *War without Mercy*.

SELECTED BIBLIOGRAPHY

Manuscript Collections

American Friends Service Committee Archives, Philadelphia
  American Friends Service Committee Records
Balch Institute for Ethnic Studies, Philadelphia
  Marian E. Potts Papers
  Muriel Shapp Papers
  Sumiko Kobayashi Papers
Bluffton College Archives, Musselman Library, Bluffton College, Bluffton, Ohio
Columbia Foundation Papers, San Francisco
Franklin D. Roosevelt Library, Hyde Park, New York
  Eleanor Roosevelt Papers
Gettysburg College Archives, Gettysburg, Pennsylvania
Hartford Seminary Archives, Hartford, Connecticut
Haverford College Archives, Haverford, Pennsylvania
Hoover Institution, Stanford University, Stanford, California
  John W. Nason Papers
  National Japanese American Student Relocation Council Records
  Thomas R. Bodine Papers
Lafayette College Libraries, Easton, Pennsylvania
Library of Congress Photoduplication Service, Washington, D.C.
  Camp Papers, 1942–45
Marriott Library, University of Utah, Salt Lake City
National Archives, College Park, Maryland
  Records of the Department of State
  Records of the Provost Marshal General's Office
  Records of the Wartime Civil Control Administration
National Archives, Washington, D.C.
  Records of the War Relocation Authority

Nisei Student Relocation Commemorative Fund, Portland, Connecticut
  Newsletters
Oberlin College Library, Oberlin, Ohio
Robert E. and Jean R. Mahn Center for Archives and Special Collections, Ohio University, Athens, Ohio
Personal collection of Thomas Bodine, Bloomfield, Connecticut
  Trudy King Papers
Presbyterian Historical Society Archives, Philadelphia
  Presbyterian Church Records
State Historical Society of Wisconsin, Madison
  Howard K. Beale Papers
Swarthmore College Archives, Friends Historical Library, Swarthmore, Pennsylvania
University Archives, University of Oregon Libraries, Eugene
University Archives and Records Center, University of Pennsylvania, Philadelphia
University of Cincinnati Archives and Rare Books Department, Cincinnati
University of Washington Archives, Seattle
Watson Library, Wilmington College, Wilmington, Ohio
Wilson Library, University of North Carolina, Chapel Hill

Other Sources

American Friends Service Committee. The Eleanor Roosevelt Connection. http://www.afsc.org/hist/roosevelt.htm.
American National Biography. http://www.anb.org.
Austin, Allan W. "'A Finer Set of Hopes and Dreams': The Japanese American Citizens League and Ethnic Community in Cincinnati, Ohio, 1942–1950." In *Remapping Asian American History*. Ed. Sucheng Chan. Walnut Creek, Calif.: AltaMira Press, 2003, 87–105.
Barstow, Robbins. "Help for Nisei Students." *The Christian Century* 59 (July 1, 1942): 836–37.
Blanshard, Frances. *Frank Aydelotte of Swarthmore*. Middletown, Conn.: Wesleyan University Press, 1970.
Brokaw, Tom. *The Greatest Generation*. New York: Random House, 1998.
Chang, Gordon H. *Morning Glory, Evening Shadow: Yamato Ichihashi and His Internment Writings*. Stanford: Stanford University Press, 1997.
Clark, Burton R. *The Distinctive College*. New Brunswick, N.J.: Transaction Publications, 1992.
Columbia Foundation. About Columbia Foundation. http://www.columbia.org/aboutcolumbiafoundation.htm.
Conte, James T. "Overseas Study in the Meiji Period: Japanese Students in America, 1867–1902." Ph.D. diss., Princeton University, 1977.
Daniels, Roger. *Asian America: Chinese and Japanese in the United States since 1850*. Seattle: University of Washington Press, 1988.

———. *Concentration Camps, North America: Japanese in the United States and Canada during World War II.* Malabar, Fla.: Robert E. Krieger Publishing, 1981.

———. *The Politics of Prejudice: The Anti-Japanese Movement in California and the Struggle for Japanese Exclusion.* 2d ed. Berkeley: University of California Press, 1978.

———. "William Jennings Bryan and the Japanese." *Southern California Quarterly* 48 (September 1966): 227–37.

———. "Words Do Matter: A Note on Inappropriate Terminology and the Incarceration of the Japanese Americans." Seattle: University of Washington Press, forthcoming.

Daniels, Roger, Sandra C. Taylor, and Harry H. L. Kitano. *Japanese Americans: From Relocation to Redress.* Salt Lake City: University of Utah Press, 1986.

Dower, John W. *War without Mercy: Race and Power in the Pacific War.* New York: Pantheon Books, 1986.

Drinnon, Richard. *Keeper of Concentration Camps: Dillon S. Myer and American Racism.* Berkeley: University of California Press, 1987.

Dykeman, Wilma, and James Stokely. *Seeds of Southern Change: The Life of Will Alexander.* Chicago: University of Chicago Press, 1962.

Eisenhower, Milton S. *The President Is Calling.* Garden City, N.Y.: Doubleday, 1974.

Fisher, Edgar. "The Relocation of Japanese American Students." *The Educational Record* 23 (1942): 451–52.

Fisher, Galen M. "Our Two Japanese-American Policies." *Christian Century* 60 (August 25, 1943): 961–63.

———. "Our Two Japanese Refugees." *Christian Century* 59 (April 1, 1942): 424–26.

———. *Public Affairs and the Y.M.C.A., 1844–1944, with Special Reference to the United States.* New York: Associated Press, 1948.

———. "Unsnaring the Nisei Tangle." *Christian Century* 61 (November 1, 1944): 1285–88.

———. "What Race Baiting Costs America." *Christian Century* 60 (September 8, 1943): 1009–11.

Franks, Joel S. *Crossing Sidelines, Crossing Cultures: Sport and Asian Pacific American Cultural Citizenship.* New York: University Press of America, 2000.

Girdner, Audrie, and Anne Loftis. *The Great Betrayal: The Evacuation of the Japanese-Americans during World War II.* New York: Macmillan, 1969.

Gleason, Philip. "Americans All: World War II and the Shaping of American Identity." *The Review of Politics* 43.4 (1981): 483–518.

Graybill, Ann. "Nisei—Good Citizens, Good Students." *The Intercollegian* 63 (1946): 109–11.

Greenberg, Cheryl. "Black and Jewish Responses to Japanese Internment." *Journal of American Ethnic History* 14, no. 2 (1995): 3–37.

Hall, Jenness Evaline. "Japanese American College Students during the Second World War: The Politics of Relocation." Ph.D. diss., Indiana University, 1993.

Hayashi, Ann Koto. *Face of the Enemy, Heart of a Patriot: Japanese-American Internment Narratives.* New York: Garland, 1995.

Higham, John. *Strangers in the Land: Patterns of American Nativism, 1860–1925.* New Brunswick, N.J.: Rutgers University Press, 1955.

Hill, Kimi Kodani, ed. *Chiura Obata's Topaz Moon: Art of the Internment.* Berkeley, Calif.: Heyday Books, 2000.

"Historical News and Comments: Howard K. Beale Obituary." *Mississippi Valley Historical Review* 46.4 (1960): 774–74.

Honan, William H. "Lucille Petry Leone, 97, Recruiter of Nurses during World War II." *New York Times,* 5 December 1999, sec. 1, 62.

Inada, Lawson Fusao, ed. *Only What We Could Carry: The Japanese American Internment Experience.* Berkeley, Calif.: Heyday Books, 2000.

Inouye, Frank T. "Odyssey of a Nisei: A Voyage of Self-Discovery." Ms. University Archives, University of Cincinnati, n.d.

Ito, Leslie A. "Japanese American Women and the Student Relocation Movement, 1942–1945." *Frontiers* 21.3 (2000): 1–24.

———. "Loyalty and Learning: Nisei Women and the Student Relocation." Honors thesis, Mount Holyoke College, 1996.

James, Thomas. *Exile Within: The Schooling of Japanese Americans, 1942–1945.* Cambridge: Harvard University Press, 1987.

———. "Life Begins with Freedom: The College Nisei, 1942–1945." *History of Education Quarterly* 25 (Spring–Summer 1985): 155–74.

Japanese American National Museum. Press release. http://www.janm.org.whatsnew/p_obata.html.

Jeffries, John W. *Wartime America: The World War II Homefront.* Chicago: Ivan R. Dee, 1996.

"Joseph Conard." *The Phoenix,* 5 April 1965.

Lewis, Paul. "John W. Nason, Educator Who Helped Japanese-Americans, Dies at 96." *New York Times,* 22 November 2001, sec. D, 9.

Linehan, Thomas M. "Japanese American Resettlement in Cleveland during and after World War II." *Journal of Urban History* 20.1 (1993): 54–80.

Maki, Mitchell T., Harry H. L. Kitano, and S. Megan Berthold. *Achieving the Impossible Dream: How Japanese Americans Obtained Redress.* Urbana: University of Illinois Press, 1999.

Matsumoto, Toru. *Beyond Prejudice: A Story of the Church and Japanese Americans.* New York: Friendship Press, 1946.

Matsumoto, Valerie J. *Farming the Home Place: A Japanese American Community in California, 1919–1982.* Ithaca: Cornell University Press, 1993.

———. "Japanese American Women during World War II." *Frontiers* 8.1 (1984): 6–14.

McKay, Susan. "The Problem of Student Nurses of Japanese Ancestry." Ms., 2000.

Moriyama, Alan Takeo. *Imingaisha: Japanese Emigration Companies and Hawaii, 1894–1908.* Honolulu: University of Hawai'i Press, 1985.

Murata, Kiyoaki. *An Enemy among Friends*. Tokyo: Kodansha International, 1991.

National Japanese American Student Relocation Council. *Directory of Students of Japanese Ancestry in the Higher Schools, Colleges, and Universities of the United States of America, Including Students Currently Working but Intending to Enter College*. Philadelphia: NJASRC, 1943.

———. *From Camp to College: Story of Japanese American Student Relocation*. Philadelphia: NJASRC, 1943.

———. *How to Help Japanese American Student Relocation*. Philadelphia: NJASRC, February 20, 1944.

Nisei Student Relocation Commemorative Fund. "To Extend Helping Hands Once Offered Us: Nisei Student Relocation Commemorative Fund." Portland, Conn.: Nisei Student Relocation Commerative Fund.

"Nisei Students in Junior Colleges: A Symposium." *Junior College Journal* 14 (September 1944): 5–11.

"Nisei Students Speak for Themselves: A Symposium." *Junior College Journal* 14 (February 1944): 243–52.

Noble, Antonette C. "Masaye Nakamura's Personal Story." *Magazine of History* 16 (Spring 2002): 37–40.

O'Brien, Robert W. *The College Nisei*. Palo Alto, Calif.: Pacific Books, 1949.

———. "Reaction of the College Nisei to Japan and Japanese Foreign Policy from the Invasion of Manchuria to Pearl Harbor." *Pacific Northwest Quarterly* 36 (1945): 19–28.

———. "Selective Dispersion as a Factor in the Solution of the Nisei Problem." *Social Forces* 23 (1944): 140–47.

———. "Student Relocation." *Common Ground* 3.4 (1943): 73–78.

Okada, Dave. *Japanese American Relocation*. Oberlin, Ohio: Oberlin College Publicity Bureau, 1943.

Okihiro, Gary Y. *Storied Lives: Japanese American Students and World War II*. Seattle: University of Washington Press, 1999.

Park College. Nisei: Japanese-American Student Transfer Initiative. http://www.park.edu/nisei.

Pickett, Clarence E. *For More Than Bread: An Autobiographical Account of Twenty-two Years' Work with the American Friends Service Committee*. Boston: Little, Brown, 1953.

Pickett, Clarence E., and Homer L. Morris. "From Barbed Wire to Communities." *Survey Midmonthly* 79 (1943): 210–13.

Provinse, John. "Relocation of Japanese American College Students." *Higher Education* 1 (April 16, 1945): 1–4.

"Recent Deaths: Howard K. Beale." *American Historical Review* 65.4 (1960): 1047–48.

Robinson, Greg. "Admission Denied." *Pennsylvania Gazette* online document, http://www.upenn.edu/gazette/0100/robinson.html.

———. *By Order of the President: FDR and the Internment of Japanese Americans.* Cambridge: Harvard University Press, 2001.

Ruiz, Vicki L., and Ellen Carol DuBois, eds. *Unequal Sisters: A Multi-cultural Reader in U.S. Women's History.* 2d ed. New York: Routledge, 1994.

Russell, Madeleine H. "Furthering the Public Welfare, 1929–1991: Oral History Transcript." Regional Oral History Office, Bancroft Library, University of California, Berkeley, 1995.

Sittser, Gerald L. *A Cautious Patriotism: The American Churches and the Second World War.* Chapel Hill: University of North Carolina Press, 1997.

Smith, Mildred Joan. "Backgrounds, Problems, and Significant Reactions of Relocated Japanese-American Students." Ed.D. diss., Syracuse University, 1949.

Smith, Page. *Democracy on Trial: The Japanese American Evacuation and Relocation in World War II.* New York: Simon and Schuster, 1995.

"Still the Greatest Country." *Pennsylvania Gazette* online document, http://www.upenn.edu/gazette/0100/0100pro5.html.

Takahashi, Jere. "Japanese American Responses to Race Relations: The Formation of Nisei Perspectives." *Amerasia* 9.1 (1982): 29–57.

———. *Nisei/Sansei: Shifting Japanese American Identities and Politics.* Philadelphia: Temple University Press, 1997.

Tamura, Eileen. "Asian Americans in the History of Education: An Historiographical Essay." *History of Education Quarterly* 41 (Spring 2001): 58–71.

Tanaka, Hank. "Earlham College: A Place of Caring People." *The Grains of Rice* (newsletter of the Cincinnati chapter of the Japanese American Citizens League) (March 1997): 4–5.

Taylor, Sandra C. *Jewel of the Desert: Japanese American Internment at Topaz.* Berkeley: University of California Press, 1993.

Uchida, Yoshiko. *Desert Exile: The Uprooting of a Japanese American Family.* Seattle: University of Washington Press, 1982.

U.S. Department of War. *Final Report: Japanese Evacuation from the West Coast, 1942.* New York: Arno Press, 1978.

U.S. Public Health Service, Federal Security Agency. *The United States Cadet Nurse Corps, 1943–1948.* Washington, D.C.: Government Printing Office, 1950.

U.S. War Relocation Authority. *The Evacuated People: A Quantitative Description.* Washington, D.C.: Government Printing Office, 1943.

———. *Relocating a People.* Washington, D.C.: Government Printing Office, n.d.

———. *Relocation of Japanese-Americans.* Washington, D.C.: Government Printing Office, 1943.

———. *The Relocation Program: A Guidebook for the Residents of Relocation Centers.* Washington, D.C.: Government Printing Office, 1943.

———. *W.R.A.: A Story of Human Conservation.* Washington, D.C.: Government Printing Office, 1946.

University of Washington. Interrupted Lives. http://www.lib.washington.edu/exhibits/harmony/Uw-new.

Van Sant, John E. *Pacific Pioneers: Japanese Journeys to America and Hawaii, 1850–80*. Urbana: University of Illinois Press, 2000.

Watson, Sheppard Arthur, and Florence Potter Watson. *Our Life Together: The Life Story of Sheppard Arthur Watson and Florence Potter Watson*. Montezuma, Iowa: By the authors, 1975.

Weglyn, Michi Nishiura. *Years of Infamy: The Untold Story of America's Concentration Camps*. Seattle: University of Washington Press, 1976.

Welker, R. Todd. "Utah Schools and the Japanese American Student Relocation Program." *Utah Historical Quarterly* 70 (Winter 2002): 4–20.

Wertheimer, Andrew. "Admitting Nebraska's *Nisei:* Japanese American Students at the University of Nebraska, 1942–1945." *Nebraska History* 83.2 (2002): 58–72.

Wiesenberg, Mark. "Japanese-American Students and the University of Utah." Ms., 1997.

World Student Service Fund. *Design for Peace: The Story of World Student Relief, 1937–1946*. New York: World Student Service Fund, 1947.

Worthen, Dennis B. "Nisei Pharmacists in World War II." *Pharmacy in History* 45.2 (2003): 58–65.

———. "The Nisei Students." *St. Louis College of Pharmacy* 13 B.1 (Spring 2003): 6–9.

Yoo, David K. *Growing Up Nisei: Race, Generation, and Culture among Japanese Americans of California, 1924–49*. Urbana: University of Illinois Press, 2000.

Yu, Henry. *Thinking Orientals: Migration, Contact, and Exoticism in Modern America*. New York: Oxford University Press, 2001.

INDEX

ABHMS. *See* American Baptist Home
Mission Society
Abington Hospital (Pa.), 113
Adrian College (Mich.), 117–18
AFSC. *See* American Friends Service
Committee
Albright, Opal, 124
Alexander, Will, 18–19, 181n27
Allegheny College (Pa.), 80–81
"ambassadors of good will": examples
of, 3, 15; National Japanese American
Student Relocation Council on, 2, 34,
38, 42, 63, 82, 94; students on, 16, 17,
61, 62, 94, 169; WSSF on, 45
American Baptist Home Mission Society
(ABHMS), 41, 43, 45
American Civil Liberties Union, 103
American Friends Service Committee
(AFSC): early involvement, 24, 28;
funding of relocation council from, 65;
returnee project, 126; and relocation
council's second plenary meeting, 99;
role of, in organizing relocation council, 33, 164; students' memories of role
of, in student resettlement, 116, 171;
at University of Washington, 7, 13
American Legion: opposition of, to student resettlement, 15, 29, 65, 77, 81–
82, 93, 109; support by, for exile and
incarceration, 10
Amerman, Helen, 121, 123, 132, 150
Anderson, Leila, 37, 182n33

anti-Japanese movement, 4–6
Antioch College (Ohio), 52–53
Army Specialized Training Program
(ASTP), 151
Asado, Chiya Veronica, 62
Asbury College (Ky.), 85
Ashland College (Ohio), 56
Ashland Junior College (Ky.), 78
assimilation: dispersal and, 20, 57–58;
National Japanese American Student
Relocation Council and, 86, 137, 167–
68; students on, 86, 87, 168–69, 172;
WRA and, 132
Association of American Colleges, 99
ASTP. *See* Army Specialized Training
Program
Aydelotte, Frank, 27, 51, 184n64

Baba, Saburo, 120
Bard College (N.Y.), 86
Barstow, Robbins W.: biography,
185n70, 188n12; cautious approach
of, to student resettlement, 43, 51–52;
65; correspondence of, with college,
82; on dispersal and assimilation, 57–
58; early involvement of, in student
resettlement, 29, 31, 35; on student
resettlement and democracy, 4; and
tensions within relocation council, 33,
39–41
Beale, Howard K.: biography, 188n12,
197–98n24; correspondence of, with

Washington University (St. Louis), 14–
15, 54, 95
Watanabe, Mary, 120
WCCA. *See* Wartime Civil Control Administration
WDC. *See* Western Defense Command
Webster College (Mo.), 94, 121
Wellesley College (Mass.), 37
Western College (Ohio), 62
Western Defense Command (WDC), 10,
14
Western Reserve University (Ohio), 142–
43
Wharton School, University of Pennsylvania, 87, 144, 218n81
Wheaton College (Ill.), 166–67
White Cross Hospital's School of Nursing (Ohio), 112
Whittier College, 31
Wilkins, Ernest H., 58, 102
Willis Santa Monica Business College
(Calif.), 138
Wilmington College (Ohio), 79
Wilson College (Pa.), 86
women and student resettlement, 89–90,
170
Woodbury College (Calif.), 138
World Student Service Fund (WSSF),
135, 165; and financial support, 22,
45, 63, 139, 149, 154; and student
returnee project, 126
WRA. *See* War Relocation Authority
WSSF. *See* World Student Service Fund

Yale University, 38
Yamada, Frank, 159

Yamada, Hana, 123
Yamaguchi, Geo., 9
Yamashita, Kay: correspondence of, with
colleges, 111, 142; on the draft, 119;
and newsletter, 122–23; relationships
of, with students, 121, 157; in Topaz
concentration camp, 98
Yamate, Sasato, 115–16
Yamauchi, Dorothy, 139
Yamiguchi, Harry, 58
Yankton College (S.D.), 86
Yano, Masao, 120
Yasutake, Shigeki, 119
YMCA. *See* Young Men's Christian Association
Young Men's Christian Association
(YMCA): in camps, 95; early involvement of, in student resettlement, 7, 10–
11, 17–18, 19, 22, 33, 179n4; and
financial support, 65; and importance
of support, 165; and placement in
trade or vocational schools, 104; and
returnee project, 126; works with colleges, 57, 79
Young Women's Christian Association
(YWCA): early involvement of, in student resettlement, 10–11, 17–18, 19,
22, 33; and financial support, 65; and
importance of support, 165; and returnee project, 126; works with colleges, 62
YWCA. *See* Young Women's Christian
Association

Zacharias, Ellis M., 75
Zook, George, 27

ALLAN W. AUSTIN is an assistant professor of history at College Misericordia in Dallas, Pennsylvania, and a contributor to the edited collections *Last Witnesses: Reflections on the Wartime Internment of Japanese Americans* (2001) and *Remapping Asian American History* (2003).

The Asian American Experience

The University of Illinois Press
is a founding member of the
Association of American University Presses.

Composed in 10/13 Sabon
by Jim Proefrock
at the University of Illinois Press
Designed by Dennis Roberts
Manufactured by Maple-Vail
Book Manufacturing Group

University of Illinois Press
1325 South Oak Street
Champaign, IL 61820-6903
www.press.uillinois.edu